New World Beginnings

Also by Olivia Vlahos

The Battle-ax People: Beginnings of Western Culture
African Beginnings
Human Beginnings

New World

Indian Cultures in the Americas

Beginnings

by Olivia Vlahos

Illustrated by

George Ford

The Viking Press/New York

To Gilbert McAllister

Copyright © 1970 by Olivia Vlahos

Viking Compass Edition
Issued in 1971 by The Viking Press, Inc.
625 Madison Avenue, New York, N.Y. 10022

Distributed in Canada by
The Macmillan Company of Canada Limited

SBN 670-50839-x (hardbound)
670-50840-3 (library binding)
670-00320-4 (paperbound)

Library of Congress catalog card number: 70-106921

Printed in U.S.A.

Second printing December 1973

Author's Note

About Indian peoples of the Americas, there are three stories that can be told: of the past, of the present, of the future. Many authors have written with sympathy and understanding of the conquests, the tragic dispossessions, which have left Indians today all too often rootless, forever stranded between a hostile world and a dying one. Others have offered proposals for the future, proposals ranging from the assimilation to the revitalization of American Indian cultures. This book is concerned, not with what is or can be, but with what has been—with the record of bone and stone, with the living record of living men still following the ancient ways. Perhaps those who are wiser than I may find use for this record in other tenses.

Men who search for the past are more richly rewarded in the two continents of the New World than almost anywhere else. What the archaeologist uncovers here often finds illumination in the patterns and beliefs of living people or of people who retained their traditions long enough to attract the attention and study of ethnographers. Even so, the picture changes slightly from yea. to year as new discoveries are made, new peoples encountered in the South American rain forests, new field work accomplished. Occasionally specialists differ in their interpretations of cultural materials.

I have tried to indicate that the past contains few absolutes and may be approached from any number of angles.

In preparing this book I have leaned most heavily on the writings of Gordon R. Willey for North American archaeology, Michael D. Coe and Richard MacNeish for Mesoamerican archaeology, and Betty J. Meggers, Clifford Evans, and Edward P. Lanning for South American archaeology. I have followed G. L. Trager's classification of North American and Mesoamerican Indian languages, that of Joseph H. Greenberg for the Indian languages of South America. In describing the life ways of living American Indians, I have tried to reflect faithfully the viewpoints (sometimes varying) of specialists who did the field work. Their names are indicated in the text and the accompanying bibliography.

It is with pleasure that I thank Dr. Irving Goldman for reading the manuscript. He brought to the task not only wisdom and an acute critical sense, but a wealth of personal knowledge of American Indians ranging from the Alkatcho Carriers of British Columbia to the Cubeo of the Northwest Amazon.

George Ford has once again, with his vivid illustrations, breathed life into my words, and I thank him warmly.

To Professor Joseph Campbell, whose kindly interest has long sustained my ventures, I offer my continuing gratitude.

Contents

Part III
GATHERERS

Part IV
FARMERS

Part V
EMPIRE BUILDERS

List of Maps

Peoples of North America

CARIBBEAN SEA

CHIBCHA   YANOMAMO

MOCHE

INCA

NAZCA   MOJO

SIRIONO

PACIFIC OCEAN

DIAGUITA

ATLANTIC OCEAN

PUELCHE

TEHUELCHE

Peoples of South America

ALACALUF   ONA

YAHGAN

Prologue
When The People Came

The New World! That is what the continents of this hemisphere have been called ever since Columbus proved that the earth was round and that on its global underside lay, not the nether shore of India, but an astonishingly vast land, a land whose existence had been hitherto unsuspected and was therefore "new."

In the geological scheme of things, it certainly was not new. It had not burst in cataclysmic birth newly from the ocean depths. Neither was it new in terms of animal life. The most ancient of earth's amphibians had long since left their fossil record in American rocks. Dinosaurs had once roamed American marshes and plains. Early mammals had skittered through forests of pulpy American trees. Here once lived the most primitive of man's primate relatives, though his later close cousins, the great apes, were never to evolve on these shores.

It is only for man himself that the continents of this hemisphere have always seemed "new." They were new to the Vikings, who left behind only the dimmest and most enigmatic records of discovery. They were new to the sailors of the *Niña*, the *Pinta*, and the *Santa María*. And to the ancestors of the people who were there to meet the Scandinavian and Spanish ships, the Americas had also once been new. For man did not begin in the New World. Always man has come to it as an immigrant—willing or unwilling, buoyed by hope or driven by despair.

The first immigrants came in family bands, in wandering hunting parties following game animals over Beringia, the wide land bridge which, during glacial periods, links Alaska to the Old World. Later, it seems, he came in canoeloads borne by the currents which sweep Pacific waters to the east and then, near American coasts, turn in great circles north and south. A few specialists believe man also came in canoes across the Atlantic while its stormy waters bore the floes, the floating islands, the drifting white debris of a great glacier in retreat. Certainly he crossed the Atlantic in later times, traveling in sailing ships that first brought explorers, then adventurers, then settlers, who multiplied, expanded their territory, and exploited men whose ancestors had been among earlier arrivals. Today men fly to the New World in airplanes, thinking still to find here—for all that the land is crowded now and busy with people—a place of refuge and a new beginning.

About the voyagers after Columbus we know a great deal. There are written records of all kinds to tell us exactly who came, and when and why. And if this is not enough, we can see in the faces of living Americans, north and south, yet another record of travel. For the earliest immigrants, however, there is no record beyond the fragmentary story told by bones and stones and potsherds buried in the ground. We cannot know what the first Americans thought when they arrived here or even if they knew they had stumbled into a different land. We cannot know exactly what they looked like or exactly when they came. Archaeology cannot reveal all. But what it has to tell us can be considerably enriched and enlivened (on these continents as almost nowhere else) by studies of living American Indians, their life ways and their languages. Sometimes these studies are available only in the documents of the earliest European explorers and missionaries, for the people whom they met and wrote about have long since died away. After all the digs and studies, those gaps that remain must be filled by the imagination.

A hundred years or so ago, imagination was virtually all anyone had to work with. There was indeed some recognition of the physical similarity of American Indians to peoples of East Asia. Thomas Jefferson thought that much might be learned by comparing New World languages with those of Siberia—a practical suggestion not to be followed up for many years. The most popular theories about New World peoples, however, hinged on lost continents and mythical travelers from Egypt, from the Holy Land, perhaps from across the Pacific. How otherwise were the great civilizations of Mexico and Peru to be explained? And then there were other theories. After the discovery in South America of the bones of men in association with those of extinct animals, some specialists claimed that man must really have begun in the New World.

In the early 1900s all speculations ground to a halt. Dr. Aleš Hrdlička, the most prestigious physical anthropologist of his day, pointed out that, however intriguing the circumstances of discovery, all the bones of men found in the New World looked exactly like the bones of men today. They could not, therefore, be very old. In fact, said Dr. Hrdlička, it was highly unlikely that man had arrived in this hemisphere much before a very few thousand years ago; he had certainly made the journey after the melting of the glacial ice, and he had come by way of Siberia. And that was that.

For a long time afterward, few scientists were much tempted to look for real antiquity in New World men, or if they were, it was not mentioned officially. Nobody suggested the possibility of travel across the oceans either, or of travelers whose faces and forms might have been different from those now to be found in northeast Asia.

But whatever the official attitude, the problems remained,

the little contradictions in the finds that said more and more insistently: old, old and different. More and more bones began to turn up, bones that, while certainly modern *Homo sapiens* in type, did not very much resemble the bones of modern American Indians. They resembled those of modern Asians even less. Physical anthropologist W. W. Howells ventured the thought that they represented an early, unspecialized type of Mongoloid.

To Dr. Earnest A. Hooton the bones seemed somewhat more European than Asian, with perhaps a touch of Australoid thrown in. He did not mean by this suggestion to add yet another clot of travelers to the original pioneer group trekking eastward into Beringia. The Ainu, a group of people who seem to be European in type, still populate the northern Japanese island. Their ancestors, Dr. Hooton thought, could easily have joined the migration. But there was certainly no notion of true Australian Aborigines unaccountably shunted north. What Dr. Hooton seems to have had in mind for *his* first Americans were northern peoples who were already very much mixed in terms of race and had been for a long time. In both interpretations of the bones, there was implied antiquity. Early type—whether unspecialized Mongoloid or the result of some archaic blend —had to mean ancient arrival. Was that possible?

In addition to the puzzle of the bones, there remained the puzzle of living men. How was the observer to explain the wide variety in size, shape, color, and stature to be found among the peoples of the New World? One had only to look at the tip of Tierra del Fuego, that frigid, snow-laced land, to see neighboring peoples who differed by at least a foot in height and who displayed an altogether disparate distribution of girth. Could one account for these differences by environmental selection alone—and could such selection have acted in the short span of years allotted by Dr. Hrdlička for man's tenure here?

Two additional problems demanded consideration: blood

types and languages. Blood groups of today's central Asians differ markedly from those of today's American Indians. And as for languages, even with most careful study and with every attempt to consolidate families of spoken words, the differences in American Indian languages were just too great to support the notion of recent arrival and short-term stay. If the first immigrants had appeared no earlier than six to seven thousand years ago and then spread out to occupy the two continents, one ought to be able to trace their word connections—the resemblances in sounds and meanings and language structure. It is by a study of such resemblances that the affinities of the languages of Europe and India have been traced. And it is by the study of degree of difference among related languages that the time of their separation can be plotted. In the matter of American Indian languages, where resemblances can be noted and the separation times plotted, the results say old, old—older than the five or six thousand years that lie between the most divergent of the Indo-European languages. There are in the Americas, moreover, many major language groups, each as distinct, as different from the rest as the Indo-European language group is different from the languages of Asia.

To linguistics specialist Dr. Morris Swadesh, these differences suggest waves of incoming people, the earliest of whom must have arrived at least 30,000 years ago. These earliest immigrants, he thinks, probably spoke languages which were lost as newer waves of arrivals rolled in. Certainly there existed in Newfoundland's recent past, and still exist in South America, small isolated groups of people whose languages, like that of the European Basques, do not even remotely resemble the languages spoken around them. Are these people and their languages remnants, perhaps, of those earliest migrations? For a long time, one could not ask.

Just as the quest for antiquity in New World beginnings had been banned, so had the quest for origin points other than Siberia. The possibility of canoes across the Pacific, for example, had been dismissed from scientific speculation, or so it was thought. Actually the speculations continued to appear, defying dismissal. For there were to be found in the cultures of living American Indians certain ideas, customs, and items of manufacture bearing unmistakable similarity to ideas, customs, and items of manufacture in use or once in use among peoples of the Pacific and beyond. There was the use of the blowgun, for example, Panpipes, and bark cloth. In South America, Indians chewed coca leaves with lime, as in the Pacific islands betel nuts were chewed with a lime-bearing leaf. Archaeological excavations revealed and have continued to reveal countless artifacts and themes in art and religion that persistently call Asia to mind. How could the interested observer account for the similarities? Was he simply to marvel at the coincidence, again and again?

Continuing excavation and new dating techniques have at last begun to resolve some of the contradictions and answer some of the questions. The association of human bones with those of animals long extinct in the New World has appeared all too frequently to be explained away or ignored. Again and again amid the ancient bones have been found the hunters' weapons—long, beautifully flaked projectile points, sometimes embedded in the very bones themselves. There have been found, as well, other sorts of weapons, thicker, more crudely flaked than the projectile points. Did they belong to men still older than the projectile-point makers? More and more specialists are willing to concede the possibility.

In the 1950s it became possible to date the remains of once-living things—bones, shells, leather, the coals of old campfires. All living things are composed in part of carbon atoms, some of which consist of a radiocarbon isotope created in the atmosphere by cosmic rays and absorbed by living tissue. When an organism dies, the turnover of carbon atoms—exchanged in respiration—stops, and the radiocarbon in its tissues begins to diminish by radioactive decay, slowly and always at the same rate. Because the rate of decay is constant and therefore measurable, bits of wood or bone can be traced back to the time when the particular tree was cut down or the animal died. The radiocarbon dates obtained for sites containing projectile points have centered around 10,000 B.C. Sites bearing the older-looking tools have sometimes contained datable materials, sometimes not. The few dates available, obtained from the charcoal of old campfires, have supported the ancient appearance of the tools. The earliest campfire found in the New World seems to have been laid at least 38,000 years ago.

Clearly, unmistakably, man did not begin in the New World. But just as clearly, just as unmistakably, he has been here a very long time. No wonder his remains and his living descendants do not entirely resemble the present peoples of Asia. Around 40,000 years ago, the Mongoloid type may have only begun to develop. Undoubtedly, man in the New World has had time enough to spread out, to adapt to new environmental conditions, to be selected by those environments for certain physical shapes and sizes and capacities. And, undoubtedly, the first arrivals were as mixed a bag of physical types as there were in Asia at that time.

Theirs was a trek destined to be repeated many times over the long years, whenever the waters covering Beringia were locked in glacial ice or after the invention of boats permitted island-hopping across the channel. The ancestors of modern Eskimos seem to have been among the most recent arrivals, advancing from Siberia sometime around 3000 B.C. They seem to be more Asian in type than most other American Indians, and the structure of their languages differs markedly from those of others in the New World. The same may also be said of Athapascan-speaking Indians who inhabit the interior of Alaska and the Canadian Northwest, and who are represented in our West by the Apaches and Navajos.

Their ancestors seem to have been late-comers as well, though certainly they preceded the Eskimos by at least a thousand years.

Time and new discoveries have even begun to rescue and rehabilitate the old theories of trans-Pacific travel. Archaeology has recently uncovered likely evidence for such voyages perhaps as early as 3000 B.C. To be sure, these would not have brought immigrants, but unwilling visitors—sailors blown off course. What new ideas they brought with them could not materially have affected the growth and course of the great New World civilizations, but surely added to and enriched them, presenting new skills and artistic themes on which endless variations could be played. There was, it seems now, time for it all.

There was time for all the Old World processes of development and elaboration to be re-enacted, time for most of the skills, the social forms, the religious ideas to be invented and practiced anew. There was time for plants to be domesticated and for the knowledge of farming ways to travel north and south. There was time for people to learn how to live together ever more closely in ever more compact settlements, to find means of making common purpose and achieving common ends. There was time for great temples to be built and writing to be invented. And as some people changed and elaborated their ways of life, there were always on the fringes those who remained untouched, living much as the first arrivals must have lived long ago, preserving in their fastnesses north and south the habits, ideas, and ways that were once common to all men of the New World.

Part I
HUNTERS

The Record of Bone and Stone

The story of man in both New World and Old is also the story of ice. Man came into being at least two and a half million years ago and matured with the ebb and flow of great glaciers in the polar north and alternating deluge and drought in southern lands. During the first of the glaciations (the first of the great rains southward), the earliest sorts of men lived in Africa. They were toolmakers, upright in posture though small in size and small in brain. Sometime during the second great ice advance, which began more than a million years ago, a larger, improved sort of man appeared —a man whose brain approached in size the lower ranges of our own, a skilled maker of tools and weapons, a fire builder,

a family man and hunter, a wide traveler in the Old World. We call him *Homo erectus*. The third glacial age belonged to the first men of our own sort, *Homo sapiens*, including the stumpy Neanderthals of northern Europe. And with the fourth glacial advance, true modern man, *Homo sapiens sapiens*, came into his own.

This fourth glaciation, which has been called "Würm" in its European manifestation and "Wisconsin" in America, began its advance perhaps 150,000 years ago, perhaps only 70,000 or less—scientific opinion varies. At its height, the European ice sheet covered all of what is now Scandinavia and much of Germany, leaving exposed only the southern coast of England. In America, the southern edge of the glacier invaded Kentucky. Northward it locked in ice the waters which, during warm times, form the Bering Strait. The land exposed was wide and glacier-free, as was part of Alaska at that time, and over this bridge, this broad highway, came man the hunter.

One highway the ice opened, but another one it closed. The great American glaciers have always had two points of origin: one in the North Pole, spreading down through Hudson's Bay; the other in the western mountain range which curves like a great spine down the coastline of the Americas. Together these two glaciers formed massive double doors. Frozen shut, they barred man's way into the New World. It was the fact of the Wisconsin barrier that prompted Dr. Hrdlička to declare that man could not have entered the New World until after the melting, the retreat of the glaciers. (For surely man with his simple, Old Stone Age technology could neither have crossed the naked ice nor lived upon it.)

Now, however, it begins to appear that man indeed did something of the sort. All over both continents of the New World have been found camp and kill sites in which are jumbled the remains of very ancient mammals such as mammoths, glyptodonts, camels, and horses along with tools of a crude and antique type. Made from lumps of stone with just enough flakes removed to produce a cutting edge, these rough tools seem to have been used mainly as cleavers and choppers. Some are what the specialists call "burins." Narrow, chisel-like tools, burins may have figured in the manufacture of wooden weapons such as darts and spears. Altogether, the crude stone implements remind us of shapes and styles popular among toolmakers in Asia all through the Old Stone Age. Now and again, the coals from old campfires are found with burins and bones. Of course, there is always the possibility that the old fire may not have been man-made, that later deposits may have intruded, or that the original remains may somehow have been disturbed. Even granting wide margin for error, however, these ancient-looking sites have yielded some very early dates— 38,000 years ago for one site in northeast Texas, 30,000 for another in California; and there are others. In South America the dates of similar sites are a bit later, but the catalogue of contents remains the same.

Man arrived, it would now seem, before the great melting. Sturdy and unafraid, he had surmounted the glacial barrier to take possession of the land beyond. A thrilling notion, surely, fit for a newspaper headline: *Man Conquers All!* But let us not give the hero more than his due. Perhaps he could have surmounted the twin obstacles of ice and sea; very likely he did not have to. The Wisconsin glacial stage seems to have been punctuated by a number of warmer periods called interstadials. It appears that, during these times, the waters narrowed but did not altogether cover Beringia, the wide bridge between Siberia and Alaska, and that the ice doors to the continent were set ajar. It must have been during one or perhaps several of these interstadials that men slipped through the ice gates and into the lands beyond.

It is only fair to say that however many the sites, however consistent the type of crude tool, however different that type from the tools of later men—this early appearance of man in the New World some 40,000 years ago is still considered chancy and controversial among scientists. Bones of the earliest hunters themselves are yet to be found. And until 1967 the early tools had all been found in weathered surface sites, never buried beneath the artifacts of later men —one of the essential conditions for establishing unquestioned time sequence.

In 1967 Dr. Edward P. Lanning and Dr. Thomas C. Patterson did at last discover in Peru an undisturbed layer-cake order of artifacts at what had been long ago a quartzite quarry and workshop. In the bottom and therefore earliest layer, thought to be about 14,000 years old, were found the familiar choppers and burins. Two layers above them lay long leaf-shaped points. Struck in large, thin flakes from glassy stone lumps, they had been carefully finished on both sides. They were, to use the specialist's term, bifacial. Bifacial flaking is the hallmark of later craftsmen, craftsmen who, in this area, lived some 11,000 years ago. Still higher levels, containing tools of even later vintage, give this site great value. Since men came first to the northern continent, a layered site there—when and if it is found—should yield even earlier dates. The picture grows clearer every day. But further proofs are needed.

We can be absolutely sure of man's residence in the New World around 15,000 years ago. His rugged bones and his skull caps, long rather than round like those of men today, have been uncovered in several sites. The most ancient of these dates back 17,000 years. Certainly his bifacial weapons have turned up everywhere in the New World, frequently in clearly layered sites, frequently embedded in the very bones of his prey—mammoth, mastodon, giant sloth, and the Ice Age bison, long-horned and huge. New World men of 15,000 years ago were big-game hunters, and they killed in quantity. Organizing themselves into great surrounds, yelling, waving torches, rushing from the line of advance to wound a great beast, they effectively stampeded groups of mammoths and whole herds of bison over cliffs, or into swamps where they were conveniently mired, or into narrow arroyos where they could be slain at leisure. The record of many such stampedes and mass kills has been uncovered, most often in the Great Plains. Sometimes the picture is so clear, so complete that the archaeologist has been able to estimate the direction in which the herd had been driven, the way the wind had been blowing on the fatal day, the month of the year, and the number of hunters in on the kill.

No doubt it was the use of fire in surrounds and the tight organization of hunting parties that allowed the men of 15,000 years or so ago to thrive and spread themselves quickly over the New World. But it might also have had something to do with their weaponry. Craftsmen then made, as we have suggested, projectile points of glassy stone, carefully flaked on both sides to make flat, broad, wicked blades altogether different from the crude chopper-cleavers of the earlier folk. And yet, do the newer weapons simply represent an evolution from older types of New World manufacture? Or were they borne by a later wave of people out

Folsom points   *Clovis point*   *Simplest willow-leaf design*   *Magellan point, South America*

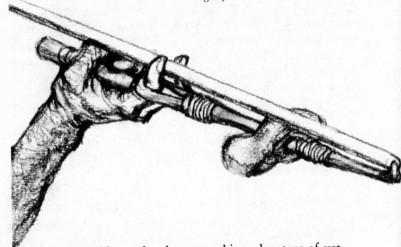

Atlatl *(spear-thrower); note "banner stone" weight for balance in throwing.*

of the Old World, people who were taking advantage of yet another interstadial open door?

Both theories have their champions. Professor H. M. Wormington believes she can trace the progress of bifacially flaked tools and weapons from an origin point in southwest Siberia where less advanced tool manufacturers could have come in contact with people who had developed the techniques of bifacial flaking and followed the big-game hunting tradition. For neither had developed in eastern Asia itself. From southwest Siberia, Dr. Wormington believes, the new techniques spread by way of Lake Baikal into the zone of choppers and cleavers. There old and new styles mingled, and the hybrid tool types were then carried to the Lena River and from there eastward, ever closer to Beringia. Interesting sites in Siberia and in Alaska lend strength to the theory of an Old World origin for American bifacial tools. One group of tools and weapons, uncovered by Dr. Robert L. Humphrey in 1966, mingled fluted points with blades surprisingly similar to a type made in Europe during late Paleolithic times.

Whether brought to the New World, however, or invented in it, American bifaces soon developed characteristics which were uniquely their own. In the mountains of the northwest a point shaped rather like a willow leaf became fashionable. Made in what is often called the Cascade style, this type of point seems to have traveled by way of the mountain chain into South America. Tools associated with the Cascade point suggest a life way which involved a good deal of fishing and gathering as well as hunting. The whole culture can be styled the Old Mountain Tradition.

The big-game-hunting way of life seems to have had its center on the Great Plains. It was here that another distinctive style of point was developed from the bifacial prototype —the Clovis point, so called because it was near Clovis, New Mexico, that such weapons were first uncovered. Typically about four inches long, the Clovis point is distinguished by its concave appearance. Once a point had been properly shaped, the craftsman liked to finish it off with fluting. About a quarter of the way up from the base on both sides he tapped off several large flakes. This operation made the center of the point almost as thin as its outer edges. Some specialists believe this fluting was intended to provide the kind of blood channel one sees on hunting knives today. Others feel it made for easier hafting, probably to spear shafts whose deadly thrust was given extra power by the spear-thrower. Many millennia later, when conquistadors invaded Aztec Mexico, they quickly learned that spears driven by a spear-thrower, or *atlatl*, could pierce armor. In Clovis times such spears pierced mammoth hides, for spearmen on the Great Plains then were almost exclusively mammoth hunters. But when the peculiar Clovis techniques spread eastward they seem to have been carried by men who chose to hunt the forest-dwelling mastodon. At the height of its popularity, perhaps 12,000 years ago, the fluted-point tradition seems to have been followed by hunters nearly everywhere in North America and down into Mexico.

Clovis hunters were successful at their trade—altogether too successful. Shortly after 9000 B.C., the lumbering, slow-breeding mammoths, the camels, and the horses vanished from the New World—hunted to extinction, perhaps—and hunters took to using projectile points more suited to other game beasts. The most popular game on the Great Plains became the bison (*Bison orientalis*), a breed smaller than the older *Bison antiquus* but, even so, more formidable than the still-to-come *Bison bison*, which would be hunted by the Plains Indians of more recent times.

The new projectile points were smaller and more finely flaked, perhaps with the use of pressure, a method almost never used in Clovis techniques. Best known is the Folsom style, so called because the first of its type was found near Folsom, New Mexico. Folsom points were definitely wider at mid-section than at the base, which was often shaped to give a suggestion of ears. The art of fluting had been improved so much that the Folsom craftsman was able to remove the very large central flake with a single tap. The Folsom style in its heyday (probably 9000 to 8000 B.C.) was never widely popular the way Clovis had been. It was rarely used in the east, and even on the Plains other unfluted points were manufactured as often as the elegant Folsom ones.

Flaked points in South America were never fluted and are often more reminiscent of the old Cascade points than of the Plains hunting arsenal. It may have been by way of the western mountain spine that people using bifacial points made their way south. By at least 9000 years ago, people using fishtail-shaped bifacial points had certainly reached Patagonia and Tierra del Fuego at the tip of South America. Such points have been found in a cave there, very clearly in association with the bones and dung of the ground sloth and extinct horse. There were other weapons in use as well—the bola, for example, a rounded stone with the center area grooved to hold a long leather thong. The use of bolas seems to have been general, though spotty, all through the

Americas. Always a second line of defense at that time, the bola would one day become the favored weapon of later hunters of the South American plains.

Hunters using weapons of the newer, smaller, bifacial types were no less successful than their Clovis predecessors had been. So plentiful was the game, so organized were the hunting surrounds, that some groups were able to settle down in permanent villages on the Plains. The remains of one such village have been found near Albuquerque, New Mexico, on the shores of a now-vanished lake. To Dr. Frank Hibben, the excavator of the site, the round floors of Folsom living areas look for all the world like the rings left on the ground by the tipis of later Indians of the Plains.

The long season of plenty was not to last. Whether there was a change in the climate, as some specialists suggest—a progressive drying out beginning sometime around 8000 B.C. —or whether it was again man's efficient capacity for over-kill, most of the remaining big-game animals gradually died out. The human population of the Great Plains dwindled too, its remnants clinging fiercely to the old ways of life long after the need for change had become acute, long after others had moved in different directions.

By 5000 B.C., in what archaeologists call the Archaic Period, technology everywhere had undergone yet another transformation. In the North American woodlands, smaller projectile points, beautifully shaped, notched, and tanged, had been developed. For by then men had taken to hunting birds and small game and to fishing and wild plant gathering, and they needed tools and weapons on a less heroic scale. At some later time, too, came the momentous invention of the bow and arrow, which also required a small stone projectile point. Ornaments of polished bone came into vogue, and later stone itself was polished and ground. In South America, too, the change to small projectile points suggests their use on small prey.

Toward 2500 B.C., the appearance of grinding stones attests to the importance of seeds and nuts in the diet of America's populations. In very few places was there the kind of year-round abundance that had permitted Folsom hunters to settle in villages. Most men now wandered seasonally and would continue to do so in the Canadian woodlands until long after the Europeans came. They were well fed, it is true, but never in the princely quantity of the big-game-hunting days, and never without hard labor every day.

Sometime after 2500 B.C. conditions improved. Yet another breed of bison thundered along the old Plains trails worn by the hoofs of the vanished herds that had preceded them. The bow and arrow, so lethal and efficient, traveled west, and suddenly out on the Plains the old big-game-hunting ways—never entirely forgotten—were revived. The dog, perhaps brought to the Plains from the eastern part of the country or by newer people migrating from Asia, was adopted as a beast of burden and a help in the hunt. Again the great surrounds were brought into use; again herds were stampeded over canyon rims or into man-made pounds.

And then came the Spaniards, who brought back to the New World an animal long extinct in it—the horse. On the grasslands of both continents, men who had hunted on foot became mounted hunters leading again a life of plenty based on a single game animal. Lords of the Plains they were, warriors and wanderers so proud and free that their image has become in our minds the image of all American Indians.

The Blackfeet

Lords of the Northern Plains

They travel like the Arabs, with their tents and troops of dogs loaded with poles. . . . When the load gets disarranged, the dogs howl, calling some one to fix them right. . . . They are a kind people and not cruel. . . . They do not live in houses but have some sets of poles which they carry with them to make some huts at the places where they stop, which serve them for houses. They tie these poles together at the top and stick the bottoms into the ground, covering them with some cowskins [buffalo skins] which they carry around. . . . All their human needs are supplied by these cows, for they are fed and clothed and shod from these. They are a people who wander around here and there, wherever seems to them best.

This is what Coronado, the Spanish explorer and conquistador, saw in 1540 when his expedition reached the southern edge of the Great Plains. The grasslands there were black with "buffalo"—a species smaller than the ancient breeds of bison which had been tracked, surrounded, and stampeded by Clovis and Folsom hunters, but still quite formidable enough to be reckoned big game. As in the ancient days, buffalo were the prey of men who staked their whole existence on what Coronado called "these cows," and not bare subsistence alone, but all the amenities of life—clothing, shelter, implements, and perhaps, as in later times, some things of religion as well.

If there is much in Coronado's report to illuminate what archaeology reveals of ancient life on the plains and of the successive groups of hunters who made it home, there is also much to illuminate the ways of hunters who lived after Coronado's time, men we know as the Plains Indians of our own time. The Spaniard's report, for example, speaks of what would one day be called pemmican:

> They dry the [buffalo] flesh in the sun, cutting it thin like a leaf, and when dry they grind it like meal to keep it and make a sort of sea soup of it to eat. . . . They season it with fat, which they always try to secure when they kill a cow.

All the Plains tribes of later years knew how to preserve meat in this manner. Dried, ground, mixed with fat and sometimes pounded chokecherries, packed tightly in hide containers, pemmican constituted the ideal iron ration, indispensable on the march and when hunting luck ran out. It was both nutritious and delicious (doubtless we would find it a taste that needed cultivation) and was as prized by tribes outside the Plains as by the plainsmen themselves. Gladly the outlanders traded sinew-backed bows and other useful items to obtain it. At least, this was true enough in the early days of Plains trade relations.

After Coronado's visit and as settlers from Europe landed along American coasts, more and more tribes poured onto the Plains—lured by the promise of the big-game-hunting way of life, perhaps also pushed by expanding tribes behind. All the major language groupings of North America eventually claimed representatives there. Some specialists call the major language divisions *phyla*. In biology, the term *phylum* describes a group of plants or animals which is, in its basic plan of organization, radically different from every other basic life plan. It is impossible, for example, to find evolutionary connections (except at the most distant and elementary level) between winged insects and animals with

ESKIMO-ALEUT

NA-DENE
Northwest: Haida, Tlingit, etc.
Athapascan: Chipewyan,
    Navajo, Apache, etc.

ALGONQUIAN-MOSAN
Algonquian: Ojibwa, Blackfoot, etc.
Mosan: Kwakiutl, etc.

MACRO-PENUTIAN
Penutian: California languages
Azteco-Tanoan: Many languages
    of Southwest, Great Plains,
    Great Basin, and Aztec civilization

HOKAN-SIOUAN
Includes some languages of Southwest, East,
    and Plains, notably Iroquois, Sioux, and Natchez

MAYOID
Possibly part of Macro-Penutian

MACRO-OTOMANGUEAN } Small independent

TARASCAN } major groups in Mexico

*Major Language Groups
of North America*

(*Source: G. L. Traeger;
map based on C. Coon*)

backbones. Each represents its own phylum. And so it is
with the major language phyla of North America. Each has,
or seems now to have, a radically different plan of organization—in sound, structure, and meaning. Each has its subdivisions, called superfamilies by many specialists, which we
shall term simply groups. There are currently thought to be
four major language groups, or phyla, in North America
(not counting the more recent Eskimo-Aleut). A few
small ones in Middle America may some day wind up as
subdivisions of one of the big four.

Not only were there representatives of the major language groups to be heard on the Great Plains, but there were
many mutually unintelligible languages within these major
groups. It was as if speakers of English, French, and Russian
(representing the Indo-European major language group) had
somehow opted to live alongside speakers of Turkish (representing the Ural-Altaic major group) and speakers of
Chinese and Burmese (representing the Sino-Tibetan major
group). Imagine all these different sorts of people, speaking different languages, but sharing a single way of life, a
hunting way of life, identical in all its parts. They shared
the same sort of dress and portable shelter (the tipi), the
same means of transport (dog power or woman power at
the time of Coronado's visit), the same ideas about religion
(the sun dance, the quest for visions), the same ideas about
warfare (the raid), the same sort of social organization
(family hunting bands, congregating as a tribe for a great
summer hunt), and the same dreams of glory (attaining
highest war honors, which could be demonstrated to all in
a special headdress). Imagine this, and you begin to see what
life on the Great Plains was all about.

All the many Plains tribes—so different from one another
and yet so much the same—were forever encountering one
another, fighting, trading, and forming short-lived and shifting alliances. And through it all, no common spoken language was ever devised; plainsmen were too proud to desert

their mother tongues. They did manage to communicate, however, by a system of gestures—the solemn sign language familiar to Boy Scouts and devotees of movie Westerns. According to Coronado, the Plains people were already using this form of communication when he arrived ("They are able to make themselves very well understood by means of signs"). Presumably the need for some sort of universal language was even then as great as it would be in later times. Converts to the Plains way of life would never be lacking as long as the buffalo remained.

Exactly which of the southern tribes Coronado encountered on his journey we do not know. He moved in an easterly direction from what is now New Mexico. Perhaps he saw the Texas Caddo, or the Tejas, who lived at the Plains' edge; perhaps he met the Pawnee, a village people who hunted only part of the year. Perhaps he saw the Kiowa, whose language has no close relatives either in or outside the Plains, or the Comanche, moving steadily down from the Rockies. No matter. The meeting was fateful, whatever tribe he encountered, for it gave the Indians their first glimpse of the horse—an animal that was to quicken and intensify the Plains way of life, if not to transform it altogether.

Within a hundred years, the foot Indians of the southern Plains had become equestrians—mounted warriors, almost centaurs. Although new to the skills of horsemanship and new to the demands of animal husbandry, the Indians quickly learned to do things with horses the Spaniards had never dreamed of doing. They could break animals easily, gentle them to quiet obedience, and put them through paces. They could stick on a horse's back without benefit of saddle or stirrups, all the while thundering after a herd of buffalo, hands busy with bow and arrow, thoughts locked on the prey. In battle they learned to use their mounts as shields, hanging from their lee sides and shooting from under their necks. They learned to retrieve their dead and wounded from the field without ever dismounting, sometimes without even breaking stride.

With the advent of the horse, Plains life moved at a faster pace and on a grander scale. No longer did the Indian, unmounted and slow, have to compensate with guile for the buffalo's speed and elusiveness; the horse became the great equalizer. Even during the summer hunts (echoes of the old ways), when a rigid hunting discipline was enforced by camp

police, each man could hunt on his own and kill his own buffalo, to be later identified by the feathers of the fatal arrow. Earning a living became not only easy but joyous. There was abundance for all, and many tribes moved out onto the Plains to have a share. Such peoples as the Cheyenne and Sioux, gatherers who had turned farmers, became in turn hunters; they were joined by Great Basin gatherers such as the Nez Percé and the Shoshoni, and other Plains villagers, some of whom discarded farming altogether for the buffalo chase.

With the advent of the horse, the nature of Plains warfare also changed. The thin lines of opposing infantry slugging it out from behind rawhide shields gave way to mounted cavalry attacks. Attention focused on the individual warrior and his courage, even his bravado, and the appearance of guns in the West only intensified the trend. Guns

made killing easy, too easy for the man bent on acquiring renown. Soon it became far more honorable to carry into battle a bow rather than a gun, a lance than a bow, a hatchet or war club than a lance. Bravest of all was to go armed only with a harmless twig. Simply to touch a better-armed enemy with this twig and leave him alive earned a warrior far more credit than to kill and take many scalps for trophies. No matter how pressing the battle, men were never too busy to notice exactly how many braves counted coups (touches, light blows) on the same enemy. Some tribes allowed three men to touch, some four—and woe to the man who later boasted about a questionable coup or one counted out of order!

Men fought in battle for honors, but they went on raids for something very different. In the old days, the prehorse days, they had taken enemy women as prizes. In later days, they raided for horses, a feat of honor thought to be nearly as worthy as counting coups. This was because the horse soon became something much more than a big dog, useful in transport, hunting, and battle. The number of horses a man had (and the prodigality with which he gave them away) demonstrated at once his wealth, his courage, his capacity for wise and generous leadership, even the quality of his spiritual power. When a man died, his horses were sacrificed to accompany him in death. When a man wished to marry, horses were given to his prospective in-laws to show his bounty and to honor his intended spouse. When a man held a grievance against another, horses satisfied the debt.

The way in which plainsmen regarded the horse differed, as one might suppose, according to the ease of their acquisition. In the South, where the soft Spanish forts and the rancherias of the Spanish colonials made easy pickings for the Kiowas and their allies, the Comanches, personal horse herds of a hundred animals or more were not at all uncommon. And among the Kiowa, men born to high rank not only possessed many more horses but had ample opportunity to augment their herds. Ranking families could each afford to maintain a "beloved child"—a spoiled youngster on whom and in whose name horse wealth was squandered in displays of conspicuous waste meant to ruin ranking rivals and their own "beloved children." Kiowa and Comanche horses were given away in droves. The Comanche were extremely partial to young horse for dinner, and even the Kiowa were not above occasional feasts of horseflesh (something the northern tribes would have considered scandalous). Little care was given to the lamed horse or to aiding the natural increase of the herds. And why should it have been? Easy come, easy go.

Among tribes of the central and northern Plains very different attitudes prevailed. The Cheyenne, and to a lesser extent the Crow and the Plains villagers, had to concern themselves with herd increase and with the capture of wild strays as well. Raids on the rich Kiowa and Comanche herds required long travel. The big horse centers were far to the south, and the northern winters were long and cold. And there was trade to be had close to home—trade with white men at the forts and posts. For horses and furs, the white men were willing to give guns and metal pots, glass beads and blankets, and best of all, whisky. No wonder the Cheyenne soon ignored the middlemen of the villages and began themselves to buy and sell throughout the Plains. To them the horse soon became, not a mark of prestige, but quite simply, cash.

If the horse was honor to the Kiowa and money to the Cheyenne, to the Blackfeet of the northern Plains it was something of a love object. Perhaps this was because the Blackfeet had had their mercantile talents awakened by the fur trade. They were shrewd bargainers over pelts and industrious hunters and trappers of fur-bearing animals (except for beaver, which were sacred to the Blackfeet). Blackfoot women were even more industrious, busy day in and day out with the dressing of the pelts. In the interests of increased production, Blackfoot social organization underwent something of a change. In the old prehorse days, a Blackfoot warrior had been wont to take only one wife, at most two. But with the demands of English traders around Hudson's Bay for more and more furs, some canny Blackfeet accumulated squads of women all turning out processed pelts in factory style.

Blackfoot horses had dragged many a fur-laden travois to the trading post, but they had never figured in trade and never would. The courageous, intelligent buffalo horse, the steady battle mount, and the brood mare were treated with special tenderness, to be sure, and many a Blackfoot wept openly, uncontrollably, at the death of a favorite. But all the horses in a man's herd (perhaps forty or fifty for a well-to-do brave) were, as anthropologist John Ewers tells us, personally petted by the owner at least once a day. If a horse broke a leg, he was not shot but treated, kept for a pack horse if his leg healed properly, for a pet if he limped. Even old horses, past their years of service, were affectionately tended until they died. Much care and forethought was devoted to breeding, gelding, and doctoring horses. There were general tonics, tonics precautionary against chills, tonics for colic and distemper, and strong stimulants. There was even a Horse Medicine Society, a powerful and secret cult whose members—men or women—could heal both horse and human ailments and were empowered to give magical protection in battle. Herbs and powders, both magical and practical, were used in the curing rites, but the most powerful of all their procedures was the Horse Dance, in which initiates imitated horses, prancing around an altar and consuming special foods.

As men imitated horses, Blackfoot horses were also made to imitate men in the Riding Big Dance. When a comrade's death cried out for vengeance, whenever a large scalp raid was planned, then the drums beat a special cadence, sum-

moning the warriors out of the darkness and into the leaping
firelight. They would converge on the camp from the cardinal directions, painted, armed, and feather-crowned, riding
their favorite mounts, as painted, as bedecked as themselves.
As the drum songs grew wilder, the men dismounted to
dance on foot—each warrior beside his horse, each horse
stepping, prancing, keeping pace beside his man.

The identification of man and mount was a familiar theme
in Blackfoot lore. They believed that as men survived death,
as men possessed spiritual powers (some more than others),
so too with horses. The horse, they said, dreams as a man
does and may transmit power to a man through dreams. It
was a usual thing for plainsmen everywhere to fast and pray
for dreams, dreams in which their own talismans, their own
"medicines," their own sacred emblems were revealed. Men
often traveled long distances alone, tormenting the body,
offering the sacrifice of finger joints and hair to the great
powers of earth and sky and animals, praying to learn what
potent objects and symbols should be collected in a personal
"medicine bundle." The Blackfeet went on dream quests
too, but some among them claimed to have learned from
their own horses how to dream, how to grow strong and
brave, and how to attract supernatural protectors.

It was sometime around 1730, according to tradition,
that the Blackfeet first saw horses, and they still remember
the circumstances. A war party of Shoshoni attacked them
on horseback, killing many young braves. The Blackfeet
called on their Cree and Assiniboin allies who were in contact with traders and could bring guns to equalize the
Shoshoni advantage. Soon after the battle that followed,
the Blackfeet had their first leisurely look at a horse—
leisurely because the animal was dead. They marveled and
admired and at last gave it the name Elk-Dog, because it was
large and beautiful like the one and domesticated like the
other. Soon after that they acquired horses of their own.
Whether the horses were captured from the Shoshoni or

bought with buffalo hides and pemmican from Plateau tribes to the west, no one knows. But one thing is certain: with the acquisition of horse and gun, the Blackfeet soon became the absolute lords of the northern Plains, feared and avoided by all.

Just how and when Blackfeet came to the Plains is not known, but it is safe to say that they are old-timers there. It is possible that Blackfeet had anciently held the north at a center not too far from the land they came to occupy in later times—a long arc from the Montana Rockies into Saskatchewan near the Eagle Hills. Now it is also true that the Blackfeet speak one of the Algonquian languages, a group of some prominence in the eastern woodlands. Other Algonquian speakers on the Plains were the Cheyenne, Arapaho, Plains Ojibwa, Plains Cree, and Gros Ventre, all of whom are known to have been woodland migrants of recent or more ancient arrival. Perhaps the Blackfeet had also traveled west. Moreover, there is a persistent tradition of rough pottery, and the certainty that Blackfoot men had once (before trading days) planted tobacco to be cere-monially smoked in pipes of soft stone. This might suggest a village background somewhere in the forest or on the Plains' edge. It might, however, merely indicate the spread of influences from the farming East, just as certain games, slat armor, and the sinew-backed bow almost certainly came to the Blackfeet from the Plateau folk to the west.

To counter the suggestion of village heritage, there is the fact that Blackfeet are not known ever to have planted any-thing other than tobacco and have no tradition of settled homes, canoes, or burial mounds. There is also the matter of Blackfoot language. Though it belongs to the same group (Algonquian) as Cheyenne, Arapaho, and Gros Ventre, it is rather different from them and from the other Algon-quian languages spoken farther to the east. Some of the Blackfoot linguistic traits are to be found in Kutenai, a

Plateau language belonging to the Algonquian-Mosan major group but forming a subdivision all its own. Differences and similarities, taken all together, seem to indicate for the Black-foot language a long separation from its sister languages to the east and for speakers of Blackfoot a very long residence on the Plains.

Always they have called themselves *Siksikauwa*, which means "the Black-footed People." Nobody knows just how the name came to be applied—black-dyed moccasins per-haps, or merely muddy feet. Plainsmen are much given to nicknames.

The Blackfeet have been historically divided into three tribes: the Blood, the Northern Blackfeet, and the Piegan—always the cutting edge in any southern foray. The three groups rarely met save in time of need, for there was no political machinery to bring them together. The word "tribe" when applied to plainsmen indicates a shared lan-guage and a common body of customs and ideals—not a formal government run by formally empowered leaders. Indeed, there were few political forms of any sort among the Blackfeet (or among any of the plainsmen, for that matter)—no hierarchies of chiefs, no hereditary sachems. What leadership there was fell to men of superior courage or wisdom, or to men possessing great horse wealth, and even then such a leader could only influence, never rule. Everything was accomplished through the advice and con-sent of various groups of able men, and this custom was as binding for the summer "chieftain" of the tribe as for the leader of a family band.

The band was the basic unit of residence, the cooperative work party, and the wandering group a man called home. It was family, though not rigidly so. Based on related men, the band nevertheless welcomed sisters and their husbands, cousins, various in-laws, and even those for whom no stretch of the imagination could produce a relationship. These groups called themselves whatever they liked, names such as "Sharp Whiskers," or "They Don't Laugh," or even "Skunks."

In October each band moved from the open plains into its own chosen river valley, its own patch of woods, seeking the cottonwood bark on which its horses could survive and protection from the blizzards to come. When the ground lay thick with snow, Blackfoot band members hunted afoot more often than not, driving the buffalo (as in ancient times) over cliffs or into pounds made of sticks. But as horses became more numerous, this technique, even in wintertime, fell into disuse. Animals besides the buffalo were hunted: deer, elk, bighorn sheep, and pronghorn for their fine supple skins, their horns, and their meat; the grizzly for the strong medicine of his claws (*never* for meat); the eagle for his sacred feathers; the weasel for his fur, used in decorating headdresses; and many other animals whose skins were used in trade, but whose flesh was not considered fit food for a Blackfoot. Fish and fowl, amphibians and reptiles were also taboo as food. To the Blackfeet only buffalo meat was "real" food, nourishing food; and fortunately there was plenty to go around.

In the wintertime men passed the weary hours with gambling and with games played with rackets and balls. Boys coasted down snowbanks on strips of hide. Girls played with dolls that had real horsehair on their heads.

When the first geese began to fly north again, when the buffalo began drifting out of the valleys, then the Blackfeet themselves moved joyfully back toward the open plains. All winter the flesh of cows and calves had been preferred, but in June the bulls were prime, and the Blackfoot bands gathered together in their tribal groups, eager for the great summer hunt.

Women pitched their tipis in a great circle, each band in its own allotted section. Nightly each age group would come together to dance and to recount brave deeds. There were seven of these age groupings. At the proper time a young man, or his father in his behalf, would buy membership in the first group, the Mosquitoes. Then every five years or so thereafter he would buy a new membership from a man in the next higher grade. Successive "graduations" were purchased, and so it was that a man progressed through grades in the school of life, learning new duties, acquiring new honors, yet always accompanied by his original group of boyhood friends, who purchased their own "graduations" at roughly the same time.

During the time of the summer encampment, the tribal chief (usually the head of the largest band) would ask one or two of the age groups to act as police, keeping order in camp, maintaining discipline on the hunt, and leading in the war parties that were nearly always part of the summer schedule. Here was a foreshadowing of political organization; sporadic of course, seasonal, plagued by intergroup rivalries, but in its limited way effective.

In early August came the Sun Dance. Now, among the Blackfeet the sun was considered one of the great spirits but in no way a god. The Sun Dance was not held in honor of the sun, though the dancers did stare heavenward a good deal. Nor was it held in honor of Old Man, a trickster god who had in the beginning brought up lumps of clay from the watery deeps, formed them into men, and then gone away, laughing at his little joke. The Sun Dance was simply a ritual of great power. Properly performed it could heal and it could bind.

Always the Sun Dance was sponsored by a good woman of unimpeachable reputation who wished to cure a loved one, to win some mighty purpose, or to fulfill a vow. In her honor and to honor themselves, young men suffered the skin of their chests to be slit, to be fastened by skewers and ropes to the great lodge post of the Sun Dance House, built of brushwork and open to the sky. And around this post they danced night and day, jerking at their bonds until they broke free. During the week-long ceremony, minor social dances were also held and minor rituals observed. Men met at this time to buy and sell powerful medicine bundles, those precious talismans assembled under the direction of dreams or perhaps obtained from other men. During the Sun Dance period young people met and marriages were arranged.

The Sun Dance came late to the Blackfeet, who learned it from the Arapaho and Gros Ventre. Was it an old ceremony or a new one? Was it the invention of the Plains village people or of the nomads themselves? Had it been present, in one form or another, during the old prehorse days, or had it developed as an expression of the new life— the more abundant life that the horse had made possible? There are only guesses to be had, not answers. All that is known for sure is that the Sun Dance, in one form or another, became common to nearly all the Plains tribes. Among them, it was the power of the Sun Dance, the great summer hunt, and the summer raids that called bands together after the long winter separation and made them truly one.

True to Blackfoot tradition, the horse was a participant in many rituals of the Sun Dance. He was a valued friend, and he is still a friend to the Blackfeet. The last buffalo has gone; most of the land has been lost to the white man in Montana and Canada. Many Blackfeet have left the Plains and are strangers to its ways and its ancient heritage. But for those who remain, the horse remains—still a thing of beauty and a joy forever.

3
The Tehuelche
Lords of the Patagonian Plains

In South America there are also great plains divided (as the North American plains are divided) in two parts, one flat and lush with grass, one more hilly and arid. The land between the Argentine Río Negro and Río de la Plata is broad and level and green in the January warmth. Farther south the land rolls at the edge of the plateau. There are hills, and far in the distance one can glimpse the Andes, rising like white spires against the sky. There is seldom much grass, for this is steppe country, in some parts arid and everywhere cold. Two seasons are known there (so said an English traveler long ago)—a hard winter and a bad spring. Sleet falls often, even out of season, and yet, in the midst of the uninviting plains, here and there are sheltered valleys in which grow bushes and trees filled with the cooing of hidden doves.

Both the southern and the northern portions of this Argentine plain once swarmed with game: the rhea, a large flightless bird very like an ostrich, and the guanaco, a wild relative of the native llama standing three to four feet tall at the shoulder and weighing 200 pounds. Ferdinand Magellan, the Portuguese nobleman whose ships first circumnavigated the globe, claimed the guanaco was "like unto a mule with the body of a camel and the tail of a horse." Others have added, with truth, that it also has "the wool of

a sheep, the feet of a deer, and the swiftness of the devil."
Disconcertingly, its jaws sport two large, un-camel-like tusks.
Preying on these furred and feathered herds was the puma,
the native American lion. And preying on all three was the
South American plainsman.

In the northern regions, called the Pampas, there once
lived several tribes of wanderers: the Querandi, the Charrua,
and the Puelche. On the cold southern plains lived the
Tehuelche, whose outsized feet were to give their land a
name. It was in 1520 that Europeans first encountered the
Tehuelche. Magellan's sailors had dropped anchor at an inlet
they named Port St. Julian. Down to the shore trooped men
of gigantic stature, "larger and taller than the stoutest man of
Castile," wrote Antonio Pigafetta, Magellan's chronicler.
They were dressed in cloaks of skin and wore hide shoes
that left so large a print in the sand that the sailors dubbed
the people Patagones, "Big Feet." And to this day, the land
from the Río Negro to Tierra del Fuego is known as
Patagonia.

Pigafetta also noted the Tehuelche tents of hide and
sticks, their painted faces, the swiftness with which they
ran, their tools of sharpened flint, their guanaco decoys, and
their bows and arrows. Later, in one of those small acts of
violence that seem, unhappily, always to characterize the
meeting of cultures, two of the Indians were captured and
taken on board Magellan's ship, no doubt to be exhibited
back home. The remaining "giants" attacked the Spaniards
and were driven off with much difficulty. All the while they
and their lost comrades aboard piteously cried out the word,
"Setebos, Setebos!" The Spaniards thought Setebos must be
the name of their god. This bit of early ethnographic information traveled quickly around the Renaissance world and
later appeared in Shakespeare's play, *The Tempest*, in which
the crude and aboriginal Caliban says of his master Prospero,
"He could command my dam's god, Setebos."

The Tehuelche were not seen again until 1578 when Sir

Francis Drake, making landfall in Patagonia, declared they were not much taller than living Englishmen. (Later parties, bearing yardsticks, would establish 5 feet 10 inches as the Tehuelche average, but with some men towering over seven feet.) In 1579 the Spanish sea captain Pedro Sarmiento de Gamboa saw the Tehuelche; this time they were mounted on Spanish horses and were using for hunting weapons, not the bow and arrow, but the lance and the bola.

Three hundred years later they had become, like Indians of the North American plains, horse herders, horse raiders, and formidable warriors. Unlike the northern plainsmen who had, because of the horse, come to emphasize the prowess of the single hunter pitted against a single beast, the Tehuelche had adopted the ancient techniques of the surround. A hunting party liked to spread out in a wide arc with knots of mounted hunters strung like beads along the line of shouting women and children. The arc was closed, fires were set to hold the game at bay, and the hunters dashed in to fell the trapped animals. Whether the surround was newly learned by the Tehuelche or whether it was part of the southern hunting heritage is not known. Its forms and techniques were duly reported, however, by the first man from the West to live with the Tehuelche. He was George Chaworth Musters, late of Her Majesty's Navy, and the year was 1871.

At that time all England was agog at Charles Darwin's adventures in the H.M.S. *Beagle* and at his subsequent writings. Everyone wanted to see primitive South America with its "savages," but while the coasts and their tribesmen attracted a respectable contingent of the curious, very few got into the interior. Musters was one of the first who did, and he stayed there nearly a year, traveling with the Tehuelche as they circled through their hunting grounds.

There exist only sketchy outlines of life on the North American plains in prehorse days. Such records are sketchier still for the Tehuelche, but in one respect, at least, we are fortunate. Until the early 1900s cousins of the Tehuelche lived on Tierra del Fuego, the one very large island at the tip of South America; they lived, moreover, in utter innocence of the ways of Western intruders or even of the newfangled notions of their northern relatives. These were the Ona, a tall, muscular people, hunters of guanaco, Indians lacking both canoe and horse, but bearing in their heritage persistent memories of large flightless birds and of horned animals (Spanish cattle, perhaps?)—both unknown in Tierra del Fuego.

Though the Ona and Tehuelche could not have understood one another's speech, the languages are closely allied. And the Ona live (though fewer than two hundred remain today) much as the Tehuelche must have lived in prehorse days. They hunted on foot. Part of their island was mountainous and heavily forested, though a small interior section was reminiscent of the Patagonian plain. The Ona stalked their chief prey, the guanaco, with the help of well-trained dogs. They butchered game on the spot, dividing it in prescribed ways between the hunter and his helpers (always the brisket to the chief hunter). The guanaco was all in all to the Ona, as was the buffalo to the hunters of the North American plains. From sewn guanaco skins was fashioned their shelter, called *kawi*. It was little more than a windbreak, sometimes three-sided, sometimes not quite that. (The Tehuelche shelter made of hides, called *kau* in the early days and later *toldo*, was scarcely more elaborate, though with horses available to carry the heavy skins from camp site to camp site, it could be much larger.) The Ona mantle was fashioned from sewn guanaco skins. The pelts were carefully prepared and treated and the skin side painted in bands of color or in geometric designs. The Ona wrapped himself in his mantle with all the dignity of a Roman senator. Because of the rain, the fur side was often turned out and the painted side in. Apart from this mantle, the well-dressed Ona wore little else save for his coronet of guanaco skin; his moccasins

*Major Language Groups
of South America*

*(Source: Joseph Greenberg's scheme as
presented in J. Steward and L. Faron)*

☐ UNKNOWN

■ HOKAN (Apparently related
to HOKAN-SIOUAN
major group of North America)

▥ MACRO-CHIBHAN
Chibchan (including Chibcha)
Paezan (including Atacama, and
Warrau of the Orinoco Delta)

▨ GE-PANO-CARIB
Macro Ge (Many languages of the forest
and Matto Grosso)
Macro-Panoan (including Charrua)
Hambicuarra (spoken only by one
group of hunters)
Huarpe (spoken only by a South Andean group)
Macro-Carib (once spoken in Lesser Antilles)
Taruma

▦ ANDEAN-EQUATORIAL
Andean (languages of Patagonia and
Tierra del Fuego, and those of
the Inca Empire)
Jivaro (spoken by people of the Montaña)
Macro-Tucanoan
Equatorial (including Arawak, spoken by Mojo, etc.;
Tupi, spoken by the Siriono, people of Paraguay,
and several others)

(in bad weather a large extra pair stuffed with grass served as overshoes); sometimes leggings ("quiver of the leg"); and his pubic covering. Made of foxskin, it was a sort of sporran, a detachable pocket in which were kept a spare bowstring and arrow makings, a supply of oily red paint used to protect his skin from chapping, a knife, and of course the flint, iron pyrites, and dried-fungus tinder with which he made fires. The Tehuelche, even in horse days, dressed similarly and painted their mantles. However, in the interests of good horsemanship they tied the mantles securely to their waists, and in the interests of saddle comfort, wore an undergarment, a sort of loincloth, which came very close to being short pants. High boots gartered to the waist were worn, though whether in imitation of the Spanish boots or as a derivation of the Ona-type leg quiver is not known. Over these in wet weather went moccasin overshoes, but neither was worn in camp, where men walked barefoot on the often sleety ground.

To complete the family costume inventory, Tehuelche women wore modest knee-length shifts of soft animal skin. Both Ona and Tehuelche women liked to paint their faces in tasteful designs. Tehuelche fashionables also doted on blue beads and silver trinkets, and extended their black braids with horsehair switches. Babies and young children were dressed in little or nothing—part of the toughening process, perhaps.

The Ona warred savagely, though on a small scale, in stubborn feuds that might last for years. Revenge or the capture of women—always in short supply—was the object. The Ona attitude toward women was always ambiguous, to say the least. They were wanted and needed, but also feared and, one suspects, hated a bit as well. Women were thought to be witches responsible for illness, misfortune, and death. It was women, said the Ona, who long ago had held the whip hand over the men. One day, so the legend goes, all the adult women and all the grown girls were slain by their resentful husbands and fathers. Only the small girl children were left alive. These, say the Ona, were brought up to respect men. To make sure this attitude prevailed forever, the Ona invented a series of frightful monsters. The men impersonated these creatures in solemn rites, called *Klokten*, emerging, horribly masked, from the forbidden recesses of the men's house to terrify the women and keep them in line. Boys were initiated by being whipped and tested and at last shown the secret of the masks, finding their manhood in becoming the monsters they once had feared.

One suspects that the Ona borrowed bits and pieces of this ceremony from their smaller fisherman neighbors, the Yahgan, who had somewhat similar ceremonies and ceremonial masks, though Yahgan women were far too important in the business of group survival to endure the nonsense prescribed by the Ona men's society. The Tehuelche, however, had no initiation ceremonies for boys and no frightful masks, but the onset of puberty for girls was celebrated in many pretty ways. The rite for girls seems to have reflected the prevailing attitude toward women. Unlike the Ona, Tehuelche men took only one wife at a time and were not given to wife-beating. Musters has told us how tender and indulgent they were with their women and how inconsolably they mourned a wife's death.

The Ona seem to have been made of sterner stuff. They tried not to laugh or cry, to accept with equal indifference both the cares and the joys of life. Elaborate decorum was required. Men did not interrupt one another, did not allow the visitor to show hunger or ask for food. Even ball games were played circumspectly. And in wrestling, the favorite sport, strict rules were in order: no gouging of eyes or ears, no hair pulling, no kneeing, no scratching, no biting. The man who got a grip with his teeth would be humiliated by loud cries. "Is it a dog?" the spectators would inquire.

In the hunt, the Ona used bow and arrow, though, as anthropologist Samuel Lothrop believes, there was some use

of the bola in later times. He sees this as evidence of an idea's trickling down from the north. Among the Tehuelche after the coming of horses, we know that the bow and arrow was discarded altogether in favor of the bola. Had this new weapon been in use all along—not so popular as the bow and arrow, perhaps, but available? Dr. Lothrop believes the use of the bola had been confined to the Charrua and Querandi of the Pampas. From them, he says, it passed to the Puelche among whom it was noted in 1599. With newer ways of hunting, the bola rapidly regained popularity and passed quickly to the Tehuelche in the south.

Musters, on the other hand, thought the bola (especially the single-ball variety) to be the original Tehuelche weapon. There was not enough usable wood about, he reasoned, to permit the manufacture of bows and arrows on a grand scale. Furthermore, though he saw many ancient bolas on the ground or in diggings, few ancient arrowheads were in evidence.

Archaeology seems to support both views. Certainly, says anthropologist Julian Steward, bolas were not in universal use in the Americas, but they have been found here and there in sites ranging from Alaska to Tierra del Fuego. Always in the layering of the earth the remains of blowguns and darts, bows and arrows lie above bolas, spears, and spear-throwers and are therefore later additions to man's ancient arsenal in the New World.

Certainly the bolas, both the two- or three-ball variety meant to trip the running feet of the hunter's quarry and the single-ball *bola perdida* with which one dispatched one's prey, were extremely useful in hunting the swift, agile guanaco and rhea (one cannot imagine using bolas for hunting buffalo). They were also used against pumas. From these three animals came the material staples of Tehuelche existence—weapons, musical instruments, clothing, shelter, the wherewithal for games and ornaments. But without doubt the rhea was esteemed as their favorite food, and in more ways than one. During certain seasons there were rhea eggs to be found, just one of which would provide a satisfactory meal for a hungry man or two. An egg was simply propped up with sticks in a small fire, a small hole was made at one end for the insertion of a stirring twig, and presently there was an omelet. The birds themselves were plucked, split, and trussed. Hot stones were placed in the body cavity and the whole laid on the fire. When the meat was done, one had only to untie the halves, each of which made a convenient platter for the broth within. Rhea fat was combined with dried, crumbled strips of guanaco meat to make something resembling the pemmican so prized among plainsmen of the northern continent.

While the conservative Blackfeet limited their preferred menu to buffalo meat, however, the Tehuelche liked variety. They shared with the northerners a common distaste for fish, but they very much liked horsemeat, especially the flesh of young mares. It is true, of course, that horses were eaten only when ceremony made sacrifice permissible—at the death of an owner or of his kin, at the puberty rites of a maiden, in thanksgiving for a deliverance from illness or misfortune. But, said Musters, excuses for ceremony were soon being invented. Even a boy's cut finger could provide an opportunity for horsemeat. It was particularly desired after a big party featuring rum taken from Spanish colonies at the plains' edge. Men who were thereby rendered unable to hunt indulged in an orgy of horse killing and horse eating, and everyone celebrated.

One might suppose that horses came always from the same source as the rum. The Tehuelche, like the Blackfeet, were raiders, fierce and feared. In vain did the Spanish, and later the Argentine, governors send uniforms to the chiefs of bands along with promises of rank in the Argentine army. The raids went on all the same.

Actually, there were often as many wild horses on the

plains as in the Spanish settlements. Over the long years many had escaped, had bred and multiplied. The very tall Tehuelche preferred these wild horses as mounts. They were bigger and speedier than their tame brethren in the settlements. Whether or not horses were loved and petted in the Blackfoot manner, they were certainly well trained. There must be, Musters thought, a sort of instinctual bond between the Tehuelche and his horse, for, said he, one never saw an Indian horse that was not perfectly quiet and biddable, except at the approach of a white man. Even the smallest child could ride his father's war mount with perfect confidence. Of course Tehuelche children, both boys and girls, learned to ride before they walked. The Tehuelche knew well how to tend sick horses, though they were not nearly as tenderhearted about it as the Blackfeet. Musters found the variety of horse gear impressive. All the items bore Spanish names (as did those used on the North American plains), but many were made in styles of Tehuelche invention.

As among Indians of the North American Plains, horses meant wealth and prestige, though women could own them as well as men. It was a man's pride to deck his horse in as grand a fashion as he did his own person. When groups of strangers met formally (their arrival having been heralded by messengers), they assumed their grandest array, rode straight at one another, and charged round and round the camp, shouting and shooting off their Spanish rifles until all possible antagonisms, all possible tensions had been quite worked away.

It is likely that the charging display had yet another, more religious significance, though Musters did not elaborate. It may have been intended to drive away the demon of ill luck and discord that ever attends the encounter of potential enemies. For it was by noise and by violent action that the Tehuelche sought to avert misfortune. Shamans, medical and religious practitioners, often directed a man's relatives to beat on the back of his skin shelter, screaming hideously all the while so that Gualichu, the demon who lives at the back of the *kau*, would be frightened away. Sometimes a parent might put his sick child naked on a horse and drive him up hill and down dale through wind and sleet, for Gualichu, said the Tehuelche, is essentially a lazy good-for-nothing who loves solid comfort. Take that away and he departs.

In the year that Musters lived among the Tehuelche he saw no prolonged religious ceremonies other than these and the puberty rites of young girls. He thought there might have been others in the Tehuelche tradition, and he was told that old men used to recite the history and lore of the people, but none of them did so in Musters's presence. It was not that the Tehuelche lacked interest in their beginnings. During their restless travels they showed Musters "God's Hill" with its many caverns from which, they said, all the living things on earth had first emerged. But after the creation, said the Tehuelche, God went away, careless of his creatures here below, leaving them to the malicious whims of Gualichu or of one another, for men died by the demon's hand or by the sorcery of their peers. When evil wishing was revealed by the local shaman, the named suspect was likely to be speared or shot, and a blood feud began that would endure for many years.

Musters called the Tehuelche "bright and open-faced" (and all the old records speak of their friendliness), but they were also suspicious, proud, touchy of their honor, and vain of their individuality. And they did not forget. A man with a score to settle might very well worm himself into a family's good graces, biding his time until the return blow might be struck and revenge taken. Fighting was the order of the day. Animosities blew up suddenly and for no apparent good reason (at least, none that Musters could understand). The guest who left a party early often took a circuitous route home in case some careless word spoken during the evening had invited ambush along the way.

Though etiquette was rigorous—one did not approach a family's tent without a small gift, never spoke a man's "real name," and always avoided one's father-in-law—social groupings were tenuous. If one did not like the headman of one's group, if he was highhanded and bossy, one simply joined another band where one had relatives. The chiefly title usually went to a man with many horses or to the most capable huntsman or war captain, but it was an empty title all the same. Because no one could agree on what leadership could or should be, groups larger than the band of a hundred persons or so seldom coalesced, and only in the event of war. They could not agree because always and forever each plainsman was a law unto himself. As one warrior cried, drawing himself to his full height though pierced by spears, "I die as I have lived—no chief orders me!"

A Blackfoot brave would well have understood that cry and the defiance behind it—the defiance of a man who, like the wind, may move where he will, the man who, fearing the Evil One though not other men, fights both to his last breath. All things considered, the plainsmen of both continents had much in common. Both knew the art of hide processing and preparation. Both wore large mantles of fur and painted the skin sides, though the southerners knew little or nothing of the tailoring applied to some skin garments in the north. Plainsmen both north and south made fire with iron pyrites and flint, while the forest and desert folk in between used fire drills. North American Plains Indians had used leather armor in the prehorse days, and the Patagonians were still doing so when Musters visited them. Plainsmen of both continents sent smoke signals. Both made pemmican. Both wore moccasins, though the forest folk between wore sandals. Like most peoples of the New World, they grew or collected tobacco and used it (smoked or licked from twigs) in solemn ceremonies, often in the cause of peace. Like most, they played games with balls made of rubber or of skin. Plainsmen, north and south, cut their hair and gashed their legs as a sign of mourning, but only the Charrua and Querandi of the Pampas cut off finger joints as did the Plains Indians of North America. The men of the Pampas are also said to have taken enemy scalps as trophies.

How are these similarities to be explained? An exchange of ideas between the two plains peoples is hardly to be imagined, for they had been separated since ancient times by oceans, by parts of two continents, by intervening peoples whose life ways had long since advanced beyond the hand-to-mouth existence of the hunter. For all its hardships, the hunting way is tenacious. People committed to its demands, people who have fully learned to exploit its possibilities are loath to change. They will, if necessary, suffer themselves to be pushed by more "progressive" groups into barren, out-of-the-way places that farmers do not know or cannot use, and there they persist in spite of all. The links between the plainsmen north and south may well represent a once common cultural chain that stretched between the Americas and included all the most ancient folk of the New World.

There is one more thing to be said. Men of the North American Plains and of the Pampas and Patagonia in the south lived and hunted in similar environments. The southerners acquired horses nearly a century before the northerners, but both adjusted in similar ways to the new wealth, the new, enlarged horizons that the horse made possible.

They also came to similar ends. Bit by bit, each was pushed back by encroaching white settlers and cattlemen. Each was decimated by the white man's diseases—northerners by smallpox, southerners by measles and influenza. Each at last massed for a final blow against the newcomers, and each was shattered in that effort for good and all.

What Tehuelche remain have no doubt been absorbed into the ranks of Argentine gauchos who, mounted on hardy Spanish ponies, work cattle over the wide and rolling plains where guanaco and rhea once fled the fire circles of mounted hunters. Yet at every gaucho's saddle hangs a reminder of those other men and their ways—the imperishable bolas.

The Ojibwa

Solitary Hunters of the Northern Woods

In the middle of northern Canada there is a language divide
—not the one which separates the French- and English-
speaking Canadians today, but one more ancient. To the
west of the divide (roughly in the Canadian state of Manitoba) one could hear in bygone times (and can still hear
today) languages of the Athapascan group, and one could
see (and can see today) men who seemed much more Asian
in appearance than the Indians on the eastern side of the
divide. It is likely that the Athapascan-speaking peoples came
late to the New World (perhaps after 3000 B.C.) and, like
their predecessors, pushed the older inhabitants aside or
moved past them.

Some speakers of Algonquian languages seem to have
been shunted east and south. Whatever the picture, life on
both sides of the language divide—all along the great arc of
woodlands, between the Eskimos of the polar north and the
farmers living to the south of the Great Lakes—life was
much the same everywhere and remained so into modern
times. It was a hunting life, though not exactly like that of
the big-game hunters. Men eagerly tracked moose and bear
but often had to settle for lesser prey. The animal luxuriance
of Great Plains and Pampas was absent in this forest arc; so
was the abject penury of the southern desert. There was
food to be had, though, and men worked hard for it, learn-

ing the while to relish a variety in nourishment that big-game hunters could never abide: fish, fowl, and rodents; the seeds of grasses, the sap of trees, and soups made of berries and lichens. Variety in diet demanded variety in the tool kit and hunting arsenal. Before the white man and his metals came along, people of the woodlands had used small projectile points, harpoons and barbs made of bone, and stone grinders and pounders. Before the first rough pottery appeared, there had been vessels of birch bark in which liquid could be made to boil by the addition of hot stones. So it had been in Archaic times just after the climate changed and the big-game animals died away. And so it was still with hunters in the Canadian woodlands when the English explorer John Cabot discovered Newfoundland.

There he encountered the Beothuk, whose language may not have been Algonquian at all but one of those remnant tongues recalling migrations so ancient as to be part myth. Certainly there were some odd and different things about the Beothuk—the shapes they gave their canoes, for example, or the designs they scratched on grave goods and personal ornaments—so different that at least one scientist of later times would suggest for the Beothuk a primary origin, not in Siberia, but in Paleolithic Europe. It is a possibility that can never be fully studied. Under the combined pressure of enemies, both European and Indian, the Beothuk died away.

On the mainland were the Algonquian Micmac, mortal enemies of the Beothuk. There were also the Abnaki, the Montagnais-Naskapi, the Penobscot, and scattered bands known simply as Algonquins. Along the center of the linguistic divide ranged the versatile Cree, some of whom ventured onto the plains and took up big-game hunting. In the middle, stretched along the upper Great Lakes from Niagara to Minnesota, were the strong and numerous Ojibwa.

Ojibwa means "people whose moccasins have puckered seams," an Algonquian word that in English or French sometimes sounded like and was spelled as Chippewa (it still is). The Ojibwa were great canoemen and great travelers, and being ideally situated at the crossroads of news and ideas, they were well acquainted with the various peoples around them. They knew well (and tended to imitate) the fierce Sioux, some of whom they had pushed out of the wood-lands and onto the plains. They had even heard of plains-men farther west, the "people whose feet have black soles" (the Blackfeet) and the "stone medicine men" (the Assini-boin). To the southeast lived people like the Huron who were more often friendly than not. To the southeast there were also enemies. All tribes of the Iroquois Federation were feared, but the Mohawk ("people who pursue in canoes," the Ojibwa called them) were especially hated. If the Ojibwa borrowed dances and deportment from the big-game-hunt-ing Sioux, they wanted something quite different from the farmers to the south. They wanted corn and precious to-bacco in trade for their own maple sugar. The idea of farm-ing itself did not appeal to the foot-loose Ojibwa; they were not moved to imitate Iroquois ways of grubbing a living from the land. Having developed their own hunting and gathering techniques to utmost efficiency, they were not about to begin all over again with something new.

The Ojibwa, widespread and numerous as they were, had gradually collected into four territorial groups, each having slightly different ideas and habits. There were the Ojibwa of the Lake Superior region, the "people of the large river mouth" around Manitoulin Island, the Ottawa of the Georgian Bay region, and the Potawatomi, "people of the place of fire," on what is now the Michigan side of Lake Huron. Beyond a community of ideas and outlook, beyond a shared language, these groups had no ties, political or other-wise, to bind them. Even among the bands in each of the four local groups, little more than nodding acquaintances prevailed. There were no age-grades as there were among the Blackfeet, no big yearly festival to bring people of a tribe together. There was only the clan system to give a vague sense of unity. Every Ojibwa belonged to his father's clan, bore clan names, wore clan markings, and honored the clan *dodam*, or totem, the special animal or plant that was its emblem. The outsider in a community stayed an outsider, ignored by all, until he could establish (or invent) clan connections. All a man's life he was supposed to feel especially close, to be especially kind, to fellow clansmen, and though real blood kinship was usually more imagined than real, he could never marry a clanswoman. As a result of this last rule, representatives of the various clans became rather evenly distributed throughout Ojibwa territory. Everywhere the clan had a good deal to say about a member's choice of spouse. If that member preceded his spouse in death, his fellow clansmen made very sure that the widow behaved herself. Beyond this general supervision of marriage, however, the clan had no responsibilities as a group. There were no specified clan leaders to order people about, no leaders even to offer clan prayers.

The band itself was merely a loose collection of families who chose to live closely together in the summertime. They did not work together, and there was no ruler to decide that they should. Each band had a chief, it is true, a brave or generous man who might be related to former chiefs. But he was neither manager nor judge—merely a sort of honorary mayor. In the long run, decent behavior among band members resulted from fear of supernatural punishment or very real threats of revenge. One thought twice about murder; the man's brothers were sure to start a feud.

The real core of life was the small, nuclear family—father, mother, growing children (real or adopted), perhaps a grandparent or an aging aunt. All others were to be counted strangers. Even in-laws were considered strange and potentially hostile. And why not? When a man died, his immediate family and his near clanmates declared that his wife had "destroyed" him and should therefore compensate his clan, laboring all by herself for several years to accumulate the death dues. Only then could she put off mourning clothes, wash carefully, and comb her hair. Only then would her husband's kin provide another husband. Should she remarry without permission or should she skimp the death dues, her slighted in-laws would punish her with humiliation and destruction of property.

No wonder, then, that parents prefer their children to marry cross cousins (or did in the old days). Anthropologists call the children of sisters or of brothers "parallel cousins." These, say the Ojibwa, are the same as real sisters and brothers. "Cross cousins" are the children of a mother's brother or a father's sister. They belong to different clans and are therefore not to be considered relatives at all—or are, at least, relatives of a rather different sort. A girl must always be "shy" with a brother (or male parallel cousin), minding her words and behaving with utmost reserve. But with her mother's brother's son, a girl can joke and bandy about the sweet nothings the Ojibwa call "talking cross cousin."

In the old days, the cross cousin was quite likely to be the first eligible male a girl encountered after reaching puberty, and therefore her first husband (though usually not her last). She and her family were isolated on their hunting grounds from November to March. Her nearest neighbors were usually her nearest kin—aunts and uncles and their families —though even they were not often in evidence. The families might manage to keep in touch only by signs: birch-bark pictures left in trees, pointer boughs broken on a bush, live coals sent flying on arrows like shooting stars in the night. In the snow and bitter cold of the northern winter, when men hunted hopefully for bear and beaver and moose, the game—even the small running things—were wary, snug in their dens, and hard to find. Too many hunters together could all too easily frighten the animals, and that would mean starvation for hunting families. Thus it was that a boy learned early to hunt by himself, bringing his game to a young sister for dressing in much the same manner as he would later bring it to his wife. And thus it was that winter hunting and trapping lands were individually owned. They could be inherited; they could be claimed from virgin woods; they could be loaned. But they were certainly not free to all. A hunter trespassed at peril to his life. It was not only the winter land that was privately owned—but also the winter fishing sites where men or their wives set nets into holes in the ice, and also the groves of maple trees from which they collected the precious sugar sap.

It was not always so, some specialists believe. The Ojibwa bands had not always dispersed and withdrawn into their constituent family groups, dependent on no one else. Before the white man came with his insistent demand for furs, the game had been more abundant. Then the Ojibwa had ranged farther in their rounds lest Shadow, who is the eye of Soul in all things great and small, warn the animals about man. In those times, say some specialists, each Ojibwa band had been more of a community, living and traveling together. Winter hunting lands had been band-owned, parceled into family holdings by the chief.

Other experts disagree. The isolation of Ojibwa families, they believe, is an aboriginal condition in the woodland north, as it still is among many of the polar peoples. They point to certain long-standing habits of sturdy independence which, among the Ojibwa, seem to go beyond isolation of the family to isolation of the self. Much of life has been and still is cast in terms of personal ownership and individuality —even when cooperative effort is clearly involved. The game a man kills is his own until he gives it to his wife to dress, at which point it becomes hers to dispose of as she will—theoretically, of course. Nobody will go hungry, but everybody knows it is *Mother's* food they are eating. In the

Ojibwa family, nothing is used, not a child's toy or a father's knife or a strip of hide, without first obtaining the permission of its owner.

The manner of Ojibwa life before the white man came may never be completely known. The fur trade was in full swing by the early 1700s. With it came European guns to use instead of arrows and steel knives instead of stone ones, and there were few careful observers around to record what changes followed. By the time anthropologists began to study groups of Ojibwa, individual male ownership of hunting grounds had long since become customary.

However much or little the traditional patterns changed with time, there was one thing that, for the Ojibwa, never changed: the long, harsh, inexorable northern winter. To survive it, Ojibwa women carefully wrapped and hid away some of the maple sugar made in March, carefully dried the catch of happy summer fishing, and diligently gathered berries to be pounded into thin sheets and dried. In late August they harvested the river-grass seeds we call wild rice. The first family to arrive at a likely stand of grass claimed it for their own, but nobody wanted to appear greedy about the sites they chose. Whether the yield from any given site was not sufficient for the number of people harvesting there or whether the wild rice itself was not nourishing enough, the fact remained that by bitter February, Ojibwa stores were nearly always exhausted. And then, unless Father could find meat, starvation faced each little family on its isolated trapping land.

A dearth of game in dead winter was never seen as a natural calamity. It was, said the sorely beset family, the work of a powerful medicine man, some shaman who had been offended by one of their number—by a pretty daughter who had refused his romantic attentions, by a father too quick to snub. It was he who had sent starvation to camp at the door of their round birch-bark wigwam. Starvation or worse. For, in Ojibwa eyes, there *was* something worse. The evil shaman could send *Windigo,* that terrible, grinning ice-skeleton who, working his way into a cursed man's heart, could make him long for human flesh, the flesh of his own close kin. Often enough in starvation winters men had turned to cannibalism, so the Ojibwa knew *Windigo* as a very real threat.

He could come, they said, not only at a shaman's bidding, but by his own evil design. Men and women of shaky mental stability might dream of *Windigo,* dream that they themselves were becoming *windigoes*—human representatives of the great cannibal giant. From both myth and fear were fashioned the form madness took among the Ojibwa. It was said that the potential human *windigo* could be recognized by his greedy eating habits and his lust for overmuch fat. Later such a one could be expected to fall into deep melancholy, emerging from it finally with a violent urge to kill and eat his relatives, who looked to him, every one of them, like lovely, fat beavers. In times of starvation, people feared their own families and feared that they themselves would turn cannibal. "Run, run!" a distressed young mother might cry out to her children. "You all look like beavers to me!"

Approaching madness, even in the summer months, caused many an old grandparent to demand death from his children. "Kill me quick with the hammer and burn me in my wigwam, or next winter I shall surely eat you." The *Windigo* could be killed, really killed, only by fire. It was the one murder nobody wanted to avenge.

However dread the winter, the Ojibwa were not without joy, without ceremony and rich seasons of revelry. Every autumn, led by its chief, the band celebrated a kind of All Souls' Day, honoring the dear departed with feasting, burnt offerings of food and drink, dancing, and merry games. Parents gave feasts to honor a son on the occasion of his first kill—however small it happened to be, however accidental the fatal shot.

Weddings were not celebrated. Indeed, the transition from the unmarried to the married state was so gradual as to be scarcely noticed. A boy earned permission to court his girl, visited at night, and gradually took up temporary residence with her parents until he could establish a new home. With the arrival of babies, however, naming ceremonies were staged that quite made up for the absence of a bridal feast. Old people known for the power of their spirit guardians were invited to name the new child. Like the good fairies at the christening of Sleeping Beauty, each old man or woman came to the cradle and whispered a name of power and accomplishment. These real names were never used in polite Ojibwa society, but the name emblems were hung like mobiles over the baby's head, encouraging dreams, encouraging the new little Shadow to see well what good things were in store, and to teach well what was expected of the new little Soul.

In spring there were all-night wakes for the winter dead (kept frozen until the ground was soft enough for digging graves). Men were buried with tobacco to pay their passage over the river of death and with food for the journey.

At graveside a great bonfire was built to light their way. Some men were given dogs to accompany them—always a white dog for a chief. Archaeology today reveals in the woodland graves of Archaic times the skeletons of men and dogs—even then sent together on the last journey.

Summer was the time for dances, often "owned" by individuals who made it possible for others to participate. In summer came the gambling, fierce and competitive, and the foot races (more gambling), and games—lacrosse for the men (lacking nothing of modern football's exertion and brutality), and for the women a kind of squash (no picnic, either).

At summer's end there were offerings to the sun and moon—pinches of tobacco, the fragrant smoke of ritual pipes, and the sacrifice of white dogs. Then, too, came meetings of the Grand Medicine Society, the fraternal order of curing which anthropologist Diamond Jenness thinks was peculiar to the Ojibwa, though granting that the age-graded soldier societies of the Plains people may have had some influence. For the Grand Medicine Society had grades of advancement, each with its successively more difficult lore and technical instruction, up to the final grades in which the rich and unscrupulous man (or woman) might learn to make medicine for evil.

Anyone with the requisite fees and the willingness to undergo initiation, sweat baths, and long apprenticeship could join the society. Sick people cured by society members were automatically inducted; their medical bills were simply paid as initiation fees. Powerful shamans also joined the society, not because they really approved of group practice, but because the society was something to fall back on when their own supernatural powers were on the wane. When in good form, they preferred to make house calls alone—always with the fee firmly settled in advance and with the understanding that additional treatment would entail still higher fees. Each shaman usually chose to specialize in a certain curing technique. At the bottom in terms of prestige was the herbalist. More admired was the shaman who relied on sound effects or who sucked from his patient's body the foreign object thought to be causing the illness (an object which, of course, had been previously secreted in the shaman's mouth). The diviner was surely the most admired of all. In a trance he learned which evil shaman had separated the patient's Shadow and Soul and let sickness in. For, in Ojibwa thought, Soul ordinarily lived somewhere near the heart and was exceedingly vulnerable in its mantle of earthly flesh. It relied on the tutelage of Shadow who resided behind the eyes and saw all. After the body's death, Soul lived on in happy realms, while lonely Shadow lingered forever near the body's grave. But in life Shadow and Soul had to be inseparable lest their common body sicken and die. For the shaman who reunited Shadow and Soul in a young girl nothing was too good, including the girl herself. Her life had been placed in his hands, and she could scarcely refuse marriage, however ancient her savior might be.

Hardly anybody, in fact, dared to say "No" to a shaman. In a society where men were touchy of their pride, seldom smiling and given to imagining insult in another's most innocent gesture, where men sought immediate revenge (actual or spiritual) and asked questions later, the shaman was the Ojibwa male at his most potent and most powerful. A careless word, a giggle, or insufficient respect might seem, to the shaman, ample grounds for sending paralysis or *Windigo*. Usually the victim was informed that such-and-such a punishment was on the way, and expectation would guarantee results.

Of course, the shaman paid a price for power, as all men must in one way or another. Evil, said the Ojibwa, rebounds in time against the sender of evil. Nobody was surprised when the children of shamans died in bad ways, when their babies were stillborn, or when they were left childless. And when a string of such tragedies occurred in the wigwam of a powerful shaman, people knew that he had been practicing sorcery on the sly.

Among the Ojibwa it was always men and the duties and activities of men that were most honored and extolled. From birth a boy was taught to be brave, to be willing to risk his life for things unessential to survival. He was taught to be industrious, sensitive to slight, overbearing in triumph, and shamed in defeat. From birth he was urged to dream. He soon learned to deny himself food so that hunger might encourage dreaming. For it was in dreams, said the Ojibwa, that the powers of earth and sky made their wishes known to men, took pity on them, and granted them boons. A boy, they said, was born an empty vessel; it was his dreams which filled him and made him a person—particularly the dreams he had at the time of his entrance into manhood, at the time of his dream-fast and dream-seclusion.

Girls were not encouraged to dream, although no one forbade it. When they went into long puberty seclusion, it was not to ensure a vision of their talents and aspirations, but to protect others from their ritual uncleanness. Nobody praised women's work—not the fancy beadwork, the fine tailoring of deerskin leggings, or the fringed shirts with their tie-on sleeves. Certainly no man would have been caught doing any of these things. A girl was expected to be virtuous, though she received little help in remaining so. Any untoward event that happened in her courting days was considered more her fault than her suitor's. Her education was haphazard. In fact, little notice was taken of her at all. And yet, precisely because she was not noticed, she could often be in many ways freer than her brother. Sometimes an indulgent father taught her to hunt and set traps so that one day she could, if she chose, support herself and her children with no husband to order her about. Sometimes she was taught the shaman's techniques and, if her dreams were favorable, she could become as respected and feared as any male specialist.

Here, says anthropologist Ruth Landes, lay the essential contradiction in the Ojibwa way. Women, said the Ojibwa, were clearly of little account. And yet, so admired were industry and skill that the individual woman who proved herself as hunter or shaman was called, not an odd woman, but simply "shaman" and "hunter" as any man would be. She could even be called "warrior." Fathers of pretty daughters regularly recruited war parties by promising their daughters to the bravest men. Naturally, the girls had to go along to help with the selection. They not only returned with brave husbands; they themselves were "braves," entitled to wear the golden eagle feather awarded to warriors.

Girls competed with men in races and never thought their speed unfeminine. Even the proper, stay-at-home woman, submissive and quiet, had her limits beyond which she would not endure. Ojibwa custom permitted (and prestige required) a man to have several wives—if he could keep them. Usually he could not. Women were shamed by the appearance of a rival in the home and frequently took a knife to the hated face and decamped, never to return. Only shamans could control several wives at once. Having married because of fear, shamans' wives regarded one another as companions in misery.

Whatever the trials of this world, the Ojibwa believed, they were not man's alone to suffer, just as he himself was not unique in nature or separated from it. With all things above and all below—sun, thunder, rocks, trees, animals— he possessed the power of purpose and of being, something of the *Manido*, the greatest power, which had brought all into being and then departed. Like all other things, man lived in a shell of substance that would one day decay and vanish. But, like them, he also possessed sensitive, flickering Shadow and steadfast, immortal Soul. So, too, did things unseen— the guardian *manidos*, the spirit masters of all things seen and known. Therefore the Ojibwa spoke respectfully to the objects and beings in his world—to his strong birch-bark canoe whose bow cleaved the waters as it bore him home; to Nokomis, Grandmother Earth, when he tore a bush or tree from her bosom; to the animals he killed for life itself. Where an animal's dying blood entered the earth, there too went its soul, one day to return alive and warm for yet another hunt. To kill cleanly and without pain was to show respect. The Ojibwa never tormented animals. They never tortured human captives, either, though the Iroquoian tribes to the south of them delighted in doing so.

The hunter took special care when his prey was beaver or bear. The Master Beaver required careful protection of beaver bones. But because the bear walked on two legs like a man, he had to be greeted as a man. One apologized for killing him, and one carried his body home on one's back— with the help of an assistant hunter, perhaps. Never could the bear be subjected to an undignified dragging through the snow. His eyes had to be removed and buried with a pinch of tobacco; his skull had to be painted red and honored at a feast. Only then would the Great Bear Soul be content.

Across the Pacific, the Ainu of Japan were hunters and gatherers in their heyday. Once they, too, honored the bears they killed and the master spirit of all bears in ceremonies much like those of the Ojibwa. So did men during the Old Stone Age in Europe. Their relics and the paintings in their caves tell us something of their feelings for the bear. The Ainu and Ojibwa link us to that other time, that early morning of human history when man was merely one creature among equals, when what he took from life had to be returned to life, and all things were in balance on the earth.

The biochemist and the physicist and the geneticist tell us today that all the universe is one, that the atoms in the heart of a star are to be found in our own bodies or in any stone, that all living beings meet in the ultimate ancestry of the primordial cell. But what we accept with our minds, the Ojibwa knew in his very soul. And that is a very different thing.

We know [a woodland hunter once told Diamond Jenness] what the animals do, what are the needs of the beaver, the bear, the salmon, and other creatures, because long ago men married them and acquired this knowledge from their animal wives. Today the priests say we lie, but we know better. The white man has been only a short time in this country and knows very little about the animals; we have lived here thousands of years and were taught long ago by the animals themselves. The white man writes everything down in a book so it will not be forgotten; but our ancestors married the animals, learned all their ways, and passed on the knowledge from one generation to another.

The Siriono

Longbows in the Rain Forest

Mention the English longbow and the mind's eye, tutored by the plays of Shakespeare, tales of Robin Hood, and half a hundred pseudohistorical Hollywood movies, summons up visions of Crécy and Agincourt, of sturdy yeomen driving back the flower of French chivalry at the point of a cloth-yard arrow.

And yet, in the swamps and forests of eastern Bolivia there are today living archers whose bows would make the famous English weapons seem almost puny by contrast, for they are, some of them, ten feet tall. When one considers that the bowmen themselves rarely exceed five feet four inches in height, the contrast is all the more striking. These little Bolivian bowmen are the Siriono, a name which neighboring groups have given them. They do not know what the term means, and neither does anyone else. They call themselves Mbia, meaning simply "people," but Siriono they are to the outside world and Siriono they will undoubtedly remain.

Since 1693 they have inhabited the forests of eastern Bolivia. At least that was when their presence there was first noted by an explorer priest. Despite all the sometimes harsh efforts of soldiers and missionaries to settle them elsewhere, they were still to be found in their old haunts, their ways largely unchanged, in 1940 when the American anthropologist Allan R. Holmberg went to live and wander with them on their ceaseless migratory rounds.

Despite the heroic proportions of their bows, not even the most sympathetic imagination would find the Siriono bowmen romantic. Not a shred of clothing—neither hide nor hair nor leaf nor fiber—dignifies their spindly frames, though sometimes they do glue bright feathers in their carefully bowl-trimmed hair or paint red designs on brows plucked clean of hair. They are short, sometimes potbellied, and always hungry. People greet one another, not with good wishes and felicitations, but with a plaintive "What have you got that I can eat?" When a family does manage to get a good dinner, its members eat until they almost burst, bolting the food rapidly with head down, so that requests for handouts will not be unduly annoying. Anything left over is usually consumed stealthily by night when the eater can be sure of a little peace and solitude. There are, to be sure, taboos designed to enforce sharing. The flesh of harpy eagles and howler monkeys is reserved for the old. (As they can depend only on leftovers, they might not otherwise get anything.) A hunter is not supposed to eat what he himself kills, but must give away his portion to one of his wife's relatives and wait until they supply him in return. Most often, however, rules are honored in the breach unless there is a superabundance of food on hand.

Nothing is preserved, nothing stored—except for living tortoises, which are often tied up in vines and dispatched at need. For the most part, men simply hope that the nourishment of one good meal will tide them over lean times, and these come regularly. Not so often or for such prolonged periods as to cause actual starvation (there is no *Windigo* in Siriono lore) but often enough to make men perennially empty and able to think of little but food. The fact is that although the Siriono are superb huntsmen, the game is not as plentiful as one might suppose. Hunters hope to bag jaguar, puma, tapir (a 400-pound dangling-nosed creature, distant cousin to both horse and rhinoceros) capybara (a 160-pound rodent), or peccary (a wild pig). But more often they bring home opossums, bats, anteaters, alligators, waterfowl, or buzzards. And even for these the Siriono must work hard and skillfully. Hunters everywhere have learned the use of decoys, but the Siriono know how to lure. They can call a mother alligator from her water hole by imitating her baby's cries. They whistle at monkeys (their most frequent prey) until those gregarious creatures gather to join in the conversation and are shot. Most curious, and therefore most vulnerable, are the capuchins. Spider monkeys are slow, easily bagged, but almost impossible to retrieve; around the branch from which his dying body falls, the monkey's prehensile tail wraps in an iron grip not to be released for twenty-four hours. The man who shoots a spider monkey is in for a long climb, a long wait, or a lost dinner. When hunting howlers, the bowman aims for the dominant male, assured that the attendant females will be paralyzed by their lord's death and therefore easy pickings.

The Siriono have developed an entire whistle language with which they communicate on the hunt. So effective is the system that one anthropologist, after an extremely cursory visit, stated that the Siriono could converse in no other way. Whistles, it is true, can be used for all sorts of intricate instructions. Whistles can bring group arrows flying in the direction of an animal which only one of the hunters can see. With whistles a hunter high in a tree can order a fresh supply of arrows; his partner on the ground will shoot some upward for the man above to catch in mid-air.

As important as meat to Siriono existence are the vegetable foods. Most may be gathered by both men and women without any sort of restriction, except for the *motacú* palm. The heart and fruit of this tree are not only plentiful and good to eat but are hallowed as well by some ancient and forgotten magic. Only women sanctified by the offering of blood from their arms may gather from the *motacú* palm.

The *chonta* palm is important to men, not for its magical power, but for the circlet of hard wood it hides beneath its pulpy exterior—the wood from which is made the precious longbows. Not every *chonta* palm will do. A man might search for days and days before finding just the sort he wants. The tree must then be felled, in the old days by fire. Quickly, before the wood dries, the bow must be shaped with a mollusk shell. Periodically thereafter its resilience will be restored by a good soaking in a nearby stream. Bowstrings are twined by women from the inner bark of the *ambaibo* tree. Long reeds provide the arrow shafts, and the heads are made of bamboo, for in this swampy land there are neither stones nor metals to be had.

Nobody knows why the Siriono make their bows so long. For short men who must perforce hunt through underbrush and drooping vines, the tall bows seem a nuisance. Dr. Holmberg suggests that the chonta wood might snap with the tighter pull of a small bow. One suspects, however, that the Siriono bow simply represents an outsized status symbol, a fad that escalated out of sight. Certainly it is true that the Siriono hunter never possesses more than one bow at a time. It is his constant companion, his pride, his mark of manhood. When questioned about the possible inconvenience of the big bow, he merely shrugs and says that a small one would be "no good."

Bow and hammock and the only "things" upon which the Siriono lavish much effort. A traveling life does not permit the accumulation of possessions, does not give time or even energy for many crafts. Even so, the Siriono do not covet goods or ornaments from the outside world. Unless a foreign mechanism proves useful in the eternal food quest, it is rejected out of hand. (Dr. Holmberg's rifle, for example, was very much admired.) It is certainly true that the Siriono like the hunting-gathering way of life and are loath to change or be changed.

And yet there are things about the Siriono that suggest some susceptibility to outside influences, coming to them perhaps from their neighbors, the farming Mojo and Paressí. The Siriono, for example, occasionally make rough pottery. They know well the uses of fire, though they cannot ignite it with twirled stick and tinder. They claim once to have had that skill but forgot it somehow. Whether or not this is so, fire nowadays is carefully tended and preserved, for the Siriono will not eat raw meat. Whenever the band moves, one woman from each family makes it her business to carry live coals from the old camp site to the new one. Some notion of farming ways has also come to the Siriono but has never achieved any importance in their lives. A small plot may be unceremoniously burned over at any time of the year, scratched idly with a digging stick and planted to corn, manioc, tobacco, or calabashes. The plants are then left to grow as they may. The family will return only at what they gauge should be harvest time. Tobacco, Dr. Holmberg was told, had come to the Siriono during the lifetime of the oldest men of the band. All other plants, they said, had been gifts of the moon.

Other aspects of Siriono life suggest a stubborn clinging to outworn habits, however many innovations may be made by neighboring folk. In a land of water trails and water traveling, the Siriono make no canoes. They swim across water barriers or fell trees for bridges. Language relatives of the Siriono all live more complex lives in terms of ceremony and are richer in material things. Dr. Holmberg himself suggests that the Siriono may represent the last of an ancient people pushed by more aggressive invaders into the backwaters of life.

There may be today many more such people than we realize. In 1968 a group of hunting-gathering people, the

Wama—isolated, nomadic, still using stone axes—was discovered in Surinam jungles near the southeast coast. "Re-
discovered" may be the better word, for they had been
briefly sighted thirty years before, but all missionaries and
anthropologists familiar with the area had thought them
long since dead. Yet it seems they had merely made themselves "dead" to the rest of the world, especially to dangerous neighbors. Siriono traditional history suggests a similar
story. Never themselves a warlike people, they have been
and are still preyed upon by marauding neighbors from
north and south. The Siriono call both tribes impartially
Kurukwa, meaning "monsters."

Though the Siriono retreat timidly from fierce neighbors,
they manage to quarrel a lot with one another, mostly over
food. *He* doesn't share. *She* eats at night. *They* hoard their
food in the forest and sneak out for snacks. A woman in-
dulges in jealous sulks when she suspects her husband of
philandering—not for fear of losing his attentions (philandering among the Siriono is permitted, in any case, with anyone who can be defined as husband's brother or wife's
sister), but because he is diverting food to the new favorite.

The quarrels and resentments actually come to blows
only during drinking bouts. Now and again wild honey is
fermented into a kind of beer, and the man who has braved
countless stings to procure the raw material invites his
male relatives and friends for a spree. His wife has one
for her women kin at the same time. Only very old men
and women may drink together, mixing the sexes with
perfect propriety. The uninvited sit around and watch as
hungrily as they watch cooking in progress, and they are
rewarded with a spectacle. As the men grow drunker, their
suppressed resentments erupt in wrestling bouts which go
on and on until the antagonists collapse in an alcoholic
stupor.

There is always an audience for everything, whether it be
quarrel or childbirth or death, because, unlike the Ojibwa,

the Siriono believe in and practice togetherness. The whole band of eighty to a hundred lives in one house, a slapdash double lean-to thatched with palm fronds. There are no windows or doors; people simply wriggle in through the thatching, and rain pours in the same way. Only falling twigs find the roof a barrier, and because of all the tiny smoky fires within and the tobacco fumes from many pipes (Siriono men never smoke outdoors), insects are effectively discouraged. Nobody bothers to clean. When messiness offends, the band moves on and builds another house.

Inside the house are strung tight clusters of hammocks, centering around that of the chief. In this instance only does he occupy the Siriono limelight. He does not settle quarrels. He does not choose the building site for the communal house

or decide when moving day will be. He is merely the best
hunter, the biggest drinker, the most generous man in the
band. His rewards are these: the center house post for his
hammock and the certainty of attracting and keeping several
wives at once.

The band is composed of a number of families who marry
among themselves. Strange bands are seldom encountered,
and when they are no individual would dream of changing
band affiliation. The Ojibwa hunter thought nothing of
joining another band if the new territory gave promise of
better hunting. To the Siriono such freedom of action is
unheard of. He is fated to remain from birth to death among
the same circle of relatives, to play out on a small stage
and with a small company the scenes of daily life.

It is proper Siriono etiquette for a man to leave his "home" to live among his wife's relatives. The move is not a big one—thirty feet or so across the village-house to where his wife and her parents and sisters hang their hammocks. He will spend all his life in the restricted company of his in-laws, their hammocks strung not three feet from his and his wife's, separated by the tiny cooking fires that take the chill off the Bolivian nights.

The togetherness of Siriono life does not necessarily involve comradeship or even cooperation. The men of a band do help one another in the tapir surround and feast together on the kill, staying out all night like gleeful little boys in defiance of Mother. They do work together in building the village-house—that is, each man adds the proper number of palm fronds to his part of the house. Young girls share a coming-of-age ceremony, camping together in the woods where they sing, shave their heads, and are instructed in wifely behavior by a respectable older woman. Every two years there is an all-band beer party, a sort of renewal ceremony. Band members scratch their arms with sting-ray spines and allow the blood to drip onto the ground, rather in the spirit of "out with the old, in with the new." But these activities and rites—the puberty seclusion, the party, the tapir hunt, the house building—represent the full extent of communal effort and communal ceremony.

No matter how closely they live together with the rest of the band, the absence of common joys or perhaps the daily struggle for existence tends to isolate the Siriono nuclear family as surely as the rigors of the Canadian winter set the Ojibwa family apart. A person's first care is always to feed himself and then his own. There is little time for other thoughts or fancies that might soften and vary the struggle for survival. Children have no toys, and it is a rare pet that survives the inevitable manhandling and the just-as-inevitable cooking pot. Adults have no art and little personal decoration. People clap and sing and occasionally dance in a shuffling circle, and everyone is predictably and forever exactly like everyone else. If there are no shamans to fear, neither are there shamans to help. The woman laboring to give birth has no midwife to attend her. She can count on a large and interested audience, to be sure, but no assistance. She manages everything herself, loosening the earth beneath her hammock so that the newborn little creature will fall onto something soft. She follows her baby over the side and they wait there until Father arrives to cut the natal cord. Custom decrees that he go hunting at first sign of his wife's labor—for whatever animal he kills will give the child its name. Afterward he remains in his hammock for several days, resting from his exertions (as his wife rests from hers), careful to protect the baby's welfare in every way by doing absolutely nothing.

Mere illness is not spectacle. The groans of a sick person go largely unnoticed unless, of course, he is really dying, in which case everyone wants to watch. Otherwise he is left alone with his anxiety. What has happened? Has his soul strayed from his body? Has he violated some taboo? Are evil spirits—always vague and unspecified—stealing his life? What will happen? Must he die and be abandoned in a house that will be shunned forever after? Quickly, then, eat! Beg for food and still more food, for the failing appetite is a sure sign of doom. And so it is that a man may literally eat himself to death, when with a little wholesome fasting he might have recovered.

The person unlucky enough to be ill when one of the periodic moves is in progress will simply be left behind in the house with a little food and water and fire. He may follow the band if he is able. No one entreats him to try. No one offers to remain behind with him. No one weeps or bids the patient good-by. The band troops out, and that is that.

So, too, with the old who can no longer even totter to the hunt or make a pretense of gathering in the forest.

Among the Siriono, a person's worth is exactly measured by his strength. The old are not the source of wisdom and countless merry tales, as among the Ojibwa. There are few tales to be remembered in any case, and wisdom lies in the keenness of the hunter's eye, the cleverness of his whistle, and the resilience of his bow—all things to be learned from much younger teachers. The old person is merely an extra mouth to feed. The taboos are wearying; why reserve even the harpy eagle and the howler monkey? Let the old ones go. Let those who are young and strong face the prospect of another hungry day.

It was not only in forests and on plains that the first Americans and their later descendants found a living. There was always the sea, teeming with fish and shellfish and aquatic animals. Some hunting people learned early of its bounty, moved to the shorelines, and became fishermen. The ancient record of their way of life can be traced today in bone, and even now and then in potsherds buried in the mounds of shell refuse that are always the monuments of fishing folk.

Part II
FISHERMEN

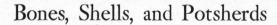

Bones, Shells, and Potsherds

Have you ever tried a nonstop shellfish diet? Oysters for breakfast, clams for lunch, and more of the same for dinner? Probably not. In our world and on our tables, the mollusk appears most often as an appetizer, perhaps as the first course of a meal, and the all-mollusk meal is a sometime thing. Not so for all worlds or on all tables. There are today coastal folk who depend on the lowly bivalve the way we depend on bread and butter. So often are clams and oysters served that beside each coastal village there accumulates a mound of shells, the refuse of a million mollusk meals. What the shell mound is now, so has it always been: the telltale signpost of a fishing way of life.

The first Americans were hunters, not fishermen. When big-game animals roamed the American grasslands and the spreading woods, people who followed them seem to have given little thought to any other way of life. At least, that is what the evidence suggests. Only one possible relic of really ancient fisherfolk has yet been uncovered. A large shell mound on the Guayas coast of Ecuador has been radiocarbon-dated as 26,000 years old. It contains nothing to indicate man's hand in the accumulation—no tools, no weapons, no manufactured objects of any kind; still, the likelihood of accidental accumulation seems remote. Perhaps the tools used for forcing the bivalves open were made of wood or some other highly perishable material. Whatever the speculation, there is no proof. Like other tantalizing indications of American man between twenty and forty thousand years ago, this one is highly questionable.

It seems plain enough that early New World men were not coastal dwellers by inclination. But even during Clovis times when game was abundant, some were beginning to settle down along the interior rivers. In the valleys of the Cascade and Coast Mountains of Oregon and Washington and British Columbia, big game was not abundant, but salmon were, and little by little, it seems, people there began to acquire a taste for fish. Settlers in the river valleys of the coastal mountains and on the plateau just behind, people who made willow-leaf points in the Old Mountain Tradition, were soon hunting a little less, gathering a little more, and fishing a lot. Heaps of salmon bones along the Columbia River and the Fraser River of British Columbia date back to at least 7000 B.C. and possibly as early as 9000 B.C.

Perhaps ancient fishermen camped there seasonally at the time of the salmon runs, putting up tipi-like brush shelters much as the Sanpoil Indians of this region were wont to do in later times. Perhaps, like the Sanpoil, men caught large quantities of fish for their women to split and dry in the sun, throwing the bones on a nearby dump heap. In winter, the Sanpoil used to move onto the plateau, where they occupied round pit houses dug well into the earth. Archaeology has uncovered in the same general area the faint remains of just such pit houses, along with even fainter marks of temporary shelters. Which type came first? Which is the more ancient? Neither, if one may judge by Sanpoil habits. Perhaps archaeology has revealed a pattern of double residence: town house and country house, winter castle and summer fishing lodge. In older times, as now, people apparently needed a periodic change of scene.

Some specialists think that the first people to take up coastal life in the Pacific Northwest may have been river fishermen, migrants from the plateau area. Leaf-shaped points dating back to 6300 B.C. have been found on the east coast of Vancouver Island. Others think that the Northwest coast was settled in later times by migrants from Siberia or even points south, perhaps people who arrived in boats. Certainly there is much about the life ways of historic Northwest coastal peoples to remind us of Pacific islanders —the use of double canoes and outriggers, for example; sails; gabled wooden houses; the family crests of carved wood which we call "totem poles"; the special rights of a family's first-born child, and many myths and religious observations.

Whoever came first and however they arrived, there was wealth along the Northwest coast to make the journey worthwhile. Not only the rivers, but the coastal seas as well, teemed with fish. Fish, shellfish, sea mammals—all were lured by the sediments and the rich plankton swept eastward on the Japanese Current, and north and west on the Alaska coastal currents. These are all warm currents, warm enough to banish much of the snow and ice one might reasonably expect to see in such northerly latitudes; warm enough to brew dense fogs and cause almost constant rains; warm enough to bring great forests marching down to the sea, and with them abundant deer, elk, mountain goat and mountain sheep, bear, and every variety of waterfowl.

It was (and is still) a land of plenty, and after 1000 B.C., fishermen were settling there in numbers. By 500 B.C. something more than shell mounds had accumulated up and down the coast. Villages had appeared and multiplied, large villages with substantial houses made of wood. There was leisure to be enjoyed, time to be spent in artistic pursuits. Here everything useful was also made beautiful, though everything beautiful was not necessarily meant for practical utility. Stone portrait heads were sculpted as well as stone bowls. Altogether, the fabric of life in these fishing villages of the Pacific Northwest was embroidered and re-embroidered by a people who became expert in its decoration.

In every place that ocean currents swept sea life toward shore on east or west coasts of the Americas, there hunters and gatherers eventually became fishermen. The trend accelerated after the mysterious disappearance of big-game animals—in Archaic times, that would be. In coastal Peru, one of the desert spots in this hemisphere, there are little river valleys and *lomas*—vegetation zones nourished by heavy fogs—where men may live in some comfort. And hunters did camp in these areas as far back as 8500 B.C.; their projectile points tell us so. Not until 4000 B.C. or so, however, did the hunting way of life give way to that of fishermen-gatherers. Then the inevitable shells began to collect in mounds, well laced with the bones of fish, seals, and sea birds. In the valley oases of the central Peruvian coast, the fishermen (or their wives, more likely than not) soon learned to domesticate and cultivate the wild squashes thereabout, perhaps beans and gourds as well. By 2500 B.C. permanent villages had been built. It was from this base of fishing-gardening villages that the great Peruvian civilizations would one day grow.

At the southern end of South America there is rain to match that of the Pacific Northwest, but it does not bring in its wake a similar abundance. For at the tip of South America one approaches the pole, and there are no warm currents to offset the cold. Fishermen live here nonetheless —have lived here for a long time. Archaeological remains on the archipelago and the record of living people there prove it. Along Beagle Channel and elsewhere nearby have been found the traces of ancient pit houses, as well as the inevitable shell mounds, some as much as ten feet in height and dating back to 6000 or 7000 B.C. Among the older shells lay crude stone tools, not pressure-flaked like the Magellan points found in a more northerly cave along with the bones of extinct sloth and horse. Even before the Yahgans, first sighted by Europeans in the early 1800s, moved or were pushed into the area, ancient people had eked out a fisherman's living here along the maze of islands, inlets, and channels that fringe the coast.

They had little time to elaborate a way of life, not in the Peruvian manner, certainly not in the Northwest coastal way. In both these favored locations, fishermen enjoyed the amenities of life usually associated only with the full practice of agriculture. In their villages of many souls, they had time to play and time to accumulate "things." But one thing the prosperous fishermen of early Peru and the Pacific Northwest never acquired was pottery. The potter's art—shaping clay and firing it to airtight hardness—is the discovery of settled folk—usually farmers; sometimes fisherfolk as well. But neither the farmers nor the fishermen of the New World invented pottery. Whether it was because their containers of bark, basketry, or wood served so well that discontent never prodded invention, whether the idea simply failed to dawn, or whether it would have appeared in time, we shall never know. For pottery in the New World seems to have been a gift—an unwitting gift perhaps, even an unwilling one, but a gift all the same—from a fishing folk of faraway Japan to a fishing folk living on the coast of Ecuador. The time: about 3200 B.C.

Digging on the coast of Ecuador in the shell-and-fishbone mound of a site called Valdivia (after a nearby modern fishing village), archaeologists Betty J. Meggers, Clifford Evans, and Emilio Estrada found a pot—or, at least, large fragments of one. The bottom-of-the-mound context of artifacts and rubbish in which it lay consisted of crudely shaped tools of stone and shell—scrapers, choppers, and stone sinkers for nets. Of the whole assortment, only certain round shell fishhooks seem to have been made with care. Considering the general level of workmanship, the pot when reconstructed was a distinct surprise, for it was beautiful, even sophisticated in form. Nowhere in known American pottery was there a shape just like it. And nowhere was there an older sample. Organic material associated with the Valdivia

Valdivia pottery and figurine: 3200–2000 B.C.

pot yielded a radiocarbon date of about 3150 B.C., giving it unquestioned priority in time. And this was the paradox. As the first New World pottery, why was it not crude and experimental as the first efforts at anything ought to be? As a first attempt, how could it possibly be better in form than the pottery of later times and of presumably more expert craftsmen? Was there perhaps a long line of development still to be located? There was not—neither in Valdivia nor elsewhere. When a paradox of this sort occurs, the archaeologist begins to think of a donor. Who had brought the Valdivia pot or the idea for it, and from where?

The castellated style of that first pot (corners worked into a shape reminiscent of towers) was not only unique to Valdivia in the early New World, Emilio Estrada recollected. It was, on this particular time level, rare in the Old World except in Japan of the prehistoric Jomon period. Jomon means "cord marked" in Japanese, and it refers to the sorts of pottery made by a fishing-hunting-gathering people (rather like those of old Valdivia) who had occupied Japan after the Ainu but long before the ancestors of modern Japanese came over from the mainland. The oldest Jomon pottery dates back about 9000 years, and its development can be traced to its simple beginnings—as the Valdivia samples cannot.

Jomon pottery (having most of the features which identify early Valdivia pottery) has been most extensively uncovered in shell mounds on the island of Kyushu. This is not only the southernmost of the Japanese islands, but the one closest to the prevailing current which, at that point, flows in a northeasterly direction at a rate of thirty-two miles per day. Kyushu is also in the direct path of typhoons thundering up from the Philippines. Even the prevailing winds blow in a northeasterly direction. It is not hard to imagine a boatload of Kyushu fishermen, out past their sheltering bay, hurled away by sudden winds and later borne onward by the currents. The Guayas coast of Ecuador, just at Valdivia, is, except for the adjacent Peruvian coast, the South American promontory which projects farthest into the Pacific. It is also the meeting point for currents flowing southward with those flowing northward —clearly the logical spot for landfall to be made. And a very welcome landfall, too. Even though the Jomon fishermen were surely wise in the ways of the sea, able to endure hardships and survive, still the end of a voyage of eight thousand anxious miles on rations snatched haphazardly from the water must have seemed glorious, whatever the harbor. As Dr. Meggers points out, the Japanese fishermen of the Jomon period were physically not nearly of such a specialized Asian type as the later Japanese. They could not have been very different from the Valdivia fishermen in looks or culture, so the settling-down process must have been relatively easy. Ideas were certainly shared (witness the pottery) and perhaps other things as well.

During the period of the first Valvivia pottery styles (about a thousand years in duration), little stone figurines began to be popular. At first these were only elongated and polished pebbles with legs marked off, but they were gradually more carefully incised. After 2300 B.C., Valdivia potters began to recreate these figures in clay. The elegant Valdivia figurines are all New World in inspiration and design. Sometimes female, sometimes without definite gender, skimpily clad but gorgeously coiffed, they were made with elaborate care. And yet, however precise the modeling, the figures seem to have been meant for short-term use. Very many were found discarded in the Valdivia trash heap. Dr. Meggers thinks they may have been important in rites meant to cure the sick, for Indians who live in the area today make wooden figurines for just such purposes, discarding them after one use.

In time the little figurines declined in elegance. Short-term use seems to have imposed shorthand methods. The once-elaborate hairdos were suggested with mere scratches, and the lines of limbs and face were unreadable to all but the Valdivian brought up a lost art. But the fad had already spread. By 1500 B.C. figurines were being made and cherished as far away as Mexico.

The idea and techniques of clay pots had traveled long before to other fishing villages in Panama, Colombia, and Peru. In Puerto Hormiga on the Caribbean coast of Colombia, the first pottery is radiocarbon-dated to about 2875 B.C. The earliest Peruvian pottery, found in coastal Guanape, has been dated to 2300 B.C.

Moving inland was yet another matter. For traveling folk, pottery is of little use. It breaks, it is heavy to haul about, and it is hard to make. Only inland people who have definitely settled down to agriculture can afford the extra trouble and enjoy the extra convenience of pottery. By 2000 B.C. pottery and domesticated plants seem to have passed one another moving north and south, to have joined forces and taken up permanent residence together through much of the New World.

The Yahgan
Living Off the Sea

"I believe, in this part of South America man exists in a lower state of improvement than in any other part of the world," wrote Charles Darwin in 1828. He had in mind and in actual view Yahgan fishermen of the isles and rocky inlets around Cape Horn. Excepted were the tall and imposing Ona hunters, with whom Darwin and the crew of the *Beagle* had been much taken. "Very like the famous Patagonians [the Tehuelche] of the Straits of Magellan," said Darwin of the Ona, concluding that they were in all respects "a very different race from the stunted and miserable wretches farther westward" (meaning the Yahgan).

Everything about these "wretches" disturbed Darwin—especially their nakedness. The Ona went naked, too, but under fur cloaks, and their skin was never bared except in time of exertion. But the Yahgans? They sat in their canoes perfectly heedless of the rain and sleet pouring down their unprotected hides and those of their babies. Occasionally one might sport a scrap of otter fur ("about as big as a pocket handkerchief," said Darwin) on his shoulder and another about the waist—nothing more. They had, moreover,

> hideous faces bedaubed with white paint, their skins filthy and greasy, their hair entangled, their voices discordant, and their gestures violent. . . . One can hardly make oneself believe they are fellow creatures.

Subsequent Yahgan behavior did not tend to mitigate Darwin's low opinion. During the *Beagle*'s first voyage of exploration (1826), four of the fishermen's children had been kidnaped—as hostages, said the *Beagle*'s captain, for the theft of a boat. The children had been taken to England, lionized, Christianized, and made thoroughly confused; and then in 1828 they were returned on the *Beagle* (with Darwin aboard) to their homeland. With their few words of English they had managed to dispense the sort of titillating information everyone wanted to hear: Yes, the Yahgans ate one another. They particularly liked old ladies who had outlived their usefulness. Yes, they would eat shipwrecked sailors too. No, the Yahgans had no god—what was "god" anyhow? (Areligious they might be, thought Darwin, but they were certainly no more superstitious than the *Beagle*'s crew.)

The young Yahgans were landed on their home islands along with some English missionaries who had hopes of converting the man-eating Yahgans. It was not to be—not then. Hounded for handouts by their prospective congregants, robbed of their clothing, and finally in fear for their lives, the clerics gave up and went home. In the years that followed, other missionary efforts were mounted, only to end in failure. One group was massacred, perhaps in retaliation for all the times European sea captains, navigating the treacherous channels of the archipelago, had dragooned native fishermen to serve as pilots.

It was not until 1863 that a mission was finally made to stick. In that year Thomas Bridges, aged eighteen, adopted son of an earlier expedition leader, determined to live alone among the Yahgan and to be accepted by them. He did, and he was, not through the power of his preaching but because he did what nobody had tried to do before: he learned the Yahgan language. It was he, in fact, who gave that language and the people who spoke it the name they have borne ever since. *Yemana* ("living people") is what they called themselves. *Yahgan* comes from a particular area in one of the channels, the most central in their territory, a spot where people liked to get together whenever togetherness was possible.

What a difference the proper words can make! We understand this very well in our world. We know that language difference can raise barriers between peoples, and we prize good translators accordingly. Even with language barriers, however, even without a handy translator, people of Europe and modern America usually manage to mingle without violence. This is because we share another sort of language, a language of polite behavior—little acts of courtesy, smiles, gestures, handshakes, winks, a collection of signals meant to put strangers at their ease. All peoples develop a silent language of friendly intent. Without it every human encounter would be fraught with anxiety or even terror. Yahgans, for example, announced their peaceable disposition with red-painted faces, bear hugs all around, and a careful avoidance of names. For the name was considered a person's most private possession, and etiquette required that it not be used in the owner's presence.

When no language of any sort is available—neither spoken words nor the silent language of custom—the stranger is apt to be feared, then hated, then destroyed, as missionaries to the Yahgans were destroyed. Even without the threatening presence of strangers, there was much in the Yahgan world to excite their fear and hate. It was a world populated by bogeymen both imaginary and real: the spirits of the drowned who rose at night to sit by lonely campfires; the bad, wild goblins of the thicketed island interiors; the tall and terrible Ona, all too ready to destroy a Yahgan camp and kidnap its women. By speaking their language, Thomas Bridges at once dispelled Yahgan fears and, with them, the disposition to murder. (In later years, two of Reverend Bridges' sons, following their father's example, would live among the Ona, learn *their* language, and be initiated as Ona men.)

Murder, as Reverend Bridges soon learned—cold, premeditated murder—was actually abhorrent to the Yahgan. Nervous and volatile by nature, they might kill in sudden anger but never (unlike the Ona) with malice aforethought. To call a man a murderer was a deadly insult. "Thief" was almost as bad a label, though thieving did occur (a persistent offender risked expulsion from the family group). If they were not murderers, they were not cannibals, either. Dear old ladies were given respectful care, though now and again a person already at death's door might be sped on his or her way.

Yahgan speech was euphonious—not at all like Ona gutturals, which Darwin had compared to a man clearing his throat or to the sounds one makes when feeding chickens. And as Reverend Bridges expanded his Yahgan vocabulary he discovered something else: the language did not fit the "primitive, hardly human" label that Darwin had pinned to the Yahgans themselves. It had a complex grammar and many rich and descriptive terms. There were terms for every imaginable sort of family relationship and for all the facts of Yahgan life. There were, for example, many words for "snow" in all its consistencies and aspects, many more for "beach." By the use of single expressions, one could describe not only the character of a given beach but the varying ways it might look to a person on land or on water, from close up or from far away, in a storm or when something obstructed the view. Among all the words for "bite," there was one, Bridges tells us, that meant "coming unexpectedly on a hard substance when eating something soft." (To us, the pearl in the oyster; to the Yahgan, merely something to break the teeth.)

Certainly Yahgans were connoisseurs of oysters and every other sort of shellfish available on the archipelago, for shellfish were the staff of life. Children were sent to gather them on beaches at low tide, and women dove for them in the icy Fuegan waters, always bringing in a good haul. Other sea creatures might be tastier but never so reliable. Fishing, however strenuous the effort put forth, often proved a disappointment. Standing in the bow of his canoe, a man might search the empty waters all day, never finding the chance to spear or harpoon a single large fish (bow and arrow were seldom used for any job). Women angled for little fish with lines made from their own black hair. Sometimes inland streams were dammed for fish traps, but the fisherman could not resort very often to this trick. After one trapping of this sort, the stream might be empty of fish for years.

Sea birds provided food, too, especially the cormorant. To catch these birds, Yahgans hid themselves under a rockface rookery and waited for the birds to come home to roost. Then at night, in the blinding flare of torches, they climbed up the cliff, wringing feathered necks before the cormorants knew what was happening.

The Yahgans of the westernmost islands and the Alacaluf, a related people, had seals to eat and sealskins for their little wraps. Yahgans around Navarino Island and on the beaches of Tierra del Fuego could occasionally kill guanaco and gain something warm to wear. But for the central Yahgan there were few animals, either in the sea or on land, to provide a wardrobe, and men had to make do with a coat of grease against the cold. (Darwin had called them "greasy," and there was certainly good reason for their being so.) The Yahgan word for "poor" was *api tupan*, which translates as "body person." There were certainly many "body persons" among the central Yahgan.

The biggest prize for the little fishermen was whale, for blubber carefully buried in the sand lasted a long while. It was the only sort of food preservation the Yahgans knew and their only real security. Whale meat was something else again. It had to be eaten quickly, a job that required many

hungry mouths. The discoverer of a stranded whale, therefore, made haste to build a signal fire. Covering and uncovering the flames with a green hemlock branch, he sent smoke clouds billowing into the sky. Four puffs in a row meant, "Whale found; everybody come!" And everybody within visual range did. It was this custom of smoke signaling that gave the archipelago and its one large island their name— Tierra del Fuego, land of fire. Some wags say Magellan called it first Tierra del Humo, land of smoke, adding, "Where there's smoke, there's fire!"

Yahgan fires were as often on sea as ashore, bobbing and winking on the waves as soon as dusk fell. For every canoe—a fragile affair made of evergreen-beech bark and shaped "like a moon of four days with raised tips"— carried its own hearth amidships. How else were the naked, seagoing Yahgan to keep warm in temperatures that never rose above sixty-five degrees in summer and in winter regu-

larly fell to ten degrees? Canoe fires were laid on pebbles, which lay on sand, which in turn rested on heavy sod. Though fire-making equipment was usually included in the boat gear, everybody tried not to use it but instead to keep the flames always alive. Good flint might be ready to hand, but the one source of iron pyrites lay in the small islands on the edge of Alacaluf territory, a long canoe trip away. Besides, Yahgans liked to keep something cooking all day and into the night so that they could eat whenever they chose.

Apart from the various baskets and bark bailers made by women (a bark canoe is a leaky canoe), all the other items, including the paddles and the canoe itself, were made by men. Even these, however, were owned or at least completely managed by women, probably because paddling the canoe was woman's work. The proper place for a wife was in the stern while her husband stood in the bow, spear poised, surveying the sea life below. Occasionally the husband took over the paddling while his wife dove for shell-fish. (Among the Yahgans, men did not learn to swim.) She never threw her catch over the side, but deposited it with care, watchful lest the shells puncture the bark of the canoe. She had to be just as careful with nighttime docking procedures. Only on the purest, rock-free sand could the canoe be beached in safety. More often she had to deposit husband and large children on a convenient pile of rocks from which they could jump and splash ashore. She then headed back to sea, back to the nearest kelp bed. There, enclosed in the weedy tentacles, her canoe was certain to be safe until morning. Most sailors fear the entangling kelp, but not the Yahgan canoewife. Neither did she fear to dive into the treacherous mass. Indeed, she had to, if she wished to go ashore. Reverend Bridges saw many a lady swimmer stoutly plowing through it even when frost coated the kelp leaves, even when babies, trying desperately to escape the icy water, climbed directly onto their swimming mothers' heads.

Once ashore, the swimmer could dry herself by the fire her husband had built meanwhile, and if the harbor and its surrounding waters looked especially promising to him, she might actually look forward to a real shelter. The Yahgan house was a round framework of saplings thatched with whatever material was available, its floor dug down into the earth for a foot or two and its hearth in the center. Darwin said that such houses looked like nothing so much as haycocks. That may be so, but the "haycocks" did offer more protection than the Ona windbreak, as any frequenter of haycocks will agree.

There might even be more than one such house in a favorable location. Brothers and their wives, sisters and their husbands, assorted grandparents, even some cousins—two or three canoeloads at most—might choose to travel together and beach together. Nice, everyone thought. Nice because the men could get together to spear the bigger fish, perhaps even the large animals like seal and porpoise. Nice because another female would be on hand to assist the woman in labor, to guide her afterward down to the icy sea for her ritual bath and for the new baby's harsh initiation into the element that would dominate all his life. Nice because someone would be around to feed father, mother, and new baby while they remained isolated in their haycock. Good, always good, to have someone else to talk to and depend on.

Fish were not so abundant as to permit large groups to remain together long, but because of the incessant moving about, Yahgan families actually ran into one another fairly frequently, and sometimes visits were planned. Bachelors, young or old, were obliged to do a good deal of visiting in order to find mates, as marriage between cousins was forbidden. Nobody objected to age differences in married couples. Men of fifty or so regularly took teen-aged brides, and young men courted older widows. Wisdom and experience were sought in a prospective spouse more often than romantic compatibility, though by marrying a widow and her young daughter as well, a man could sometimes achieve both.

However practical (and brittle) the marital arrangements, Yahgan spouses bitterly resented infidelity and often backed up accusations with blows. Far from suffering silently, as was the custom among subservient Ona women, the sturdy Yahgan wife gave as good as she got. Wasn't she, after all, an equal partner in the food quest? Didn't she manage the canoe, and didn't she own the paddle? She did, and she was not a bit loath to use it in ways that had never been intended by the manufacturer.

In seasons of real plenty (and nobody could ever be sure when they would be), groups of extended families congregated. Then ball games were organized, and opponents engaged one another in wrestling matches. For though the Yahgans were seldom over five feet two inches in height and had delicate hands and feet, they were avid wrestlers, fierce and skilled. Reverend Bridges found he had to forbid

European visitors to accept Yahgan challenges to wrestle; they were too often thrown.

Among Yahgans themselves, wrestling matches sometimes ended in death, especially when they had started in jealousy over women. The victor took instantly to his heels or to his canoe, for the dead man's family, painted white for war, could be expected to seek vengeance. As stand-in he left behind his nephew, his sister's son. Alone, this young man ("he who invites the storm to rage against him") presented himself as target for the stones of the offended party. With hands on ears, he nimbly dodged and danced until both stones and wrath were spent. Appeased by gifts, the avengers departed. Never again would they come to slay the real guilty man, though they would certainly administer a beating if ever their paths crossed his.

Illness provided another excuse to foregather. When smoke signals announced someone's distress, people appeared from miles around. They were concerned, of course, but mostly they liked to watch shamans at work. (Bridges saw one shaman walk barefoot over live coals.) People gathered, too, when the signals were for death. With black-painted faces they bewailed the lost one, scolding the Great Spirit for having permitted him to die. Everyone helped with the funeral. In summer a proper grave was dug and a rock cairn built over it. In frozen winter the remains were burned so that foxes would not worry them, and forever afterward the spot would be shunned.

Perhaps once a year many of the fluid local groups met to celebrate initiation rites. Boys and girls past puberty underwent the rites together. For weeks they had been isolated in a large oval hut, roof thatched, sides open to the weather. For weeks they had been instructed by their sponsors—two men and a woman for each boy, two women and a man for each girl. They had fasted and taken ice baths in the night. They had drunk their water through a bird bone and scratched louse bites with a special wand. They had listened attentively to the wise water rules, the rules that would insure good fishing; less attentively, perhaps, when the rules concerned behavior—be generous, be mild, respect the old, don't gossip. Their hunger-sharpened nerves had often magnified night noises outside the house into the very person of the Evil One, and the initiates had danced to drive him away, beating the hut wall with sticks and crying aloud.

There was another sort of initiation for boys only, a rite called *Kina*, which was, in many ways, reminiscent of the Ona *Klokten*. Like the *Klokten*, the Yahgan *Kina* was frankly anti-female and pro-male. Men wore peaked masks with cut-out eyes. They postured and screamed and fought mock battles with the women, but it seemed to Reverend Bridges that their hearts were never quite in it. As was discussed in Chapter 3, the Ona commemorated that glad day when men wrested home rule from their womenfolk. The Yahgan *Kina* also celebrated a male takeover, but one that had been accomplished, they said, by mutual consent. There was still another difference. In the original *Klokten* massacre, said the Ona, all the witch-wives had been slain and never afterward had women possessed that terrible power. Such an idea was never mentioned or even suggested in the Yahgan *Kina*, perhaps because Yahgan women had never lost or been deprived of their power of witchcraft. Even the male shaman, taught in the conclave of shamans and supported by his fellows, even the shaman who could kill or cure in his own right would not long contest female magic. For women were allied with the sea, had power in the sea, and could draw forth its bounty. In the Yahgan scheme of labor and life, the sexes were as nearly balanced in importance and respect as ever they would be anywhere on earth. Call it witchcraft.

Darwin called it something else. He called it equality, not only between the sexes but among the Fuegans generally, a pernicious equality that would long retard them on the way to civilized living, that was the reason for their backwardness and poverty. Not a piece of cloth, he said, could be given and remain whole. Instantly it was torn into shreds of equal size so that no one became richer than another.

> It is difficult [he said] to understand how a chief can arise till there is property of some sort by which he might manifest his superiority and increase his power.

He misunderstood much of what he saw in Tierra del Fuego. Being a child of his century, he could scarcely do otherwise. But had the *Beagle* continued to follow the Andean spine upward toward the Pacific Northwest instead of following, as it did, a westerly course, Darwin might have seen things that tended to reinforce his speculations about the Yahgans and their lack of chiefs. He might have seen the sorts of social distinctions that wealth, even in the primitive world, can bring about. He might have seen leaders whose rank was based on wealth and seen them, moreover, among another fisherfolk, one that had property to burn.

The Kwakiutl

Spending the Wealth of the Sea

While fishermen of the southern archipelago struggled and schemed just to stay alive, fishermen of the Pacific Northwest had other ends in view. What was the good of food, they said, without honor? What, after all, was a man who could not dazzle onlookers with extravagant display, display that announced as loudly as words, "Look at me! I've got so much I can throw it away!"

They could well afford this kind of extravagance. The seas from which Yahgan fishermen drew a bare living brought to the shores of the Pacific Northwest abundance beyond dreaming. Twice yearly there were runs of salmon, and the offshore waters teemed with cod, herring, halibut, and the small "candlefish," so rich in precious oil that, strung on a wick, a single dried fish would burn like a candle. Game animals of the land, also in rich supply, were often neglected. (Some of the northern fishermen actually found their flesh repugnant.) But nobody turned down the game animals of the sea—porpoise, seal, sea lion, and whale. Of all the peoples of the Northwest, only the Nootka hunted whale in its natural home. Others waited for lucky tides that left the great animals beached and helpless. Sea otters were prized for their pelts. Made into long rich mantles, these provided the status symbols for "big men." Chinese aristocrats across the Pacific would later take a fancy to such cloaks, introduced to them by European traders, creating such a demand for the dense, beautiful fur that sea otters in the Northwest would be brought close to extinction.

Drawn by the same promise of abundance that had drawn hunters into the Great Plains melting pot, many migrants settled the Pacific Northwest. All along the narrow shore-line from Yakutat Bay in Alaska to Cape Mendocino in Northern California were many sorts of people, speaking different languages, tracing different origins, and yet all sharing a common pattern of life. Among the fiords and sea cliffs of the far north lived the Tlingit whose Athapascan languages were of the Na-Dené major group. The Haida of the Queen Charlotte Islands were also Athapascan-speaking. Fierce and warlike, the Haida had pushed into neighboring islands and raided for slaves as far south as Puget Sound. On the mainland coast just opposite were the Tsimshian groups who spoke Penutian languages related to those spoken by the acorn-gathering tribes of California. Some of the smaller tribes of coastal Oregon spoke Penutian languages as well. Between the northern and southern fishermen were peoples speaking languages of the Algonquian-Mosan major group. There were the Salish who inhabited the land around Puget Sound but who claimed relatives among the Bellacoola of the north and the Tillamook of the south. There were the Nootka of Vancouver Island, and the closely affiliated Kwakiutl. The Salish people are thought to be late-comers to the region, and it is certainly true that they long retained many customs that remind one of Algonquian people far to the east—an elaborate bear ceremony, for example, somehow out of keeping with the seaward bent of most Northwest coastal peoples.

The Kwakiutl were in-betweens in more ways than the strictly geographical one. They were at the crossroads of social forms and art forms, and even of attitudes. All the peoples of the Northwest coast were wealth-conscious, rank-conscious social climbers. Among the southerners, solvency counted for more than inherited position, but it was just the reverse in the north among the Tlingit, Haida, and Tsimshian. The Kwakiutl required the ambitious man to be both wealthy *and* wellborn, and nobody could have one without the other. Nobility among the northerners descended from uncle to nephew—from a woman's brother to her own eldest son. In the south, rank and wealth tended to travel from father to son. But the Kwakiutl (and Nootka too) claimed noble connections wherever they could be found—in either side of the family or in both sides. Nobody bothered to quibble.

Never was there a people who believed more sincerely that it is better to give than to get, not because of any natural altruism, but because giving demonstrated superiority, high rank, and importance. Among all the Northwest coastal peoples, giving was elaborated into a solemn game called the potlatch, which was the Chinook name for it. It was a game in which one scored points by giving more than a rival could reasonably return. One fought, not with fists or weapons or even with a ball, but with property, and a player won by losing. In all the Northwest coast, nobody played the potlatch game with greater passion and greater daring than the Kwakiutl.

Not everybody was eligible for the potlatch game. Slaves could not play. Captured in raids, carried so far away that all hope of ransom was lost, they existed merely to demonstrate their owners' importance, generosity, and carelessness of property. They could be bought and sold and given away. They could be freed or killed on a whim, thrown into the holes in which the great posts of a house would rest, or used as rollers for the canoe of a visiting dignitary. If a master died, they could expect to be sacrificed at his funeral. In the ordinary course of events, nobody noticed the slave, and certainly nobody would marry one, however high had

been his former place in life. Forever tainted by his degrada-
tion, the slave had no hope of property; naturally, he could
not play the potlatch game.

Commoners, men without rank, could potlatch only in
fun and as a lark, never seriously. A commoner might gain
renown for his skill in canoe crafting or wood carving, but
however sought after and however praised, he did not potlatch. He might be a famous warrior (as younger brothers of
"big men" often were), leading slave raids, vengeance raids,
and raids meant to ease the sorrows of bereaved kin; still, he
did not potlatch. He might be a much-feared shaman, one
who ranked high in the shaman society, one who had the
power to influence events about him. He might engage in
duels of magic with his fellow shamans, seeking always to
win higher renown, but he did not potlatch.

The big solemn game with its grand gestures and high
stakes was for nobility only, for the "big men," all of them
first-born children of former "big men." We might call
them chiefs, though they did not operate in the usual political way. There might be several chiefs in the typical beach-
side village. Each one lived in a large plank house with slop-
ing roof (northerners liked to build gables into their roofs).
With the chief lived his *numaym*, an extended family including not only his own children but brothers and their
wives and children, perhaps sisters and their families, even
cousins' families. Altogether there might be a hundred people
in the house, each family occupying its own partitioned
space on the great earthen bank that extended around the
four walls, leaving a large communal pit in the center. The
size and beauty of the house announced the importance of
the *numaym* within. So did the artistry of the house's post
carvings, the number of its family heirlooms, its carved feast
dishes, and the majesty of its totem poles.

The term "totem poles" is actually a misnomer. Though
animal and bird figures (along with human figures) were
often carved on the poles, never did they represent creatures

sacred to the family and therefore taboo to the family table. Each figure was meant to call to mind a supernatural being in temporary animal guise, perhaps a being who had appeared to the family founder, granting blessings and boons. The figures might also trumpet achievements in the Great Game. New carvings could be added when the occasion warranted. Think for a moment of the designs, the fanciful beasts that adorned the shields of medieval knights—designs which at length became the crests identifying noble families of England and the Continent. Totem-pole figures of the Pacific Northwest were heraldic just as griffins, lions rampant, and unicorns were heraldic in Europe. On totem poles were carved the emblems which identified a particular family and were held for the family by its current head. They appeared on his house and in front of it. After his death, the totem figures were carved on mortuary poles which marked his grave. Sometimes, if a pole were large enough, it might function as the grave itself, with the noble corpse neatly tucked inside.

Chiefs were arranged in a very tight "pecking order." Whether at home or abroad, in his own village, in his own tribe, or among all the tribes of the Kwakiutl, each chief knew exactly where he stood with respect to every other chief. No two chiefs were ever exactly equal in position, but no one stayed exactly where he had begun. A man moved ahead by leapfrog potlatch jumps over his next highest rival, and his family group jumped with him.

All summer long the Kwakiutl *numaym* labored to amass wealth. Sea otter pelts were cured and stored. Fish were dried. Precious oil was pressed from cooked, rotted candlefish. Exquisitely planed dugout canoes were built, beautiful boxes carved and bound by thongs laced through borings. Blankets were finger-twined of cedar bark, painted with gorgeous designs, and trimmed with otter fur. Fanciful basketry rain hats were made, and dance skirts brilliant with paint. Though the Kwakiutl knew nothing of tailoring tech-

niques and went year-round as nearly naked as the impover-
ished Yahgan, what things they did wear were, in true
Northwest coast fashion, elaborated into works of art.

All summer long, men and women worked on the family
holdings, hurrying to bring in the wild harvest. Rights to
hunting and fishing preserves and berry patches were most
strictly observed. Even plots of clover, much liked for its
tasty root, were fenced and individually owned. Nobody
knew anything about planting and cultivation, but they
could certainly stake claims to what nature provided. The
chief of the *numaym* held all these individual rights and
claims as part of his inheritance. He was both owner and
steward of the family estates, allocating land and water rights
as need arose, taking some of the surplus as family insurance
and to support family reputation. Everybody gave as much
as possible of the fruits of his labor and skill. If a man was
close kin to the chief—brother, near-cousin, or older son—
giving made him closer still. If he was not close, separated by
age or degree and therefore a commoner, generous giving
might win him appointment as dancer to the chief, the actual
title to a mask and to the dance in which it figured. And
title, of course, meant rank—rank, at least, in the *numaym*
itself.

Family surplus, held by the chief, might be invested in
a "copper," a large shield-shaped plaque of cold-pounded
metal, beautifully incised to represent one of the mythologi-
cal beings dear to the Kwakiutl. In somewhat the way our
dollar bills each represent one hundred pennies, coppers each
represented vast quantities of blankets. The problem was
that nobody ever knew exactly how many. With every
transaction—be it potlatch or sale—in which a copper
figured, its value increased, for the last thing in any pur-
chaser's mind was a bargain. The object was to spend more
than the copper was worth (whatever that seemed to be),
thereby demonstrating the buyer's magnanimity, his superior
extravagance, and the solid buying power of his *numaym*.

Kwakiutl wooden dish
and ornamental "copper"

With the end of September all labor ceased, for the sacred season was at hand. Men dropped their workaday names and were addressed by their special winter titles. Now the chiefs of houses began seriously to consider the business of feasting, for if a "big man" failed in his social responsibilities, even his own people might in time come to call him "rotten face." After all, their reputations rose or fell with his. What occasions might warrant a round of the Great Game? Had he recently lost a relative whose memory should be honored? Had he taken one of the family titles due him? It must be validated in the giveaway. Had he a first-born son ready to have his baby hair singed? Was it time for the boy's initiation into one of the secret societies? Time for his recognition as heir? Then certainly the taking of a new name was in order, and with the name rights, a feast. In the Kwakiutl scheme of things, all names were family names and all family names were also titles—from the greatest to the least. Some were inherited, some given by the chief. Whatever the origin, name meant rank, and rank had to be validated through giving, by the newly named in his own

right or by the house chief in his behalf. Kwakiutl caution-
ary tales are populated not only by handsome princes dis-
guised as slaves, but also by unfortunate outcasts, men of low
degree, who "invent" names and are punished for their
presumption.

The chief whose eldest child was a daughter had double
opportunities to potlatch. As his heiress, she was required
to play the game—with Father's help, of course. She also had
to be given in marriage, a prospect which triggered new
bouts of giving, fresh displays of largesse. To win the hand
of the first-born daughter of a rich and powerful chief—
first in his village, perhaps first in his tribe—noble suitors
came from far and wide, from distant Kwakiutl tribes, even
from foreign peoples. They and their family groups were
then tested in the potlatch. The most daring player won the
heiress. He also won the magnificent dowry she brought—a
dowry of goods and coppers, of fishing and hunting rights,
and also wealth less tangible but no less valuable: rights in
dances, myths, and songs, rights in crests, rights to seek in
dreams the help of certain supernatural beings. Crests and
prerogatives were meant to be held in trust for the future son
of the heiress, but they were not without immediate utility.
To be the guardian of titles shed greater luster on those a
man owned himself. As guardian he acquired added power
to borrow goods (which, if he dallied a year in repayment,
might cost him as much as one hundred per cent interest).
Being a guardian gave him the excuse for even more ambitious potlatching. Many of his feasts would be given to honor
his father-in-law, who would in his turn reciprocate ("buying back the daughter," it was called) until four gigantic
exchanges had finally established her position as "great
woman."

Huge dowries were required for heiresses, but they were
proper for lesser daughters as well—perhaps eldest though
not first-born. And in these marriages the son-in-law acquired properties, even titles, that became truly his own. In

time he would pass them on to his own son-in-law. Lacking daughters, a chief might have to choose a stand-in son-in-law, marrying the young man to some part of the chiefly anatomy —a foot, for instance—so that the inheritance of in-law property might not be interrupted.

What pleased the gentry was not always guaranteed to please the common folk. When marriages of state happened to convey family or even tribal property into the hands of foreigners, local hotheads often set out to mend matters. They simply ambushed the bridal party and killed the new son-in-law. Whoever held the princely scalp also held all the rights and titles awarded to that scalp's former owner. Among the Kwakiutl, murder was thought to be as acceptable a way of social climbing as contracting a fortunate marriage. The man who killed the owner of a dance took title with life and thenceforward owned the dance himself. Of course, the murderer knew he himself faced the vengeance of the offended family, faced the threat of murder by young men of ambition equal to his own. He accepted the risk. More serious was the necessity of validating the newly won honors in a potlatch, and a big one, too. Without supporting wealth, his desperate gamble could bring him nothing whatever. But if he could potlatch, he was then home free. Nobody whispered about the truly big spender.

In the autumn, the family criers went forth from great house to great house.

> Now he is going to show his great name, the one who calls many tribes to meet . . . give presents to them . . . give again double amount, the same amount of property on top of the first amount . . . to those invited from time to time by our chief.

And the great chiefs came. To each property was given in exact accordance with his rank among his peers. It was not really so much the amount that was important, but the *relative* amount, and every guest surreptitiously assessed the haul given to every other guest to make sure that honor was satisfied. If by chance or design some chief had been slighted, then lines were drawn for battle, a battle to be fought with property. The insulted one left in a towering rage, bent on "covering his shame" with gifts and with more than gifts— with destruction. Now the heralds cried,

> Ah, do not in vain ask for mercy and raise your hands, you with lolling tongues! I shall break, I shall let disappear the great copper that has the name *K!ents!legume.*

At the return bout, the host and host *numaym* paraded their wealth. Candlefish oil was poured in great gouts into the fire so that the flames burned the roof beams and scorched the robes and eyebrows of the assembled guests. Honor demanded that they endure without flinching, without change of expression. The host might destroy beautiful dugout canoes and blankets. He might kill a slave. He might even "kill" a copper, burning it in the flames or throwing it from some headland into the sea.

The rival had no choice but to try to top this display of waste. One ambitious chief succeeded only when his two daughters offered themselves to the flames. At the crucial moment, of course, slave girls were substituted, clad in the daughters' full dancing regalia. Nobody seemed to notice the substitution or even to question when, weeks afterward, the "cremated" daughters reappeared, claiming miraculous resurrection. For the brutal sacrifice had accomplished its ends. One chief had been flattened, ruined, driven to suicide, while the victor had moved up a notch in the everlasting "pecking order" of the Kwakiutl.

The tension of feasts and dances was heightened during the highest holy days of winter. Ten days and nights were given over to sacred pantomimes performed by masked dancers from the various secret societies. The privately owned dances and songs were also performed. Each round of celebrations was sponsored by one of the great chiefs, who found in it another occasion for giveaways. During the holy days young men were initiated into secret societies. Of all the societies, none was more feared or had greater prestige than the Society of Cannibals. Its members, all first-born sons of chiefs, were served first at all feasts, given deference and seats of honor. The Kwakiutl looked with horror on the eating of human flesh; and yet the initiate of the Cannibals—and his female partner, Rich Woman Dancer—had to eat this flesh, had to consume the slain body of a slave, had to bite and raven at the living flesh of spectators and fellow dancers. Some say that smoked bear, fitted with a cleverly carved mask, was substituted for the slave, but nobody denies the reality of the frenzied biting. Too many Kwakiutl of the old days bore the scars to prove it. The Cannibal Dancer symbolized all that was most aggressive, most brutal, most violent in Kwakiutl society—the insatiable lust for glory, no matter what the cost in toil, in creativity, in human life—all wasted, thrown away.

But there was another side to Kwakiutl life, overshadowed though it was by the noise and color of the Great Game and the towering figures of its leading players. Behind the great house portals, very often carved to represent the gaping jaws and wicked teeth of a killer whale, there was not violence but fun and jokes and the tenderest sorts of sentiments. The husband, who had perhaps fought for his wife in great property duels, might call himself her "slave." The stern old grandfather, whose violent deeds in past potlatches were not yet forgotten, played with zest the little games of his grandchildren. He answered to the names "Doggy Face" and "Doggy Collar" and was disappointed if the little ones would not use these "doggy" titles. He told stories to the sleepy children, whispering sadly as the old memories came flooding back.

Sometimes, as Dr. Helen Codere tells us, children played at potlatching, and sometimes women mocked the great potlatches of their men, giving one another silly presents and making grand, empty speeches in prescribed potlatch style.

Even during the Great Game itself there were fool dances and moments of lighthearted merriment. Sometimes a whole village might stage a play-potlatch, seasoning the entire episode with practical jokes and ribald laughter. And "nobody," said Dr. Codere's Kwakiutl informant, "laughed more than the big chiefs themselves."

How can this split in Kwakiutl personality be explained? Should one draw the line between public and private life, perhaps, or between behavior expected of "big men" and commoners? One might view the competitive potlatch, as does Dr. Irving Goldman, against the Kwakiutl religious backdrop, seeing in it a reflection of that pervasive will to power that colored even the Kwakiutl's addresses to his gods. Just as there were two seasons to the year, the sacred winter and the workaday summer, perhaps there were also two attitudes about the potlatch—one ceremonious and solemn, the other comic, even satiric, a necessary relief to tensions and strain. One might, finally, consider the potlatch in the frame of war and peace, the hostile feast serving as a substitute activity for people uninterested in and too busy for warfare of the conventional sort.

Perhaps the destructive, conspicuous waste of the potlatch was something that developed very late in Kwakiutl history. In the 1890s, when the Kwakiutl were studied by Dr. Franz Boas (often called the father of American anthropology), their numbers had already been reduced by epidemics that had ravaged tribes to the east. They were, it is true, still in possession of their ancient lands. Their contacts with European culture had come late, but with those contacts had come new wealth of a quantity and a sort beyond even Kwakiutl dreaming. The already inflated economy grew more inflated still. It was the European fur trade, say some specialists, that brought on the Kwakiutl competitions of waste and destruction and created, in the process, new sorts of men. In the old days, wealth and rank had been inevitably bound together. With the influx of foreign trade (and the reduction of bona fide nobles by disease), suddenly the Kwakiutl began to see wealthy commoners brushing elbows with great chiefs. Why, some of these newly rich even wanted to potlatch, if you please! Some were slain for their pretensions, but their numbers grew. Finally a new rank had to be created. Very rich commoners were called Eagles, given precedence at feasts, and allowed to assist highborn chiefs to potlatch. They might not potlatch on their own account unless somehow they managed to wangle a title or become son-in-law to an old chief's toe. Then, what orgies of destruction!

Think of America of the nineties, and the whole Kwakiutl pattern grows clearer. Think of our legendary "big men" of that time who played with railroads and factories instead of otter pelts and coppers. Think of these same "big men" directing the labor of many workers toward their own ends. Think of them fighting games for financial control of industries—games from which the loser often emerged bankrupt. Princes of industry spent little money on one another, but they did spend and spend competitively in games called "philanthropy." Attitudes and ambitions permissible for the very rich filtered down to the not-so-rich in attenuated form and remain to haunt us.

We still recognize a status symbol when we see one: the mink coat, the ski lodge in Vermont, the racing car that will never race, the swimming pool in which no one ever swims, the vastly expensive ceremonies in which a daughter takes the title of "debutante" or "wife," the flowers and processions that honor the great man's demise. We know something about hostile gifts—the ones that have to be given and have to be expensive lest the recipient think us cheap! We know something about the competitive feast, too, the one that must be bigger, fancier, and more fun than the one *they* gave if it kills us. Oh yes, we know something about rank and something about the "pecking order," though we may not want to admit it.

The plain truth is that most of the world's people live and have lived by a double standard: the ideal and the actual. Though the Kwakiutl admired fierce competitiveness, the sort of reckless abandon that sought victory at any price, they could not altogether hide the tender sentiments they were not supposed to display. Though Americans admire tender sentiments, they cannot altogether hide an unregenerate zest for competition. No person and no culture is all one way or all the other. No one follows a single star or plays a single game. The marvel is that the Kwakiutl, a people living on what they took from sea and land, could play a game at all, play it with high art, play it for high stakes right to the very brink of civilization.

Behind the sea is the land; behind mountains, the desert. For the ocean-born clouds that water and warm the Northwest coast cannot flow inland. From southeast Oregon down through central Mexico there stretches a great trough of dry land, harsh and bare. Yet people have lived in this land for many thousands of years—have lived there and sometimes even thrived there, learning to make do with little and to use what came to hand.

Part III
GATHERERS

Baskets, Seeds, and Grinding Stones

Why people remain in bad lands after they have seen them, after they have plumbed the disadvantages and learned the terrors, is something of a mystery. Picking up the feet and moving on at once would seem the logical thing to do. And over the long years, some people did move on. The Indian populations of Central and South America bear living witness to the continuity of migration. Nevertheless, some hardy souls seem always to have remained behind, for the dry lands have never been unpopulated. Whether the stay-at-homes feared hostile tribes beyond the desert, whether they had adapted beyond complaint to desert demands, or whether

they were, quite simply, happy where they were we can never know.

The upper part of the North American dry lands (steppe as often as actual desert) is called the Great Basin because, bowl-like, it lies between mountainous rims—the Sierra Nevada and Cascades to the west, the Rockies to the east. The American Southwest, the uplands of central Mexico, and the interior of Baja California are outliers, as dry and often as harsh as the Basin itself. In all these areas the pattern of human life was for long years very much the same. Since Clovis times men have called the dry lands home. The record of their existence and their passing has been preserved in an unbroken series under the bone-dry dust of caves. In some caves of the Great Basin the record extends into modern times, into the lives of Utes, Paiutes, and Shoshoni Indians who were, until about twenty years ago, still following the old desert ways (and living in the cave homes) of their predecessors. So faithfully had they preserved the old techniques and patterns that archaeologists could connect past with present to the greater understanding of both.

The oldest people in the area (from about 9000 to 7000 B.C.) were hunters, but not of the flamboyant, big-game variety. The large spearheads of the buffalo hunter, fluted or unfluted, are not often found here. These hunters seem to have preferred the simple willow-leaf point popular on the northwestern plateau and the whole unspecialized tool kit that went with it. Already this choice tells us something about them, tells us they were adaptable, not committed to any one sort of life or diet. Whether the desert was as dry then as it is now, the fact remains that Great Basin folk lived somewhat on the fringes of things, making do with what they had.

What they had began to diminish after 8000 B.C. Whether the larger game animals were killed off by the hand of man, by some mysterious plague, or by increasing dryness is not known for certain. (Recent excavations in one of the Great

Basin caves cast some doubt on the theory of increased desiccation.) In any case, there was a change of some kind, a change for the worse. The larger deer and pronghorn antelopes thinned out. By 7000 B.C. people had taken to hunting rabbits, ground squirrels, mice, rats, and lizards and had learned to use throwing sticks, throwing clubs, and small stone-pointed darts. They had even acquired a taste for insects. Remains of grasshopper meals have turned up in the waste and trash of ancient Mexican caves, and North American Paiutes were still storing dried grasshopper paste in the early 1900s.

Ancient desert folk learned to find various sorts of roots and to extract them with the digging stick. Most of all, they took to grass seeds. (The refuse heaps in Utah caves indicate a local fondness for pickleweed seeds.) For seed preparation grinding stones must be found. The desert folk learned to use all sorts of grinding stones—flat ones, curved ones, and even mortars and pestles. For seed gathering light containers are needed, and the desert folk made such containers of tule reeds, which grow in the scattered, diminishing ponds, and of chewed fibers. In time their baskets became works of art. Tight and almost waterproof, they may even have been used in cooking as the Paiutes of historic times cooked in their baskets, bringing water to a boil by adding heated stones. Bags and carrying nets, trays, bowls, cradles, and seed beaters were also made from vegetable fibers. There were mats to sleep on, skirts to wear, and even sandals—all of them made from twined and woven fiber. Without large animals to provide really warm and durable clothing for the winters and cold nights, they learned to use the fibers combined with fragile rabbit skins. Cut into long ribbons, the fur was twined around the fiber string, the whole bound together into a blanket light, warm, and remarkably durable.

Most desert folk were poor and hard-working, but not really as badly off as they might have seemed at first glance. Though the land was dry, it was also varied, and one might

Cradleboard,
tied with yucca fibers

get a change of scene and diet simply by seeking altitude. Everywhere mountains shouldered onto the desert, mountains on whose slopes could be found pines and the tasty piñon nuts which were something of a staple of desert diet. In the highlands, too, there were occasional sheep and deer to be hunted. The trick was in knowing just when to move, when to tackle one environment and when another. It was a trick that desert folk learned early and never forgot. Every season brought new patterns of residence, sometimes in flimsy shelters, sometimes in caves; sometimes in large groups, sometimes scattered into single families.

Amid all the moving and all the harshness of life, there was still, it seems, time to play. In the strata of the caves there have been found dice and counters of various kinds. Balls used in kicking games are thought to be very old in desert cultures. Bone pipes for smoking have been found, bone rattles used in dancing, feathered wands, and medicine bags. All speak eloquently of a life beyond bare subsistence. There are even, throughout the area, seashell ornaments.

Some adventurous soul was evidently peddling luxury goods to poor folks even in those early days.

As time moved toward the beginning of the Christian era, the people in one part of the North American dry lands—the part known to us as the Southwest—took up a new way of life. Throughout what is now Arizona, New Mexico, and northern Mexico, cultivated plants from the south spread and caught on. So did settled villages. Planting ways and the plants themselves had to be adapted to soils and climates. Surely the Southwest is not the world's lushest farm land, but in the sturdy desert way, people learned to make do.

The land in which plant domestication began was no more likely a spot. In the highlands of Mexico, with its bone-dry valleys and wooded mountain slopes, there once lived people similar in every way to their counterparts in the north. Caves throughout the area record the same sequence of events. Several caves excavated by Dr. Richard S. Mac-Neish in the Valley of Tehuacán carry the story farthest of all.

As in the Great Basin, hunters had first occupied the valleys, the slopes, and the caves. Then sometime shortly before 7000 B.C. came the change, just as it did in the north —the shift to small animals and vegetable foods, little weapons and large grinding stones. All, all the same, except for one thing. Of the wild grasses whose seeds were eaten in the Valley of Tehuacán, one was undoubtedly the ancestor of corn. And two of the food plants—squash and avocado—were already under cultivation (squash probably more for its protein-rich seeds than for its thin rind).

Now avocado does not grow wild in the Mexican uplands; it is a lowland native. Was it domesticated there and imported to the highlands? Or had some enterprising highlander, visiting in the south, liked the wild fruit so much that he brought a plant or two back home? We can only guess. There has not yet been found any evidence of lowland plant domestication around 7000 B.C. To be sure, villages had appeared in what is now the State of Chiapas, but they were villages of gatherers who lived entirely on the bounty of the forest. By 5000 B.C. corn had been domesticated in the Valley of Tehuacán, and in other highland centers beans, pumpkins, and chilis were under cultivation. Lowland folk of Veracruz were, at that time, gathering shellfish in the coastal waters. They would not take to farming for a long time to come.

Why should it be otherwise? Everywhere and in all times people who are committed to a way of life that yields considerable dividends in comfort and ease, people who have invested their leisure with rich ceremony, are not ordinarily receptive to change. They do not welcome the appearance of new ideas or new inventions unless those ideas and inventions can be made to fit easily into familiar patterns. This is why farming was the discovery of poor folk who had learned to scratch for a living. It was the invention of people who were skilled at making do, people so close to bare survival that they had little time or heart to glorify the effort of staying alive. It was the invention of people who, lacking a vested interest in things-as-they-are, had eyes ever open to things-as-they-might-become.

The great civilizations of Mexico rose from the dry farms of onetime desert folk. In the pueblos of the American Southwest, farming gave yet another onetime desert people leisure to devote to religious exercises and to art. But in the Great Basin proper, the old desert way of life was to remain unchanged, unmodified by influences from the south until the advent of modern times swept it away altogether.

The Paiutes
Making Do in the Desert

People who live in dry places, if they are to live at all, must learn to imitate their animal neighbors. Not the big creatures, pronghorns or deer. It is the little animals which have most successfully come to terms with drought. It is the gopher, the pack rat, the prairie dog who know where to seek coolness and where warmth, how to store seeds and nuts against the winter, and how to hide themselves. No wonder the first trappers and explorers in the Great Basin said its people lived the most like animals of any race of beings. Like animals, they fled at the sight of a stranger. Like animals, it was said, they wore no clothing, built no shelters, and provided nothing for future wants. Some visitors even thought that Great Basin folk hibernated through the winter, crawling into warm holes from which they emerged in the spring, weak and thin, to crop the new greens like cattle or to grub for roots with their digging sticks. So often, in fact, was this simple implement seen in action that its users were universally known as the Diggers.

White settlers and travelers in the wagon trains moving west soon learned of other Great Basin inhabitants. They encountered some Indians who had acquired horses, who lived in more favorable environments, and who, to the vast approval of the pioneers, were of more cleanly habits. Snakes, these Indians were often called, possibly because some had originated around the Snake River.

Snakes and Diggers, the mounted hunter and the scratcher in the earth. This was the only distinction most newcomers were able to apply. Naturally, their observations were not always accurate. They were even less often sympathetic. An additional source of confusion lay in the Digger habit of naming scattered bands after the most plentiful food available in a particular area. Thus there were the Piñon Eaters, the Rabbit Eaters, the Cricket Eaters, down through the list of desert edibles. Whoever joined the family groups scouring these various locales became himself a Rabbit Eater or Piñon Eater, whatever his origins or speech.

And there was language variety, though certainly the Great Basin was never the sort of Babel one found on the Plains or on the rich Northwest coast. With the exception of a Hokan-Siouan tongue spoken by the Mojaves of southern California, languages of the Great Basin all belonged to one major group (Macro-Penutian) and even to a single group of that—the Azteco-Tanoan group. Such languages are spoken far down into Mexico, carried there by the Aztecs in their heyday. Of all language groupings in North America, only Azteco-Tanoan has been spoken at both ends of the cultural scale: by the urbanites of a high civilization and by gatherers who lived life at its poorest and most elemental. Azteco-Tanoan languages of the Great Basin were those of the Utes and the Paiutes (northern and southern varieties) and of the Shoshoni. In all these language clusters there were representatives of the Diggers and the Snakes. Consider the Shoshoni. By the late 1600s there were mounted Shoshoni who pushed out into the Plains to become the rich and much-feared Comanche. Others on the Basin's northeast fringes took horses to the formidable Blackfeet and suffered eventual defeat at their hands. But all the time there were other Shoshoni, like the White Knives of Humboldt Lakes, who were poorer than poor, stealing (when they could) the seed caches of burrowing animals or of each other.

The same sort of division applied among the Paiute, whose mounted warriors were known as the Bannocks. It was the same again among the Ute. The territories of the southern Ute extended into the Southwest. Unlike most Great Basin folk, who were untouched by outsiders until after 1840, the southern Ute were early in contact with the Spanish and were early mounted. They had a long history of alliances with the Spanish, first against the Apache and later against the Comanche. Still later, they served as scouts for the United States Army.

It was the horse that gave Snakes a better way of life. To most Diggers of the interior Basin, the horse was feared as a competitor for the scanty vegetation that was life itself; he was also meat on the hoof, a commodity to be dispatched as quickly as possible. But by the 1860s there were some Diggers who had stopped eating horses and had begun to ride them in lightning raids against isolated settlers. And why not? Many a Digger had been shot out of hand simply because he had been *there*, looking Indian and therefore dangerous. Many a stand of irreplaceable piñon trees had been cut down by the settler's ax, many a patch of grass overgrazed by wagon-train livestock. And many a Digger had starved in consequence.

The new predatory bands were, of course, defeated and enclosed in reservations. But there were many more Great Basin people who knew neither horses nor settlers and who remained behind to live as they always had, remote from the strange world springing up around them.

The nature of the Great Basin itself makes isolation possible. Row upon row of mountains enclose narrow, remote valleys. With any luck at all, the people of these valleys need never venture far from home—in linear miles, that is, for there is much traveling up and down. Moisture is conserved on the heights as it cannot be in the valleys, and other things can grow—different plants at different zones. Over 11,000 feet one finds mostly grass, but it is there that the wild sheep live, elusive animals who take to the crags at the first sign of pursuit. The man who would hunt wild sheep must be a great mountaineer or a wily trickster—preferably both.

Between 9000 and 11,000 feet, fir, spruce, pine, and willow grow. Many more varieties of grasses can be found, many berries, including the wax currant. From 7500 to 9500 feet the deciduous trees appear, and with them other fruit and berry bushes—chokecherry and wild rose and raspberry—and still more species of grass. At 7000 feet begin the piñon trees whose nuts, roasted and stored, can keep a

family the whole winter through. But not every winter. Piñon trees bear only once in three or four years.

Berries can be pounded into a paste and dried; so can grasshoppers. But in the long run, stored seeds and piñon nuts mattered most to desert folk. In rain years or in bearing years for piñons, families could stay alive until spring. But in really dry years, prospects of survival were dim. People sickened and died, or might even be cannibalized.

Great Basin Diggers liked to winter near the piñon stands

so that the basketed nuts would not have to be carried down-hill. They liked to stay but most often could not, for winter snows forced them down to the foothills and the warm valley floor. In other days, say the Diggers, before cattle were brought to the Basin, some grasses grew there. Now only sagebrush and greasewood, mesquite and cacti are to be found. Of course there are the various small animals and insects. Diggers kept busy all winter hunting this sort of miniature game.

The main problem for them in choosing a winter residence has always been water. In the Great Basin little rain falls, and the air is so dry, the temperature range so extreme that sometimes more moisture is lost in evaporation than remains. Whatever rain does fall and collect into mountain streams is most often lost in the sands below. And because the Great Basin is a catchall with few permanent river outlets to the sea, what moisture there is often puddles into alkaline sinks or dries into salt flats—useless to man. Wherever dependable springs were to be found or small shallow lakes, Diggers usually congregated for the winter, putting up houses of tule-reed matting.

Necessary for life, water also became sacred to desert folk, especially to the Paiutes. The reverent man prayed to Father Sun while patting water on his face. He prayed in the sweat house amid the steam. Water was sprinkled over participants at a curing ceremony, for water was "like the human's breath" and purified all. Water baths took away bad thoughts and wishes and broke the sorcerer's spell. Water brought power, too. In the few water holes that never dried up there lived the Water Babies. Wherever they were, cool breezes blew. The man who could see the Water Babies and speak to them was a fortunate man indeed, for they gave him power to call the clouds and to cure.

There was no permanence to winter refuge camps. Family groups were likely to encounter relatives there, but just as often they might not. And when spring came, each little family went its separate way. Father, mother, and two or three children, no more: this was the irreducible social unit. One did not live with one's relatives; seldom was there lots of jolly company. On the other hand, one did not, could not, live alone. Whatever fighting there was among desert folk seems to have been over women—getting them, losing them to other men, looking anew. Without both halves of the marital team, life was quite literally impossible.

Mother and girls made baskets, gathered roots and seeds, parched them with live coals on basketry trays, ground them between stones, and hunted rodents in between times. Men made flint tools, hunted larger game, made rabbit-skin blankets, and helped build winter houses and summer wind-breaks. They helped gather piñon nuts and might even lend a hand at carting wood and water.

It was a man's job to teach his son to hunt, but he helped his girls (and boys, too) in yet another way, a magical way. The first wail of a new arrival sent him out into the hills, running as far as his legs would take him. Only thus could he assure his child strong legs, sturdy legs that would never tire no matter how many weary miles there were to be walked nor how many crags to scale.

As spring turned toward summer, the desert family began to climb. Upward from greens to seeds to roots and berries and at last to piñon. Then down again—down for autumn and the only big occasions of the desert year. In harvest autumn came the get-togethers, the dancing, singing, and gambling that punctuated the year. There came also the communal rabbit hunt. For a short time, men of many families worked together as a team under the direction of an elected "rabbit boss." Throughout the summer each family had busily refurbished its net, which looked something like our tennis net but was much longer. These nets were joined end-to-end to form a great semicircle dividing a valley. Behind them, the hunters waited. From the other end of the valley came the shouts and cries of the beaters. Sometimes fires were lit to help drive the game, though desert folk dreaded the loss of vegetation that fires caused. The beaters moved forward. Before them the jackrabbits fled madly and were caught in the net, clubbed, and collected. The owners of the nets had first claim to the kill, but it was the job of the rabbit boss to make a just distribution.

Sometimes pronghorn antelope were hunted in this way, too, and were driven into pounds made of brush. Not often, certainly not every year, for pronghorns were slow to breed. Like rabbits, pronghorns could be driven. Unlike rabbits, they could also be lured, for they were intensely curious animals. Men who could run with special fleetness were thought to possess power over the pronghorn antelope, could lure them, could ensnare their souls. And it was such a man who was always sought out to direct the pronghorn-antelope drive. Days of ceremony were required, special dances and songs, and helpers who wore pronghorn-antelope disguises. But the ultimate success of the hunt depended mainly on the antelope shaman.

Whoever had power over the pronghorn, an animal who was the bringer of illness as well as a source of food, also had the power to heal human ailments, and in Paiute life with all its misery, doctors were much needed. Men became doctors informally by inheriting the techniques from a close relative, or formally through a dream. For the Paiutes the dream was all. It was not solicited as among the Ojibwa, not coerced in the way of the Kwakiutl who sent their bereaved, hysterical and suffering, out into the forest to demand visions. A dream, said the Paiute, must come of its own or it will not come at all. To the sleeper there might appear at any time hawk or weasel, fire or gun or dozens of other potent objects or beings bringing boons and instructions. Woe to the man who failed to recognize those instructions, who failed to follow his dream. A dream unfulfilled brought illness as surely as the sorcerer's wish. And yet even the sorcerer, the "eater of people," had no choice but to follow his own dream, however repugnant it might be. In Paiute terms, each life had its individual path, its individual destiny. To deny destiny was to deny life and health and happiness.

People were not supposed to tell their dreams and thus to reveal their special powers. The bulletproof hunter, the woman immune to snakebite, were to be discovered in action, not by boast. This rule, of course, did not apply to shamans, who remained silent at their own peril. No matter how shy and retiring a dream-ordained doctor might be, he had to become a public figure, exhibiting his powers for all to see, answering after sunset of the same day any call presented before sunrise. The curing spirits, it was said, took an exceedingly dim view of free treatment, and all doctors were careful to collect fees in advance.

Illness came from several sources—from bad wishing by a sorcerer, from a dream deferred or unrecognized, from contamination of the blood, or from a ghost. The shaman's first care was accurate diagnosis, obtained in a nightlong public session of song, dance, and trance. Sometimes the shaman actually had to send his soul chasing after that of the unconscious patient, wresting it back to earth by main force. Sometimes, in the time-honored New World manner, he sucked from the patient's body sticks, stones, even live frogs, placed there, he claimed, by a sorcerer's ill wishing. Even though hopelessly ill, helplessly aged persons might be abandoned to die, it cannot be said that an ordinary sufferer lacked care—the care of his relatives who somehow managed to finance treatment, the care of a shaman who was plainly skilled, who might at any time walk on live coals, summon clouds, speak to water babies and run like an antelope.

Without the support of family, the help of shamans, and the direction of visions, surely desert life would have been insupportable. But not everywhere in the Great Basin was it stripped so ruthlessly to the bare essentials of survival. In some favored spots life took on added color, a certain tone of well-being almost out of place in those bleak surroundings. One favored spot was Owens Valley in southeastern California. It is near Death Valley (surely one of the world's *least* favored places), yet it is blessed by a small but dependable river. On one flank rises the Sierra Nevada range, rain-drenched and snow-crowned. If there is not plenty in Owens Valley, there is at least enough of all that makes life livable to attract people and to let them settle down. As late as the 1920s, when anthropologist Julian H. Steward came to study the Owens Valley Paiute, there were permanent village clusters along the piñon zone. Each had a chief who supervised the building and maintenance of a sweat house which served as an ordinary men's clubhouse when the sacred sweating fire was doused. He organized the autumnal mourning rites which commemorated all village members who had died during the year just past and which released the bereaved from their mourning taboos. It was also a chiefly responsibility to arrange the harvest dances and communal hunts, or to appoint temporary leaders who would do the arranging.

Each village chief ordered the yearly treks to distant piñon stands and berry patches. He also directed an activity which seems to have been unique to Owens Valley, or at least to its northern end: a yearly irrigation project. Little streams flowing down from the mountains were dammed and diverted into a network of artificial channels which wound through and around stands of wild grasses. Now the idea of irrigation ordinarily comes to farmers already wise in the ways of plants. Ordinarily it is a late and sophisticated achievement in farm technology. And yet here were the Owens Valley Paiute, innocent of cultivation techniques and even of the notion of planting seed, doing what Mexican farmers had not learned until sometime around 800 B.C., after several thousand years of sowing and reaping.

Nobody knows how or when the Owens Valley people learned about irrigation. Nobody knows whether it was introduced from the outside or invented from within. In all of Owens Valley there is no record of a prior farming folk. To the west in California, Indians in the old days were acorn gatherers, hunters, and fishermen. To be sure, across the Colorado River in Arizona is the agricultural Southwest, but the plants grown there were never known in Owens Valley. Perhaps the idea of irrigation came late with some wandering trapper full of Yankee ingenuity and handy with a spade. Whether early or late, whether introduced or home-grown, the Paiute irrigation project reflects the same desert-bred receptivity and inventiveness that, in another dry valley far to the south, brought agriculture itself into being. In this hemisphere it was truly the meek who inherited the earth and made even a desert to blossom and to bear.

Part IV
FARMERS

Mounds, Towns, and Burials

Imagine if you can a candy bar without chocolate, or cup custard without vanilla flavor. Imagine pizza without tomato sauce, lamb stew without potatoes, Halloween without pumpkins, breakfast without corn flakes. Automatically the mind rejects this bland and cheerless prospect. And yet, had New World people remained hunters and gatherers and fishermen, our diet today would indeed be minus many delights. For tomatoes, potatoes, the cacao bean, the vanilla bean, pumpkins, and corn (or maize) are all native to the Western Hemisphere and were domesticated in the New World. There are many more: condiments such as chili peppers; among vegetables—five kinds of beans and four kinds of squashes; among fruits—avocado, papaya, pineapple, tomato, guava; among root crops—sweet and bitter manioc, sweet and "Irish" potatoes, and peanuts; even stimulants and drugs, things to chew and things to smoke—coca (from which comes cocaine), tobacco, chicle (as in Chiclets) from the sapodilla tree. Some American things grow as they will, cultivated or wild—the cinchona tree from which quinine is extracted, and the castilla tree from whose sap comes rubber for balls, hot-water bottles, and automobile tires. Some native American plants are ornamental—dahlias, bright marigolds. One at least is both useful and beautiful; that is the sunflower—the only New World plant to be domesticated north of Mexico.

The list is not exhausted, not nearly. It is true, of course, that the New World's roster of animal domesticates is short. Mention the dog, llama and alpaca (tame cousins to the guanaco), guinea pig, turkey, and duck, and you have about covered the lot. Nothing to compare with the Old World beasts of byre and burden. But in the matter of cultivated plants, and even of planting techniques, the New World clearly ranks first. Although many hunters, fishermen, and gatherers were still following the ancient ways when Columbus arrived, most American Indians were already farmers, and rather sophisticated farmers at that.

Of course, they had not all adopted the new life overnight. In some places—up near what is now Maine in North America, down through the Amazon Basin in the southern continent—the conversion to farming came very late. Neither was the complete catalogue of American plants domesticated at one stroke nor all in the same area. Potatoes seem to have had an Andean highland origin. Manioc belongs to the rain forest. Tobacco—one species, at least—seems to have been domesticated in Bolivia or northwest Argentina. None of these, however, was widely cultivated—and some not cultivated at all—until after 2000 B.C. The oldest domesticated plants (as was mentioned in Chapter 6) have been found farther north in Mexico. Perhaps it was from this "hearth" that the farming idea spread, stimulating other gathering folk to try with their own wild plants what had been already accomplished elsewhere.

If, when "hearth" is mentioned, you visualize a single tight little center of invention, that is not precisely what archaeology has revealed in Mexico. For even there, different plants were apparently domesticated in different places—pumpkins in the highlands around Tamaulipas, beans in the west of Mexico, and squashes and avocados in the Valley of

Tehuacán. Chilis seem to have been everywhere popular. All these plants were in cultivation soon after 7000 B.C.—a date which compares favorably with the date of eight or nine thousand B.C. for earliest domestication in the Old World.

For a very long time the people in these various highland centers kept their ideas and their plants to themselves. The corn of Tehuacán, domesticated by 5000 B.C., had already been hybridized with wild relatives, enlarged, and improved before anyone outside the valley learned of it. And a good thing, too, for they might have found the tiny cobs (as Dr. MacNeish says, little bigger than a cigarette filter) hardly worth the trouble of cultivation. For domesticated corn cannot propagate itself. It cannot even be sown broadcast but must be carefully placed, kernel by kernel, each in its own little hummock. At any rate—whether it was the extreme isolation of the dry valleys or the fact that, in early highland Mexico, cultivated plants provided no more than ten per cent of the diet—horticultural news and views were not widely shared. The pumpkin of Tamaulipas, for example, did not reach Tehuacán until 3000 B.C.; corn did not arrive in Tamaulipas until 2500 B.C. By this time Tehuacán people had come to depend on cultivated plants for about one-quarter of their dietary needs. Farming had obviously become an activity of importance. And important activities do tend to travel.

The making of pottery is also an important activity, and you will remember something about the way it traveled. You will remember, too, that pottery has an affinity for settled folk—fishermen or farmers. The first pottery in Tehuacán dates to 2300 B.C. and is found in the remains of small pit-house hamlets. By 1500 B.C. figurines were being modeled in clay. Whether pottery was brought from South America to Mexico by boat or by land, through jungle trails or over mountain passes cannot yet be known. What does

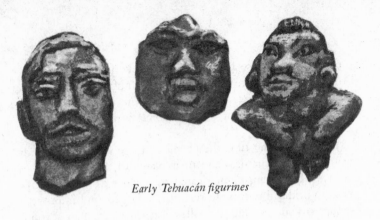

Early Tehuacán figurines

seem certain is that the traffic in ideas was not all one way. Mexican innovations and Mexicans themselves were traveling south.

Sometime around 1500 B.C. a new people appeared on the Guayas coast of Ecuador. Their remains turn up in the upper levels of shell-mound villages there—not so much in the Valdivia sites as in those of their neighbors who had adapted Valdivia styles to suit their own tastes. The newcomers brought wholly different sorts of pottery—ear plugs shaped like napkin rings and beautifully designed figurines, obsidian tools, and vessels all exhibiting a remarkable similarity in style and inventory to items recently found at a site of comparable age near modern Ocós on the southern coast of Guatemala. An ancient sea trip seems likely—a migration undertaken by people whose homes had been in or near the northern site. The Mexican newcomers combined styles and perhaps forces with the resident fishermen, and soon afterward both began settling inland, back from the coast. Now the Valdivia people and their neighbors had never farmed, but the move inland, up river valleys, suggests that a new mode of subsistence had been introduced, almost certainly by the corn-planting Mexican colonists.

Shortly before 1500 B.C. corn and apparently some of its donors as well reached the river oases of the Peruvian coast, for about this time new pottery styles came into vogue. Pottery was no surprise to Peruvians. It had first appeared in the area around 2000 B.C. Neither were domesticated plants a new thing. You will recall that squash-farmer-fishermen had been settled in the river valley coasts since 3500 B.C. or thereabouts. By the time Mexican corn appeared, native beans (Lima beans, of course), potatoes (in a few places), bottle gourds, and cotton had joined squash in domestication.

Bottle gourds and cotton are mystery plants, plants which more and more specialists believe to have been brought over the Pacific rather than domesticated on these shores. There is indeed a wild cotton native to the Americas. Its germ cell contains thirteen small chromosomes. The germ cells of Old World cotton, in both the wild and the domesticated forms, bear thirteen large chromosomes. But the seeds of *domesticated* New World cotton contain twenty-six chromosomes—thirteen of them small and thirteen large. That, any botanist will tell you, strongly suggests a case of mixing, of hybridizing the cottons, Old World domesticated with American wild. Immediately the questions surface—when and how? Perhaps, suggests Dr. Meggers, by way of the same errant canoe that brought Jomon pottery to Ecuador (see Chapter 6). It was in 2500 B.C.—several centuries after the first appearance of pottery in Valdivia—that textiles made of twined domesticated-cotton fibers appeared in a Peruvian site. Perhaps cotton was first used in fishing lines; of that there is no record.

It is fair to say that direct evidence of domesticated cotton, either the Peruvian or the Mexican species, has not yet been uncovered in Ecuadorian sites of this early period (3000–2500 B.C.). It must also be noted that cotton seed tends to rot in prolonged exposure to damp air; one surely cannot imagine a setting more damp than an open canoe on an ocean voyage. And yet, however damp the voyage, however lacking the direct evidence for such a voyage, for canoes bearing cotton seeds, we must consider the notion. It is for now the best explanation we have. Only time and hope and further excavations can finally resolve the question of how the New

ESKIMO ARCTIC HUNTERS

NORTHERN HUNTERS

NORTHWEST COAST
FISHERMEN

BISON
HUNTERS

SEED AND ROOT GATHERERS

SOUTHWEST

SOUTHEAST

MEXICAN

MAYAN

*Economy and Politics
at the Time of
European Arrival*

INCA-ANDEAN

FARMS
AND GATHERING

HUNTER-GATHERERS

FISHERS

Simple societies of
gatherers, hunters, and fishermen

Desert farm
villages

Tropical forest
farm villages

Farmers and
farm villages

Confederations
and chiefdoms

High civilization
empires

(Based on J. Steward)

World–Old World hybrid cotton appeared in this hemisphere.

By 1500 B.C. in Mexico, a little later in Peru, domesticated plants had provided the economic base from which great civilizations would soon grow. From Mexico and Peru spread not only plants and agricultural techniques, but notions of leadership and worship, of order and of art. In ever more diluted form, the influences spread north and south, sometimes clashing, sometimes mingling with strong native developments, sometimes capturing a people altogether, but always changing, adapting, forming patterns anew.

By 500 B.C. the South American farming traditions had crossed the Andes and were moving down the eastern slopes. In what is now northwest Argentina, a secondary farming center developed. The land between the great mountain rims is high and dry, its horizons punctuated by stark buttes and rocky cliffs, its floors softened only by sagebrush and cacti. The visitor can see there a geographical twin to the North American Southwest, itself a secondary center of farming traditions. Curiously similar, too, were the ways of life developed in both spots. The tools, the pottery, even the figurines are alike—shaped by the demands of similar environments and the pervasive influence of the two great centers of civilization.

The ancient people of northwest Argentina built ceremonial platforms and carved figures of stone, often using the feline theme so popular throughout the Americas. They built small separate houses of dry stone which in later years were erected so close together as to form apartment complexes. Earlier they had constructed round, communal pit houses, somewhat reminiscent of the kivas of the North American Southwest. After 1000 A.D. they took to building on mesas true apartment-house towns, ringed by walls and girded for war. The farmers of the high desert, some of them the Diaguita Indians of historic times, were surrounded by hostile hunting bands and mounted warriors, by soldiers of the Incas and soldiers from Spain, even as their northern counterparts were surrounded. Both had adopted much the same means of defense.

North of the Diaguita zone, in what is now Bolivia, farming traditions reached a lowland folk. Between the Beni and Mamoré Rivers lies the Mojos Plain, less than eight hundred feet above sea level. It is a sea of grass dotted here and there by forest islands. For seven months of the year they are truly islands, for the grass is covered everywhere by flood waters several inches to several feet in depth. In the rain forests on the fringes of this plain live the hunting Siriono (see Chapter 5). Here, too, were once found the chiefdoms of the Mojos, Paressí, and Baule Indians, their little village confederacies built—quite literally—on the achievements of their predecessors. For the first farmers in the Mojos Plain were builders. Perhaps noting how the better-drained forest islands escaped the floods, they lifted their farm lands, piling them into series of low ridges that from the air look like corduroy fabric. They built hundreds and hundreds of these mounds, enough to cover 50,000 acres of flood land. And not only planting mounds, but also village mounds and burial mounds, all interconnected by causeways, some of which stretch unbroken for as much as seven miles. Archaeological excavation has barely got under way. Nobody knows what staple crop supported the early farmers of the Mojos Plain nor exactly when the mounds were built. There are other such ridged fields in South America, meant, like the Mojos mounds, to lift agricultural land above the flood. One in Ecuador has been dated to 500 A.D., another in Surinam to 700 A.D. Are the Bolivian mounds older? There they lie, awaiting the archaeologist's spade.

In between Mexico and Peru lies Colombia, a perfect target for cultural cross-fire. Colombia has tropical forests, a hospitable coastline, and mountains that extend one arm into Central America while embracing Venezuela with the other. On the Caribbean coast are shell mounds with pottery almost as old as the earliest Valdivia samples. Inland is a 3000-year-old site (1000 B.C.) containing fragments of a rough-pottery grater—just the sort later used in the preparation of bitter manioc. For bitter manioc is poisonous in its raw state and must be shredded, wrung dry of its juice, and heated thoroughly before its prussic acid is dispelled. The Colombian grater is the oldest so far discovered. It may be that bitter manioc and its sweet cousin were domesticated in this very area.

It is in the Colombian mountains—or rather, in the high valleys between peaks—that early corn farming got under way successfully. Remains of ambitious construction have been found there—not the remains of villages but of burials, cemetery-memorials. One in particular is a sort of Forest Lawn of the Colombian highlands. Scattered over several hundred square miles near the village of San Agustin are its tombs, revealing a dizzying variety of burial styles. There are cremations and interments, urn coffins and sarcophagi hewn each from a single stone. There are burials in shafts, in stone-lined rooms, and even in stone-lined houses mounded over with earth. Whether this variety represents an exceedingly individualistic people given to expressing their

San Agustin monument

whims, a society of status ups and downs, or simply a trip through time, it is hard to say. Since the San Agustin cemetery dates back to 555 B.C. and remained in use for at least a thousand years, time may indeed account for the range in style, so thinks anthropologist Gerardo Reichel-Dolmatoff.

There are some things about San Agustin, however, that did not change, even through a thousand years. The people who buried their dead there had a predilection for statuary. Everywhere one sees stone figures—big ones twelve feet tall, little ones of midget size. They are to be found in graves and out, sometimes enshrined, sometimes not, dominating the landscape and the viewer with their squat power. It is impossible to know whether or not they were meant to be memorial portraiture, but it is safe to say that some at least represented gods, for these have the fangs and grim muzzles of the New World feline deity. There are birds of prey, too, and several serpents—also popular American religious themes. Some cannibal figures seem ready to devour what appear to be small children—the American version of Cronus and his offspring, perhaps. Most of the statues sport imposing headdresses and little else. Many hold ordinary objects in a manner so threatening that they might as well be weapons.

Remains of the houses of San Agustin's farmers, craftsmen, and groundskeepers are scattered in the hills. Plain little huts, they seem to have been, round and built of wood. Grinding stones are found in these sites, plain pottery (no time to decorate anything that was merely of everyday use), and the faint parallel furrows of ancient fields. By the time Adaqui Indians occupied the area, the original farmers were long gone. And the new people who settled in their places did not know how to honor the stone gods left behind or even what they were meant to represent.

All around the mountainous fringes of South America the farming idea traveled, penetrating the tangled rain forest only very late in time. At least, we think it was late. The forest environment is not kind to cultural remains. Slashing, burning, moving on as they must, forest farmers have, in any case, few possessions to leave behind. What evidence there is suggests the trickling of ideas down-river toward the sea, from highland centers to the forests below. Perhaps the ideas came with hopeful highland colonists in search of land and a new beginning, perhaps with soldiers bent on imperial expansion. One such ancient colony has been uncovered on an island at the mouth of the Amazon. Beginning about 1200 A.D., Andean settlers made valiant efforts to cope with forest, floods, and fields that rapidly lost their fertility. By 1500 the experiment was at an end, though it had no doubt converted many a hunting band to the new way of life. The farming idea is traveling still. Every year the numbers of hunting-gathering folk in the Amazon Basin shrink a little as one small group after another takes to cultivating the soil. And yet there remain the stubbornly unconverted who prefer the old ways, the old foods, the old uncertainties, and perhaps always will.

Farming ideas and farming techniques traveled north as well as south and at an even earlier time. Early arrival did not always guarantee quick acceptance, however. In a cave in southern New Mexico, there have been found corn cobs from Mexico, tiny, primitive, but definitely domesticated, cobs which have been dated to about 2500 B.C. No doubt the kernels were planted sporadically by people who inhabited the high, dry valley beneath the cave—a people who in every other particular faithfully followed the old desert way of life. In an on-again-off-again fashion, a patch here and a patch there, the new idea gradually spread, taking a good 2400 years to take hold. Suddenly, around 100 B.C., there were better varieties of corn available, and farming villages began to take shape, the oldest around the Mogollon Mountains. Villages next appeared in plateau country, among people whose cultural remains would later be called

Anasazi (Navajo for "the Ancient Ones"). Then, around the Gila and Salt Rivers, there developed the Hohokam Culture (again, but in the Pima tongue, "the Ancient Ones"—literally, "those who have gone away"). Later still on the hot Colorado flood plain would settle the people archaeologists call Patayan (a Yuma word for "the Ancient Ones").

The name of "Ancient Ones" is, in all instances, particularly appropriate, for there are in these areas today people who live in much the same sorts of dwellings, worship and farm in much the same ways, as archaeology has suggested for their forebears. Ties of time bind the modern Pueblo people—Hopi, Zuñi, and others—to the Anasazi area, Pima and Papago to the Hohokam, and Yuma, Walapai, Havasupai, and Yavapai to the Patayan. The earliest of the Southwest's farmers, the Mogollon people, are thought to have dispersed through the other zones, to have influenced strongly the people in each but to have left behind no living connections of their own.

The first farming villages in the Southwest were clusters of round pit houses, and so they remained until some of the Anasazi folk around 700 A.D. took to building aboveground, building no longer single houses but many-storied apartment dwellings of adobe and stone. Some were constructed in natural cliff overhangs. Others were free-standing like Pueblo Bonito in Chaco Canyon, New Mexico. Begun in 919 A.D. (as archaeologists can tell from the tree rings of preserved beams), this D-shaped town eventually accommodated 1200 people in 800 single rooms and thirty-two kivas, those round ceremonial centers which recalled the ancient pit house.

The apartment-project idea had spread early to the Mogollon area but appeared along the Gila and Salt Rivers only when Anasazi themselves came as refugees to build anew among the pit houses of the Hohokam. For times around 1275 A.D. were troubled. There was, for one thing, a severe drought (or so the tree rings tell us). There was also war. With the exception of the Patayan, the people of the Southwest seem never to have been warlike, never to have practiced a religion that required human sacrifice or human torture. And though they were able to organize themselves for big building projects and the construction of immense irrigation systems, they seem never to have been rank-conscious social climbers, either. Yet suddenly among these quiet people were warriors. The evidence is very plain. Pueblos were fortified against attack, towns were burned, the inhabitants slain and their corpses mutilated and left where they had fallen. Perhaps, some say, newcomers were to blame—incoming Navajo and Apache, Athapascan-speaking hunters and gatherers, fierce, tough, and hungry for gain. This may be so, though we cannot be absolutely certain of their presence in the Southwest until about 1500. Whoever the invaders, whatever the press of circumstance, sometime around 1300 the northern pueblos were deserted. People moved south and west, taking refuge in other apartment towns or building new ones, towns in which the incoming Spaniards would find them in 1540.

It was not by way of pueblo farms that domesticated plants were carried east. Mexican ideas that had evolved in one way in the desert Southwest took quite different forms in the woodland environment. Eastern land, after all, was so much richer because of its extended rainfall, the variety and abundance of wild foods so much greater, that people had long ago grown used to living well and with reasonable security. It is not too surprising, then, to learn that some Eastern Woodland people, hunters and mollusk fishermen who lived along slow rivers in the lower Southeast, sometime around 2000 B.C. took to using pottery without also taking to farming. Their ware was crude, fiber-tempered, in shape and style so much like the stone bowls and jars they had fashioned earlier that many specialists believe these very people must have invented the idea of pottery independently. Others see in this pottery evidence for a new wave of migration over the Bering Strait. Still others, pointing to similar (and older) fiber-tempered samples found on the Caribbean coast of Colombia, suggest a diffusion by sea, perhaps with island stopovers along the way.

Newer sorts of ceramic ware—cord-marked and grit-tempered—appeared around 1000 B.C. But pottery was not the only new thing to appear at this time among woodland hunter-gatherers. A new religious idea was born. So completely did it capture imaginations that it was to spread north to Manitoba and Nebraska, south to Florida, and to last—through several transformations—until after 1700 A.D., when the white man, his Bible and his diseases, defeated it for good and all.

Precisely what the religion was—its gods, its dogmas, its hopes—nobody now can say. Its remains (most of which are to be found in what is now Ohio) do not include anything like temples. There are merely communal burials to suggest the ideas that brought them into being. But what burials! Tall mounds, surrounded by secondary earthworks, moats, gates, and corridors. Never was the earth simply thrown up haphazardly over the graves. Each interment progressed through several stages in the open stockaded "houses" built to receive the dead. There was an initial laying out, the painting of the skeleton after a lapse of time, the burning of the stockade, and finally the careful mounding of earth over all. Funerary protocol evidently required that each mound and each individual grave within it contain certain offerings. Always there were precious things (jars overflowing with river pearls, for example); always figures, bowls, ritual pipes, and plaques beautifully carved of stone or of exotic materials brought from afar. In the early mounds (and even more strikingly in the later ones) there are to be found ornamental heads and hands cut from mica

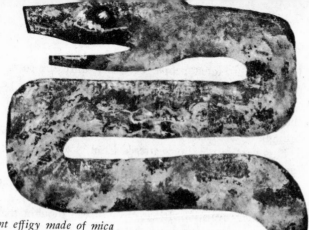

A serpent effigy made of mica

sheets imported from Virginia; plaques, pendants, and bracelets made of copper brought from the Great Lakes (where for two thousand years hunters had known how to hammer the abundant natural nuggets into weapons and fanciful shapes); grizzly-bear teeth brought from the Rockies and inlaid with pearls; conch shells carried north from the Gulf of Mexico. As archaeologist Olaf Prufer suggests, such offerings must have involved an enormous network of trade contacts. Perhaps this may explain how the religion spread so fast and so far. It would not be the first time in man's past that religion and trade have supported each other's interests.

The emphasis on death and a stylish burial may be simply one way of doing honor to the upper crust, the wealthy or high-ranking members of a particular society. But it may also reflect certain strong beliefs in an afterlife or even rebirth into this one. More than that archaeology cannot tell us. It seems very clear, however, that mound building of this very specific type spread as an idea or cluster of ideas, not as a total cultural package. One would not, for example, speak of a single widespread "Mound Culture," for the characteristic burials are to be found among the remains of people who lived very differently from one another, made different sorts of tools and houses, and undoubtedly spoke different languages. One thinks of the way Christianity or

Islam has attracted people of many different sorts, with many styles of life, and the word "religion" (or perhaps "cult") seems the only one suitable for mound building in the Eastern Woodlands and for the unknown beliefs that brought it into being.

Nowhere in the tiny scattered hamlets which surrounded each of the early mound complexes is there an indication of corn, or even clear evidence for the cultivation of squash or beans. Some specialists find this a surprising, even a disconcerting, revelation. It has always been thought that vast building projects, requiring the labor of many men and the specialized artistic direction of a few, required also a large food surplus to keep workers on the job. And a surplus, what is more, of high-bulk, high-energy food—a carbohydrate food of the sort supplied by grain. Men who must hunt or collect their meals every day or even every other day have little time for anything else. Yet here are the early mounds, apparently built by just such people. For if there were cultivated foods to be had, they must have been in exceedingly short supply. We can only suppose that the forest environment provided a greater surplus of high-energy foods than has been imagined—acorns, walnuts, and hickory nuts, for example—or else that the power of an idea overcame all natural obstacles.

The early period of mound building (1000–300 B.C.) is often called the Adena Cult. It was followed by a newer elaboration, the Hopewell Cult, so called for the Ohio farm on which the first large mound was excavated. Woodland pottery, typically marked by cord or vegetable fibers (no cotton was grown in the Eastern Woodlands), is to be found in Adena hamlet remains but not in their burial mounds. Pottery was a frequent addition to the Hopewell offerings, however, and so were ceramic figurines beautifully shaped, fired, and ceremonially "killed"—broken so that the spirit of their beauty could accompany the dead. Something else is to be found in the Hopewell sites besides pottery and an increased quantity, increased beauty of grave goods. In the scattered bottom-land hamlets where lived the builders, the artisans, the custodians of the Hopewell tombs, corn has been discovered. Extra food for the part-time workers, who congregated whenever mounds were being built, came now from furrowed fields—not, as before, from the distant woods and streams.

Looking at the burial mounds and their furnishings—the simple and elegant Adena style, the Hopewell elaborations, the effigy mounds of still later times, mounds built in the form of snakes and fanciful beasts—we wonder how it all began. Native invention, perhaps? We could hark back to the riverine people of the lower Southeast, those earliest of North American pottery makers. They liked to bury their dead in the ever-present shell mounds, accompanied by dogs and grave goods of various sorts, even imported luxury items. Did the burial-mound idea come from the Caribbean area, where mound building was also important? Adena mounds are older than those in the Antilles or on the Caribbean coast of South America, almost as old as the oldest Mexican mounds. Did the idea come from Asia, then? Again, the Adena mounds antedate the sort of chiefly barrow burial, long practiced by the Battle-ax People in central Asia. From Mexico, then? This is the likeliest prospect. Both the snake and the bird of prey—old in both Mexico and Peru—are constant decorative themes in Adena and Hopewell art. It seems true, of course, that Adena mounds were raised long before the appearance of corn in the Eastern Woodlands. And certainly corn diffused northward from Mexico. The routes of diffusion, however, are unclear. Coastal lands lying between the mound builders' territory and the farthest-known extension of Mexican influence were long held by simple hunting-gathering folk who exhibited not the slightest effect of southern ideas and ways.

Still and all, the possibility of Mexican influences at work among early mound builders of the Mississippi and Ohio

valleys is a strong one. After 700 A.D., after the distinctive
Hopewell style of mound building had died out, those influences are unmistakable. Large villages began to appear then
along the stretch of Mississippi between what are now St.
Louis and Memphis. Stockaded against assailants (the east
had its time of troubles, too), these villages sheltered farmers
whose main crops were corn, squash, and beans. Within the
walls were burial mounds (no longer crammed with treas-
ure), but these were completely overshadowed by other
mounds, huge and flat-topped, strikingly similar to Mexican
pyramids and, like the pyramids, crowned with temples or
chiefs' houses to which one mounted by way of steps or
ramps. And there were buildings of a public sort, some on
and some off the mounds. There were community meeting
halls and even sunken council chambers. One such hall, uncovered near Macon, Georgia, is round in shape with a wall
banquette marked for forty-seven councilors. Seats for three
other speakers were placed on a raised platform built in the
shape of a bird of prey, its beak pointing toward the central
fire pit. The statuary, the ornaments, the pottery designs to
be found in these southeastern towns, all speak eloquently
of Mexican inspiration. Amid the variety of symbols and
motifs there is even a suggestion of hieroglyphs.

Clearly the Temple Mound People had evolved a highly
complex culture—Mexican in its architectural form and its
religious symbols, but drawing much from all that had gone
before. Their descendants—tribes like the Natchez, for example—were still living in such towns and praying on just
such temple mounds when they were discovered by the
French.

Up toward the Great Lakes and points east, the ideas
which had inspired the mounds and towns and temples
thinned out until they reached the horizons of the northern
hunters where people did not or would not plant and to
this day are hunters still.

Pequots and Yanomamö

The Warrior Farmers

To most of us—busy as we are with the concerns of the city and its peripheries—the word "farm" conjures up visions of refuge. We think of quiet fields, tilled by an unhurried farmer at peace with himself and the world. Like all visions, this one may not be fancy altogether. It might very well apply to some farms and some farmers even in this day and age. But it would not apply to all farmers everywhere in place and time—certainly not in the Americas. In the first place, many farmers native to this hemisphere were women. And their labors provided the means by which male war games could be perpetuated. Farming and fighting are never really incompatible, of course, even when men do work in the fields. These activities simply take on seasonal character-istics, become alternating activities. When men are not bound to the land, however, when even their hunting and fishing obligations are few, then warfare becomes something of an occupation as well as a game, the only certain means of establishing one's credentials in a warrior's world. Among many farming Indians the old hit-and-run tactics—raid, ambush, and quick retreat—grew into wars of territorial conquest.

In 1614 Dutch navigators sailing north from New Am-sterdam on Long Island Sound discovered the broad Con-necticut River. Just below what is now Hartford they encountered villages of the Pequot Indians. These were, as it turned out, new villages. The Pequots had lately taken the Connecticut Valley by conquest. From the tip of Long Island (*Sewan Hackey*, "Land of Shells") where lived the Montauk, to Block Island of the Manisses, to the Rhode Island Narragansetts, the Pequots exacted tribute in shell money, or wampum. And all the tribes of the Connecticut mainland—the Podunks, the Tunxis, the Quinnipiac, and others—feared and paid tribute to Pequot ferocity and Pequot numbers. It had been sometime around 1600, according to New England historians, that the Pequots had begun to move east and south from around the Hudson River to occupy much of the coastal area of Connecticut. In the move one Pequot group, the Mohicans, had been left behind to hold the Thames River.

In actual way of life, neither the Pequots nor the other Connecticut tribes seem to have lived very differently from the Ojibwa who were their Algonquian language relatives. There was a good deal of moving about so that wild foods could be gathered: to the shore for spring fishing and mollusk gathering, to hunting grounds in the fall, to protected valleys in the wintertime. The home fields were sometime things, planted with corn and beans and then neglected until harvest-time. Men had only one activity in those gardens, and that was the raising of tobacco, considered far too sacred for women to touch and certainly too sacred for them to smoke.

Chiefs had begun to live year-round in palisaded villages which became forts in time of war, forts in which Indians from miles around tended to congregate and from which (more frequently in the Pequot case) war parties sallied forth. New England historians tell us that the office of chief was hereditary, though personal character still determined the degree of actual power any chief could exercise. Each tribal unit was rather clearly organized around the chief and his lieutenants, called *sagamores*. The Pequot high chief (or sachem) is said to have commanded twenty-six *sagamores*. In this rule-conscious, leader-controlled way of life, we are told, the chief himself might punish offenders. No longer did he lead (as among the Ojibwa) by mere example and demeanor. There was now muscle behind the customary regulations.

Ojibwa on the war path took scalps but never captives. Pequots took scalps and captives, gaining honor from both. Captives were sometimes adopted into the group to replace sons and husbands lost in war, but more often they were treated in quite another way. They were tortured to death as slowly, as ingeniously as possible. It was the captive's part to sing his war songs all the while, to defy his tormentors, and to go to his death bravely without a groan. Such a man was extravagantly admired by the Pequots even while they busily plied knife and brand. Afterward they eagerly parceled out the victim's flesh to eat, hoping that his superior courage would be absorbed along with the nourishment. The fact that there was something other than fiendish pleasure in the applied torment, that there was also a sense of ritual and a sense of honoring the brave man, suggests the influence of far-off Mexico where torment and human sacrifice were essential to religious observances.

The Ojibwa—who constitute a sort of Algonquian prototype—had never practiced torture. It may be that the Pequot and other farming Indians of New England took up the custom through genuine attraction to it. But then again they may have had no choice in the matter. Certainly neighbors like the fearsome Iroquoian Mohawk were torture enthusiasts; perhaps the farming Algonquians found it necessary to adopt the practices of their enemies.

What the Pequots may have feared in the Mohawks, other Connecticut Indians feared in the Pequots. Their wars proceeded without let or hindrance. Even in the fur-trading posts where the Dutch endeavored to keep peace, Pequots constantly violated sanctuary. Finally some defeated tribes invited the English in the Massachusetts Bay Colony to settle in Connecticut, hoping to muster some additional help against their enemies. The English came and never stopped coming. Realizing the dangerous potential in gunpowder and enemy numbers, the Pequot tried to enlist the aid of the Narragansetts and other of their former tributaries in ousting the white man. Had they forged a successful alliance, American history might now read rather differently. In 1630 guns were not all that reliable, colonial numbers not all that great, and Western notions of humanitarianism not all that superior to those of the Pequots. Europeans were enthusiastically given to burning heretics and witches, mutilating thieves, and executing traitors by drawing and quartering.

The Pequots were unsuccessful in their projected alliance, because of the efforts of Roger Williams, a religious refugee from the Massachusetts Bay Colony who had the complete confidence of the Narragansetts. By 1637, the Pequots had been utterly defeated, and they were soon extinguished as a tribal power. So were the Narragansetts who had sided with the colonists—not as quickly, perhaps, but just as surely.

The way of the Pequot warrior is known to us only from old books. It lives in the memory of no man as do the exploits of Plains people in the memories of a very few grandfathers among the Cheyenne and Blackfoot. The way of the forest farmer in South America is also described in old records, those of Spanish and Portuguese explorers and colonizers who often found themselves in the hot middle of intertribal, intervillage, even interisland raids. Indian farmers of the Amazon Basin found honor in war and in the bearing and behavior proper to the warrior. Like the Pequots with their trophy scalps, South American jungle warriors advertised their bravery by an accumulation of "medals"—human emblems of various sorts. (The famous shrunken heads of the Jivaro Indians of the western rain forest constitute one variety of emblem.) Like their northern colleagues, jungle warriors (especially those of the eastern areas) tortured captives and admired the proper show of defiance. They also ate the brave man's flesh—though sometimes rather more in the spirit of the gourmet than of the fan. Some, like the Tupinamba, went so far as to keep captives around the village, fattening them up with loving kindness for an eventual appearance on the menu.

The Tupinamba, the fierce Caribs of the Antilles, and others of the coastal area are gone now or changed beyond recognition. But the jungles of South America are still largely intact, unlike the deciduous forests of temperate North America, most of which are gone, along with the people they once sheltered. In the Amazon and Orinoco Basins there are stretches of rain forest not only uncleared but still unexplored. Living in these forests today are people virtually unknown to the outside world. On pages 84–5 we have already mentioned the Wama, hunting-gathering folk only recently encountered by missionaries in Surinam. The Yanomamö of Venezuela are another such "new" people who had their first contact with outsiders in 1950. The Yanomamö were then farming and using stone axes (when they could get stone), arrowheads of palm wood, and knives of agouti teeth. Their fields were cleared of brush with fire. Large trees were killed by slashing their bark all around. On the language map, the spot where the Yanomamö live is blank, and even now, apparently, the exact affiliations of the Yanamamö language have not been established. When discovered in 1950, they were at war—each of more than a hundred villages against the others. They are warriors still. "We are born," claim the Yanomamö, "from the blood of the moon, the fierce spirit moon who was shòt by other first beings, other spirit men, as he hunted the souls of children down below the sky. There were no women then upon the earth and no cowards, either, until they issued from the legs of a blood-born man. We know now that there are other people in the world. They must have wandered away and degenerated, until now they can hardly be counted men at all, even cowardly men. But we are still descendants of the moon's blood. We are fierce!"

It was among these fierce people that anthropologist Napoleon A. Chagnon went to live in 1964. He stayed with them a total of nineteen months, most of that time dependent on their protection and good will. There was little of either. Daily he was threatened, intimidated, lied to, cheated. Daily he was goaded. Not until he learned to live as a Yanomamö, to shout, snarl, and retaliate, not until he established a personal reputation for ferocity, was he treated with respect and even affection. Later, as Dr. Chagnon tells it, the Yanomamö of his base village reminisced fondly about his former timidity and about the time they had been able to bully him into giving away many axes and machetes.

Though there are a few *waiteri*, "truly fierce ones," in every village, much of the vaunted Yanomamö ferocity is actually a matter of astute bullying. The "front" is all. An established potential for violence may be in the long run more impressive than its actual expression. For most Yanomamö the object in life is to reap the fruits of ferocity—respect, deference, gain—without ever having to fight very hard for them. Thus it is that when a village is being attacked by a number of enemies, its own allies are often apt to join in the attack, for it is both safe and profitable to kick a former pal when he is down. (Dr. Chagnon knew of one Yanomamö village that had sustained as many as twenty-five raids in the course of the nearly two years he was in residence among them.) If a village learns that other villages—even allies—are belittling its ferocity, it must immediately (however unwillingly) raid *somebody* to demonstrate strike capability. It can announce its intention of a contest with spears—which is thought to be mildest of the real war games. It can plan an ambush, dispatching unsuspecting farmers in their gardens or attacking villages whose defenders are away. It can also stage a massacre.

For this ultimate in violence, a belligerent needs the help of a third party, an ostensibly neutral village, to "set up" the object of their mutual dislike. The neutral host village invites the intended victim village to a feast. Hidden in the jungle round about are warriors of the attacking village, waiting to strike. When the guests are sufficiently at their ease, lying in the hosts' hammocks and displaying their gorgeously painted bodies, those same hosts treacherously fall on them with clubs and axes. The attackers join in, mopping up anyone who manages to make his way over the palisade. If any fighting man of the victim village survives, then both host village and attacking village must make plans to decamp, establishing new gardens elsewhere. For retaliation will come, maybe not right away, not during the dry season in which the attack took place, not during the flood time to follow. But come it will. It must. The village that does not revenge its losses is not fierce, is not Yanomamö, is nothing at all.

Very often the raids and ambushes, if not the massacres, are instigated by the women of the village, who taunt their menfolk until the intended result is achieved. It is, after all, in their interests that the village reputation is upheld. For if the "front" slips even a little, a raid is sure to follow. And in any raid, women are likely to be carted off to be other men's wives. Even if they manage to escape that fate, if their hard-pressed village can manage to take refuge with an ally, they are likely to be doled out anyway. For the village obliged to ask for help must pay a price, and the price is women.

This, in truth, is what all the fighting is about. The Yanomamö do not fight for land. They do not take trophies. They do not eat conquered enemies (though they do consume the powdered bones of their own dead kinsmen; this, they say, makes them fierce). Women are the prizes of Yanomamö warfare. They constitute the "estate" of each

village, its negotiable assets, its currency, its means of forging alliances, which—in Yanomamö terms—involves entering into new bonds of kinship. The man with many sisters to give can always be sure of a personal political following. As negotiable assets, women can be traded, extorted, exchanged, borrowed, repaid, and stolen. The danger of this last is so real that women take their nursing infants with them wherever they go, preferring that the little ones be part of the abductor's booty than that they starve at home.

All this happens because women among the Yanomamö are in short supply. They are, for one thing, taboo to their husbands during the several years of pregnancy and nursing. For another, "truly fierce men," certainly headmen, can take and keep many wives while others must do without. Moreover, according to Yanomamö marriage regulations, a man should marry a girl who is his cross cousin, because anybody in his own line is considered a sister and is out of bounds as a marriage partner. This tends to limit choice. It also means that brothers and male parallel cousins (who, by Yanomamö reckoning, are the same as brothers) are in constant competition for the same women—married or not. And since Yanomamö men tend to be fiercely possessive about their property, they eye brothers warily and tend to be on much friendlier terms with their brothers-in-law, with whom they exchange sisters rather than competing for them.

Among some forest-dwelling farmers, even the most cruel and aggressive, the ferocity visited on the outside world must be carefully curbed at home, where etiquette and smooth good manners prevail. Not so among the Yanomamö. There is apt to be as much fighting inside as outside the village, and usually it begins over women. First there comes the bluffing to see who will be first to turn tail. If neither does, then follow the bitter insults. Calling a man by the name of his dead father is one such. The merest mention of any dead kinsman's name is actually enough to provoke rage. Then there is combat.

In-village fighting tends to be a bit less lethal than the outside kind and follows rigidly prescribed forms. Duelists may trade blows to the chest, taking turn and turn about. A man may cough up blood for days after such a bout, but he seldom dies. They may also smack each other over the head with ten-foot clubs, again turn and turn about. Most male Yanomamö skulls are laced with old scars which their owners proudly display by shaving tonsures in the middle of their soup-bowl haircuts. During club fights, the headman or headmen stand by with drawn bows to make sure nobody takes unfair advantage. Big villages of over 125 people are prone to constant club fights and challenges and usually break up into two smaller villages, friendly for a time but eventually deadly, murderous enemies in spite of their blood ties.

What the Yanomamö do not understand, and perhaps do not want to understand, is that they themselves cause the woman shortage that is at the root of the constant warfare. The girl baby who is first-born to any family is almost certain to be strangled. A man prefers his first-born child to be a son, a son whom he can teach to be fierce, applauding his baby rages and assaults on mother and sisters, even on father himself. Girls can come along later. If the life of a girl child hangs in the balance, so does that of her mother. Far from receiving the devoted care that scarce items usually get, women are all their lives treated little better than the village dogs. They are kicked, beaten with clubs, chopped with machetes, branded with torches, shot with barbed arrows (hopefully but not always in a nonvital spot), and cut freely about the ears and nose. And why? Sometimes on suspicion of adultery, but also because dinner is not ready on time, because their husbands' wants are not quickly enough anticipated, or simply because women are *there*, easy targets on which to vent passing spleen. By administering thorough and frequent wife-beatings a man may display his ferocity with little danger to himself. Other men, especially younger men, are sure to be impressed. He may even accumulate a few hangers-on, attracted by this superior *waiteri*. Of course, if his wife's brothers live in the same village, he tends to moderate the beatings lest his wife be taken from him and given to another, less ferocious husband.

This is why women feel secure in two-lineage villages, why in small villages parents promise additional daughters to a new son-in-law, hoping thus to keep him in permanent residence. For then their girls will not have to leave their natal home and the protection of strong brothers. It goes without saying, of course, that the stolen woman has no protection whatever and will have none until her sons are grown —if she lives that long.

To injury, insult is usually added. Wives do the dirty work around the village. They haul wood and water, prepare the daily meals, help in the garden. But they are not considered capable of handling important jobs. Men do the cooking for feasts. Men hunt. Men build the village—a collection of open, wedge-shaped houses, built around an open plaza and thatched into a single wheel surrounded by a high palisade. Men do the major farm work—and this in a region where, except for tending tobacco and the coca plant, men do not ordinarily concern themselves with the gardening. Yanomamö may have been farmers for only a few centuries. They know sweet manioc and corn but use them only as emergency food, much preferring the banana and plantain (a kind of nonsweet banana which, cooked green, tastes something like potato). Neither is native to South America; both were brought by the Spanish from Southeast Asia and spread rapidly in this similar environment.

The Yanomamö differ from most forest farmers in their attitude toward tobacco. Though highly prized, tobacco seems not to be sacred or even especially honorable. Everybody chews—men, women, and children. Lower lips are perpetually distended by large brown wads. Drugs are something else again. Made from the pounded bark of the *ebene* tree or from seeds of the cultivated *hisioma* tree, drugs have a special place in the male scheme of things. Late every afternoon, at a sort of cocktail hour, men take turns blowing powdered *ebene* up one another's nostrils through long cane tubes. The immediate result is not especially pleasant, but then come color visions, and men dance about chanting and inviting various hill and forest demons to "come live in my chest!" A little too much *ebene*, say the Yanomamö, makes a man uncontrollably fierce. The village shamans spend a good deal of their time under the influence of *ebene*. It is essential, they say, in the curing rituals.

Women, of course, do not take *ebene*. They do not join actively in the feasts, nor dance for the assembled company except when their husbands are away hunting and household dancing is required to make the operation a success. They may not even use the crude Yanomamö pottery in cooking, for, as their husbands say, they are clumsy and might break things. And then—woe betide!—shouts, blows, shrieks.

It is no wonder that Yanomamö women tend to be, as Dr. Chagnon says, sour, dour, and embittered creatures who count blows as marks of affection. In their eyes, that woman is blessed whose husband beats her often enough to show interest but not so often or so fiercely as to maim her for life. Such women, like their men, show off the scars in their scalps—neither deep nor dangerous, but proof that the husband "cares."

Another contradiction in Yanomamö life—a truth that can be neither recognized nor expressed—is the need for friends. No village is an island. No village can stand alone—neither the tiny one barely able to muster the minimum fighting force of ten men, nor the big one headed for fragmentation. The problem is how to get help without ever admitting a need for it. The Yanomamö manage by giving and reciprocating feasts; by giving and reciprocating trade goods like steel axes or hunting dogs or cotton string; and finally, in recognition of real friendship, by giving and reciprocating women. Even among truly close friends, however, the feast is always partly war. The goal of the host is to prepare more of certain kinds of food (ripe plantain soup, an accompanying green vegetable, and smoked meats) than the guests can possibly consume. The aim of the guest is to eat everything and still profess hunger; to trade with an air of hauteur that belittles any gift; to display a grandeur of paint and decoration and a ferocity of bearing that will dazzle his hosts. Thus may the respective "fronts" be maintained. Often a chest-thumping duel is required before honor and independence can be established to everyone's satisfaction. (The weaker the village, the greater the need to show violence.) But somehow, amid the brave, fierce show, men do become friends, embracing and chanting at one another of their needs for this and that. Somehow, though men do die in war (24 per cent of the yearly fatalities, Dr. Chagnon estimates), the Yanomamö have not achieved total self-extermination as, they say, did those first fierce men created where the moon's blood fell most thickly to earth. By shifting alliances, by a balance of fierceness, the violence is contained.

One day the violence will be stopped for good. When the laws of Venezuela and Brazil extend far enough into the jungle, the Yanomamö will be part of a larger world—a world of guns instead of arrows, of travel at the speed of sound instead of at the speed of human footfall. It is also a world of violence held in check only by its own uneasy balance of terror. And how or under whose dominion this order of violence can be ended is anybody's guess.

Iroquois and Mojo

Council Fires and Confederations

What you think of the Iroquois depends entirely on your point of view. Look at them from a 17th- and 18th-century French perspective and they become sheer military might, a force to be reckoned with and feared. For it is true that for centuries the Five (later Six) Nations of the Iroquois League held the balance of power in northeastern North America. During the so-called French and Indian War, they sided with the English and were largely responsible for making Canada British instead of French.

Look at the Iroquois through the eyes of Indians dispossessed by the League's invincible warriors, and they become fiends out of hell, smashing, killing, and cannibalizing for the sheer joy of it. The Algonquian-speaking tribes of New England never called their northern Iroquois neighbor by their proper tribal name, Canienga. They used instead the word *Mowak* (our Mohawk) which means "those who eat what has life," literally "those who eat men." The Iroquois themselves sometimes termed their military policy one of "eating the nations." And they did. In the century between 1600 and 1700 the Iroquois expelled, exterminated, engulfed, or subjected tribes from what is now New England to Illinois, from southern Ontario to northern Tennessee. They fought (and sometimes feared) Algonquian-speaking neighbors like the Ojibwa but seemed to enjoy most persecuting their own close Iroquoian language relatives in the Hokan-Siouan major group: the French-allied Hurons, the Eries, Conestogas, and Cherokees in the south. A whole year on the warpath was not thought unusual for the single-minded Iroquois soldier, provisioned with parched corn and, so the anti-Iroquois records suggest, with captives taken on the way.

This is not, of course, the whole story. Only shift the point of view, and sentiment rather more pro- than anti-Iroquois appears. The English thought well of their Iroquois allies (though they did not hesitate to abandon them to their fate after the Revolution). Some white Americans, enemies of the Iroquois, were equally impressed. Benjamin Franklin admired the organization of the League and warmly commended it to his colleagues as a possible model for the United States Constitution. George Washington was disposed to generosity on the Iroquois' behalf, offering the League favorable peace terms when he might well have imposed harsh ones. For that he earned himself a niche in the Iroquois heaven, the only white man ever to be so honored.

Many religious men—Jesuit missionaries in the seventeenth century, Quakers in the eighteenth—were impressed by the Iroquois' devotion to law, their hospitality, generosity, and care for one another, and their lovely religious rites, many of which were faithfully transcribed into French and English. All ethnographers who have studied the Iroquois in later years have found much to admire. In the founding of the League, they tell us, the aim was as much to provide a refuge from wars as to strengthen the Iroquois' hand in battle. For the League was meant to envelop all Indian nations that would accept League leadership. According to tradition, Hiawatha (not Longfellow's fictional Algonquin hero, but the flesh-and-blood cofounder of the League) offered this invitation:

And you of the different nations of the south, and you of the west may place yourselves under our protection, and we will protect you. We earnestly desire the alliance and friendship of you all.

Words of peace dominated Iroquois rituals, most of which were dedicated to quiet, planting themes. And so far separated were war and politics in the Iroquois scheme of things that a council chief had to doff his hereditary titles before joining a war party and had to purify himself before assuming them once more.

The League's later wars of extermination against the Hurons and other tribes speaking Iroquoian languages just possibly may have reflected the pique of an elder brother, frustrated in his attempts to do good, rather than sheer vindictive cruelty. There may also have been an element of economic competition. By the late 1600s the fur trade was thriving, and the Iroquois, whose own fur-bearing animals had become scarce, wanted to make sure they and they alone were the dominant middlemen between the tribes of inland hunters and the eastern trading posts.

Admirers of the Iroquois like to point to the League's gracious acceptance of refugees. There were the Tutelos, Nanticokes, and Delawares (after a long and bloody war). There were the Tuscaroras, an Iroquoian tribe driven from North Carolina in 1715 and given League lands in New York. They remind us of the kind treatment of captives adopted into Iroquois ranks. Lewis Henry Morgan, the famous lawyer-turned-ethnologist who studied the Iroquois in 1851, dismissed the torture of prisoners in a few sentences: "It is not necessary to describe this horrible practice of our primitive inhabitants. It is sufficient to say it was a test of courage. . . ." The two images of deliberative statesman and bloodthirsty marauder just do not merge comfortably in the mind's eye any more than they did in League custom.

It is never easy to accept a paradox, whether it appears in the character of a nation or in that of a single individual. We expect perfection in those we admire. Whatever lapses appear must needs be explained, excused, or skipped altogether. Otherwise admiration soon becomes loathing, fair images turn foul. And yet most nations and the people in them do present studies in contradiction, and if we are to know anything of the Iroquois, we must accept the paradox, must juggle two images in our minds, for both seem to have been true images and in a way even complementary ones. It is precisely the things that the Iroquois learned to achieve in peace that made them so formidable in war. Unlike their Huron cousins, who fought bravely and recklessly, each man his own captain, the Iroquois learned to weld together a fighting force, to give and take commands, and to devote some forethought to tactics. When the Hurons and Algonquians were armed with matchlocks by the French, League warriors quickly gave up wearing slat armor and fighting in the old ways with bows and arrows. They learned to draw the gunmen into ambush and to attack hand-to-hand with war clubs before the matchlocks could be brought into play. Later, when they were themselves armed, first by the Dutch and then by the English, they learned the fine art of sniping from cover, the value of thin-spread lines and quick, concerted assaults on command. Their own villages were always strongly fortified and surrounded by moats. The French could never persuade their Huron allies to build quite so carefully or so well.

It was not only in fighting but in living that the Iroquois practiced togetherness. Confederacies of tribes—usually short-lived, *ad hoc* affairs—were not new in the eastern United States. What was different about the Iroquois League was that it was made to last. It lasted because personal desires were somehow submerged—and submerged willingly, what is more—in a concern for group good. In the process, no class distinctions emerged. Initiative was not lost; it was merely redirected. Surely, in a land of rugged individualists, this was a remarkable achievement. The Iroquois themselves well understood the unique nature of their League and sang at their council fires:

> I come again to greet and thank the League;
> I come again to greet and thank the kindred;
> I come again to greet and thank the warriors;
> I come again to greet and thank the women.
> My forefathers,—what they established—
> My forefathers,—hearken to them!
> Hail, my grandsires!

The League began in 1475 or 1570 (depending on which scholarly opinion pleases you). It began in violence. Five of the Iroquoian tribes—the Mohawk, Onondaga, Seneca, Cayuga, and Oneida—had long been under heavy attack by their neighbors, the Algonquian Adirondacks of the Quebec region. There is even a vague and ancient tradition of war with mound builders on the Ohio. In any case, the Five Tribes were driven away to occupy lands between the Hudson and Genesee Rivers in what is now New York State. There they were discovered by the Dutch in 1609. For a long time the five tribes fought one another as enthusiastically as they raided their neighbors. Then two remarkable

leaders, Hiawatha (*Hayenwatha*, "He Who Seeks the Wampum Belt"), an Onondaga, and Dekanawidah, a Mohawk chief, conceived the noble idea of confederation. They made the idea a reality by astute political maneuver and by thorough knowledge of Iroquois social organization. All things considered, the Iroquois have probably produced more than their share of geniuses—men with long vision, able to introduce great and lasting changes in a people's way of life when change was due.

Everyone between the Hudson and the Genesee liked the new plans for peace—everyone but the Onondagas, whose chief, Atotarho, rather fancied his own autocratic power. Hiawatha and Dekanawidah got around this by loading him and the Onondagas with honors. The capital of the League was to be in Onondaga territory. The Onondagas were to be keepers of the wampum belts—those intricately worked strands of shell whose symbols were meant sometimes to remind celebrants of the successive acts of a ritual, and sometimes to validate treaties and contracts. The Onondagas were to be the keepers of the council fire, traditionally the prerogative of a leading tribal chief. They were to have more chiefs to represent them in the annual Grand Council than any of the other nations. And Atotarho was to be first in the chiefly roll call, as would all Onondaga chiefs who afterward bore his name. His would be the responsibility of convening extraordinary sessions of the Grand Council. Wisely, Atotarho exchanged power for glory. No longer was his word law, even in his own nation. The principle of absolute unanimity came into being with the League and trickled down through the village and into the smallest unit of family life. All decisions had to be agreeable to *all* chiefs before action could be taken. To forestall the prospect of endless wrangling and minority opinions at the Council Fire, the body of chiefs was subdivided into committees, each of which discussed every item on an agenda until all its members reached consensus. Later, at the Council Fire, each committee spoke as one voice and cast one vote.

It is hard for us to imagine a state run on the principle of unanimity. In our factional, diverse world, filled with dissenting voices, we feel lucky to achieve clear majority whenever we come to vote. Among the Iroquois, it was the principle of majority rule that was unthinkable. For though the League indeed constituted a state, it was a special kind of state, built on and by means of the bonds of kinship. This again was the genius of Hiawatha and Dekanawidah: to cast the League in a family mold.

> We must unite ourselves [said Hiawatha] into one common band of brothers. We must have but one voice. Many voices makes confusion. We must have one fire, one pipe, and one war club. This will give us strength.

A family shares common language, common origins, common values, and fellow-feeling. Its members know and are known by all. Since they live together, problems must be thrashed out until each member is satisfied, for resentments breed dissension, and after dissension comes separation. And the League was surely family, large but somehow intimate. It was no accident that the name for the confederation was *Hodenosaunee*, "People of the Long House." For the League was envisioned as a single dwelling sheltering all who lived between the Hudson and the Genesee, its fire in Onondaga territory and its western door on the Seneca frontier. And why not? Iroquois families themselves lived in long bark houses, each sheltering as many as 150 people. On the lintels of these houses were carved certain animal or bird figures which announced the dominant clan membership of the residents.

Each of the five tribes of the League was subdivided into a number of these clans. Certain of the clan names ran through most of the five nations, and Tortoise, Bear, and

Wolf appeared in all. The League founders carefully fostered a sense of clan fellowship and used it to bind as kin the chiefly representatives from the various tribes. All speeches were invariably begun with the words "Friends and Relatives."

Cutting across the clan affiliations was added yet another loyalty. In each tribe the various clans were arranged in moieties, or halves—some clans in one group, the rest in the other. The moieties were team opponents in all games of skill or chance, rather like the American and National Leagues in our own arrangement of athletic moieties. At all tribal councils the clan representatives seated themselves, according to their moiety affiliations, on opposite sides of the fire. When clan members in one tribal half mourned the loss of a member, it was up to their opposite numbers to offer condolences. The founders of the League extended this notion of halves and arranged the Seneca, Onondaga, and Mohawk chiefs as elder brothers on one side of the Great Council Fire, and Oneida and Cayuga (and later Tuscarora) chiefs as younger brothers on the other side. The national halves condoled with one another at the loss of a chief, complemented one another in ceremony, and fostered an air of friendly competition just as the tribal moieties were wont to do.

Once the League had been founded, once its membership had been set, no outsiders were permitted to shake its single-minded will; no alien voices spoke as voters at the Council Fire. Certain Iroquois chiefs represented the interests of refugees and subject nations, but these could not speak for themselves. Even the Iroquoian Tuscarora, added to the League as the Sixth Nation, did not vote as equals in the Council. The unanimity of the band of brothers, the original fifty chiefs, was considered too precious to be exposed to dissent. (The American Revolution did actually cause some dissent. Oneida sympathies were pro-American in spite of everything.)

Chiefs of the *Hodenosaunee* did not sit in the Grand

Council as a natural birthright but were elevated to office by the Iroquois electorate. And the electors were Iroquois women. Each of the fifty chiefly titles was the hereditary property of a certain family line in one of the local clans. In other words, each clan in each nation was represented in the Council by one or more chiefs. The bearer of a clan title was chosen from among all the men of his local clan by the clan matron, acting with the advice of her sisters and daughters. It was, furthermore, her responsibility to monitor the political performance of any newly elevated chief, to warn him if his behavior got out of line in any way, and to impeach him if he proved utterly unsuited to his high office.

It would be easy to suppose that Iroquois women were entrusted with such high responsibility because inheritance of clan name and family line descended through the mother and because, most often, young men expected to take up residence in their brides' long houses instead of the other way around. An easy explanation, perhaps, but by no means the whole of the story. Many societies which follow descent through the mother do not also accord high station to their women. The Iroquois were rather unusual in this respect; even their neighbors and language relatives thought so. Some whispered that among League members the sexes alternated in power, and wasn't that a silly way to run a nation! Like most tidbits of gossip, this one was only partly true. Men and women of the League had different responsibilities and different roles, organized to complement, not conflict. Women never meddled in the Council, never spoke out personally or put themselves forward. They could, if they chose, participate in certain medicine societies. A few were even inducted into the False Faces, a club whose members wore ugly and fantastic masks and treated illnesses of the head, eyes, teeth, and ears. They could be made Keepers of the Faith, religious leaders and guardians. They could be chosen Pine Trees, a sort of "All-American" title given to men and women who best exemplified Iroquois ideals.

For the most part, however, women kept strictly to their own sphere of life: the land, the farming, the house, the old traditions. They were entrusted with certain aspects of the cycle of rites, all of which focused on the earth and its various fruits. Especially honored were the "Three Sisters," —corn, squash, and beans—also called "Our Life" and "Our Supporters." Women arranged the marriages of their children and worked to keep young couples in harmony. They participated in dances but followed their own feminine choreography. They did not accompany war parties but did decide which captives brought home from conquest would be adopted into their families and which consigned to the torture. All in all, their world was narrow, local, and domestic, the homely core on which great events were built.

Iroquois men, on the other hand, concerned themselves with hunting, war, and politics. They lived in the expanded national family, traveled afar to trade or fight, and looked at wider horizons. Beyond helping to clear fields, they had little contact with farming, and not much more with their own children until, as grandfathers, they became "special friends" with one child or another. Because women were largely responsible for child care and knew the strengths and weaknesses of the boys growing up under their care, they were well qualified to confer titles and choose able representatives.

Togetherness was the keynote of Iroquois life. Women farmed cooperatively, did their chores cooperatively, even in a sense cooked cooperatively. For though each nuclear family had its own small cooking fire on the long house's central aisle, everybody had a taste of everyone else's dinner, and the person loath to share was apt to be thought a witch. Every year, at two of the celebrations of thanksgiving, men and women were handed belts of white wampum and urged to confess all the bad thoughts and resentments they had harbored against their fellows. This was thought to be good for the soul and also a sound guarantee of right thinking in the future.

Now, proper behavior may be subject to guarantee, but never proper thoughts. And with the extreme propriety required of the individual Iroquois, the constant pressure for harmony in family, clan, and nation, it is not surprising that private resentments festered and found outlets other than the semiannual confession. The Iroquois believed in witches, believed that certain persons were innately evil, were capable of doing evil whether they willed it consciously or no. The figure most resented and therefore most often suspected of witchcraft was the mother-in-law. After all, when mother-in-law rules the long house and son-in-law is a more or less permanent guest therein, certain conflicts are bound to surface. If quarreling is forbidden, suspicion takes its place.

Another outlet for resentment and anxiety was found in dreaming. Most Iroquoian-speaking people believed, along with their Algonquian neighbors, in the sovereign power of dreams. Visitations from on high took place in dreams; that was understood. But dreaming gave still another direction to life. Among the Iroquois and their Huron cousins, dreams were thought to reveal the hidden wishes of the soul, wishes so unformed, so deeply personal that the dreamer himself might not be consciously aware of them, so mysterious that he might not even be able to translate the shorthand symbols by which they were expressed. That was what his relatives and neighbors were supposed to do for him—much as the psychoanalyst in Western culture plumbs the hidden meanings of dreams. Once defined, a wish had to be satisfied, and a man's friends and kin vied with one another to give him all the goods, acts, or dances his soul might require for its continued good health.

Sometimes dreams were thought to be prophetic. Not surprisingly, warriors often had nightmare visions of their own torture and death. And the only way to cheat fate, they thought, was to re-enact the dream right up to, but omitting, its fatal conclusion. Sympathetic friends hastened to tie the dreamer to a stake, lit fires, and brandished knives while he sang his death song but did not die.

> I am brave and intrepid [he sang]. I do not fear death, nor any kind of torture. Those who fear them are cowards. They are less than women. Life is nothing to those who have courage. May my enemies be confounded with despair and rage.

It was by way of dreams that the Iroquois managed to survive the shrinking of their empire into several small reserves and to survive the white man's ways, and above all the white man's whisky. In 1800 a Seneca chief named Handsome Lake, ill for many years, suddenly rose from his sickbed, cured. He had been visited in dreams by three super-natural beings sent to him by the Great Spirit, the Master of Life, and he preached the "Good Message" they had given him. Nevermore, he said, must his people sell land to the white man. Never should they touch whisky again. They must farm like the white man and keep domesticated animals, for the wild creatures would soon disappear. In all other ways, however, they must keep themselves to themselves, holding fast to the old beliefs, the old brotherly feelings, the services of thanksgiving, the reverence for the League. Handsome Lake's "Good Message" took root among many Iroquois.

The Six Nations have not flourished in the white man's world; often they have been cheated and robbed of their lands. But they have not withered away as ethnographers in the 1850s feared they might. They have even found skills that give them high value in the modern labor market. As far back as 1714, visitors to the Iroquois had noted the absence among them of a fear of heights. Today, almost to a man, they work in "high steel," in the construction of sky-scrapers in New York and in the great cities of Ontario.

They climb unconcerned among the narrow girders as their forefathers strode along ridgepoles or mountaintops—Iroquois still and unafraid, having long since learned the way of changing just enough to remain the same.

The festivals of Iroquois thanksgiving were always followed by games—peach stones tossed in a bowl like glorified dice, or lacrosse, a team game played with rackets and a deerskin ball. Whether all the frenzied activity was meant to provide relief from ritual solemnity or whether the games were integral parts of the ceremonies themselves, they were certainly played with zeal and watched with passionate interest. People cheered themselves hoarse for their moiety players and made wild and reckless bets on the scores.

Rough-and-tumble ball games might almost be termed a New World passion, one which quickly infected incoming European colonists and traveled on Columbus's ships back to the Old World. The idea for such games may have migrated with the first Americans over the Bering Strait, or it may have developed with the discovery of the rubber tree and the remarkable properties of its sap. In the middle latitudes games were played with rubber balls which could be volleyed and bounced somewhat as we play tennis and volleyball with maybe a touch of basketball thrown in. In the extreme north and extreme south, balls of skin, copying (or perhaps antedating) the rubber ones, were used in shinny- or hockey-like games and even in simple circle games which required the players merely to keep the ball aloft.

In eastern Bolivia, among the mound-village chiefdoms of the Mojos Plain, ball games had their devotees as much as anywhere else in the hemisphere. Players used hollow balls molded around a core of clay (later removed) or hard balls of solid latex. Team players "served" the ball by kicking it off the ground and volleyed it with their heads. They ostentatiously cultivated swollen shins and took time out to swathe their legs and arms with protective wrappings. And no wonder. Balls sometimes weighed as much as twenty-five pounds, and a wild serve could break a man's leg. No concern was shown for the head, however; it was considered the fit and proper instrument for ball playing.

The letters of missionary Jesuits, visiting the Mojos Plain from the late 1500s onward, do not stipulate whether or not the games they witnessed had religious significance or even how the opposing teams were chosen. Perhaps players were drawn from neighboring villages, competing in games in lieu of war. The Mojo and neighboring Paressí carefully kept in repair the great roads and causeways of their ancestors, causeways which bound many villages in what may have been a network of athletic competition, of trade, or perhaps even of government. Nobody can say, for descriptions of bygone days among the Mojo are fragmentary at best. It is known that the Paressí (who spoke, like the Mojo, an Arawakan language) were organized into small federations of villages; perhaps this was true of the Mojo as well.

In early times there was quite an assortment of chiefdoms in eastern Bolivia, remarkable because they did not appear in a solid block but were widely scattered among very simply organized farming folk or even hunter-gatherers. Near the Mojo chiefdoms lay Siriono hunting grounds, conveniently close for slave-raiding parties. For the Mojo village chiefdoms, like others in the area, were for a long time in the slaving business and used slaves themselves to work their own extensive fields.

The kind of equality to be found among the Iroquois seems to have been missing among the Mojo chiefdoms. Each village was divided on strict class lines with slaves on the bottom and hereditary chiefly families on top. Chiefs were chosen by the length and nobility of their bloodline and were on the way to becoming absolute rulers somewhat in the manner of Inca autocrats on the other side of the

Andes. Each held the power of life, death, and punishment, modified only by groups of old men whose job it was to counsel mildness and mercy.

Almost as powerful as the chiefs were the curing shamans and the temple priests. Each village of small houses had at its center a large building which was temple, drinking house, and men's house all rolled into one. Here were housed the flutes and pipes which Mojo musicians played so skillfully. Here were stacked the heads of enemies taken in battle and the heads and paws of jaguars taken on the hunt. The jaguar —that fierce and beautiful animal—meant something truly special in Mojo religion. His spirit was terrible and beneficial by turns. The man who killed a jaguar was highly honored but had to be ceremonially cleansed. The man wounded by a jaguar was thought to be touched (albeit painfully) by the Power and was therefore eligible for induction into the jaguar shamans' cult.

Ordinary men, untouched by supernatural powers, un-sanctified by noble blood, went their ways—hunting, tilling, maintaining the mounds and causeways. They drank copi-ously when maize beer was to be had and, while drunk, settled disputes in wrestling matches. They liked their wives to be nice and fat and clever at dressing their husbands' hair. Girls hoped their future husbands would be good providers and handsome, too, with dark and shining complexions. Men made feather mosaics and knew how to get the colors they wanted from tame blue-and-green parrots by pulling out their feathers, rubbing certain clays into the pores, and waiting for the growth of new feathers, which would be red.

In the steady decline of Mojo fortune, it was these com-mon folk who survived. The Bolivian tribes expelled the Jesuit missionaries around 1767, but then suffered invasions of exploiters and adventurers lured by tales of El Dorado. Many times the Indians rose against them, only to be put down, and villagers who had taken slaves were themselves enslaved. When balance was once again restored, a few things still remained of the old life. Many of the Mojo religious dances and rites found their way into Christian services. Only the ball game remained unchanged—unchanged the passion for sports which long dominated the people of this hemisphere and was their legacy to the new Americans.

Hopi and Diaguita
Apartment Houses in the Desert

"White men come, white men go," say the Hopi of eastern Arizona, "but we are here forever. The modern nations may pass away, destroyed by bombs and radiation and strife, but we shall be here, safe in our mesa-top villages, ready to commence the new life, to move on to the next of many new worlds promised us by our gods."

They may be right. Already they have survived hazards enough to defeat many another people. Very early they learned how to survive the desert—how to wring from it a farmer's living, how to space the corn plants widely so that each could draw its due from the scanty rainfall, how to position plants cunningly underneath mesas and down the middle of arroyos so as to make the most of the mountain runoff and of the unpredictable flash floods. Hopi survived the depredations of Spaniards who threatened their religion and way of life. They survived the invasions of Navajo and Apache raiders who threatened their land and livelihood. They survived the white man's diseases and missionaries and government officials and gawking tourists. And so they may well survive the twentieth century and its demands.

The Hopi are today where Coronado found them in 1540, still living on three long, rocky fingers that stretch out from Black Mesa. Many of the villages Coronado saw are occupied to this day. Some have been moved higher up the mesas to more protected locations. Others have spun-off suburbs. There is one village built in 1700 by Tanoan-speaking refugees from the Rio Grande area. There are two new towns, Hotevilla and Bekavi, built around 1906 when angry factions formed and split in Old Oraibi. Oraibi itself on the top of Third Mesa is the oldest continuously occupied town in the United States. The evidence of growth rings in old trees, cut for use in Oraibi house beams, suggests initial construction in the early 1200s. Most specialists believe the town is older than that.

Hopi mesas and their desert farmlands are entirely surrounded by the much larger Navajo reservation whose people, say the Hopi, are forever trying to improve their holdings at Hopi expense. Once the Hopi claimed as promised land everything between the Little Colorado and the upper Rio Grande. And the scattered villages of Pueblo people, allied to the Hopi in custom and religious outlook though not in language, dot this whole area. The Hopi language is very closely related to that of the Northern Paiute, and it is probably reasonable to suppose that Hopi ancestors before the coming of corn were desert grubbers and gatherers somewhat after the old Paiute pattern. Along the Rio Grande, many Pueblo people speak Tanoan languages— that second branch of the Azteco-Tanoan group. The Tanoan family (you will recall) includes Kiowa, one of the Great Plains languages, and it may be that the ancestors of the Rio Grande people were originally buffalo hunters, later becoming converts to the Pueblo way of life. A number of specialists, however, give the Tanoans long tenure in the Southwest, suggesting that their ancestors may have been the builders of Pueblo Bonito, now in ruins, and the other great old towns of Chaco Canyon.

Inhabitants of other villages along the Rio Grande and points west speak Keresan languages which belong in the Hokan-Siouan major group. Ancestors of these people are usually thought to have moved from a homeland somewhere near that of the Hopi to the Rio Grande area, perhaps around 1400. In between the bigger rivers is the Zuñi, a small but dependable stream. Near it is the pueblo of Zuñi whose people speak a language totally unlike those of their neighbors in the Southwest or, seemingly, any other American Indian peoples. Very like the Hopi in way of life, they are, in terms of language, mystery men.

With all these other pueblos (*pueblo*, of course, is the Spanish word for town), the Hopi recognize a distant relationship—as they do also with the Pima and Papago farmers of the Gila-Salt rivers. All of them, say the Hopi, came in later migrations to the land, emerging into this life from underwater. And why not? Even today most of them have access to flowing water for their crops and can direct their religious thought to creature comfort and curing rites. But we, say the Hopi, must focus our prayers on rain, for our crops grow, our lives are sustained by faith and faith alone.

It is a faith which, according to Hopi traditions, has carried them already through four creations of life and three destructions—once in fire, once in flood, and once in ice. Each time, evil came because some men forgot and some denied the Creator's plan. But those who remained true were preserved safe underground with the ant people. Even today the Hopi kiva (though it tends to be rectangular rather than round) recalls in every detail the anthill refuge. It is, for one thing, underground, sunk into the town's central plaza. Its own floor is arranged in descending levels. The lowest contains the *sipapuni*, an opening which represents the hole of first emergence (such holes are to be found in all the kiva ruins of Anasazi times, mentioned on pages 161–2). Moving upward from the fire pit to the altar level, from the altar to the spectator level, and from that up the ladder which leads to the plaza above, the sacred acts of creation and re-emergence are built into the very stones. They are also built into every Hopi grave. The dead person is buried in a sitting position, facing east, so that his soul can quickly rise, grasp the stick planted beside him, and on it climb into the world to come—the world in which he will live as a cloud person bringing rain.

When the Hopi got to the Fourth World, they say, they found it to be not a bit like previous creations, luxuriant and thoughtfully provided with every convenience. This one was blocked by waters and by ice. Once the barriers were past, there were still more difficulties to surmount. For the new land was laced with deserts and marshes, punctuated with mountains, and lashed by winds that blew now hot, now cold. The Hopi were told by their gods that they must wander over this land until they could find the proper home. In the course of their wanderings, they say, they struggled through vast jungles, built cities, and left ruins behind. They see in the cliff paintings of Chaco Canyon and Mesa Verde the markings of Hopi clans and the pointers they left for late-coming clansmen to follow. They even claim to have constructed the vast snake-shaped mounds in the eastern United States. This is, of course, the stuff of myth which ever clothes in poetry the grim reality of drought, attack, and a search for fairer land. Even so, there may be some underlying truth to the Hopi claims of connections with other peoples in the Americas. Certainly these connections—of whatever sort they were—must have occurred so long ago as to be untraceable in any definite way. Here is one tantalizing hint. The priests of two important Hopi men's societies wear headdresses crowned with horns. Just such horned figures appear in rock drawings from Utah to Texas. And in the mounds of the Eastern Woodlands there have been found similar horned headdresses, obviously marks of distinction for the wearer. In the Iroquois League, elevation of a chief was always called "putting on the horns," and his death or removal "putting off the horns." On the Plains, as many drawings by frontier artists attest, a common badge of chiefhood was a headdress of buffalo horns. However it was that horns came to be announcers of prestige, religious or political, the notion was certainly widely shared in North America.

Throughout the time of wandering, say the Hopi, they did not travel as they chose but clan by clan. Through every creation the clans endured and, say the Hopi, they will endure forever. (The present diminished roster of Hopi clans does not bear out this belief, however.) Some clans became allied through shared dangers and common experiences and so they remain allied and together to this day. Most important of all clans in the Fourth World was the Bear Clan. It was first to find and settle the villages of Hopiland. It owned the crucial winter-solstice ritual, the *Soyal*. Its chief was the leading priest of that rite and therefore was, and must always be, the chief of any village inhabited by Hopi people. Other clans arrived in time and asked for land in each of the Hopi villages. Each brought its own distinctive clan deity, its secret and special rites. These were added to *Soyal* of the Bear Clan, one by one, to form at last a complete calendar of services which helped keep the world spinning aright and all life on it secure and sustained. Today, because some clans have died out, the ceremonies are "owned" in the various villages by different clans, clans which succeeded to rights of ownership through alliance with the original clans.

In November the ceremonial round began (and begins even today) with the sixteen-day festival of *Wuwuchim*, managed and presented by the four men's societies in their kivas. It is meant to encourage the germination of life, sleeping now under hard, cold ground. New fires are kindled, the stars are scanned for the right moment at which young men may be made fully Hopi. Around our Christmas season there falls the twenty-day *Soyal*, which concludes with a communal rabbit hunt. The sun must be sped upward again toward warmth and longer days, the business of life begun anew. At *Soyal* the Kachinas appear. They are men wearing masks to represent the real Kachinas, spirits and powers of animals and plants, the spirits of Hopi ancestors who have always helped living Hopi. But little children do not know this yet. They see the Kachinas as so many Santa Clauses, loaded with gifts for good children, punishments and scares for naughty ones. They handle carved Kachina dolls which help them learn to distinguish the many masked figures they see dancing, praying, clowning through the village.

When they are about eight years old they learn who and what the Kachinas really are. In February comes the festival of *Powamu* when bean sprouts, forced into premature growth in warm kivas, are distributed through the village. During this time, every four years, a new batch of children lose their illusions in a great initiation ceremony. Serious, religious-minded children are initiated into the Powamu Society (whose leading priests are chiefs in the Badger, Kachina, Parrot, and Tobacco Clans). Lively, noisy children are initiated into the Kachina Society (led by the Kachina Clan) and are whipped by what they take to be masked gods, until suddenly the masks are snatched away and the men behind them are stunningly revealed.

There is no ceremony for spring, though the old legends tell of one that required the ultimate price of death for life —a price often paid in ancient spring rites the world over. In spring, the watchers on Hopi rooftops carefully measure the position of Father Sun as he rises behind the mesas and announce to the people when it is time to plant. In July the new corn is celebrated in the *Niman* festival, and young eagles and hawks, captured in early spring, are killed, "sent home" in spirit to give messages to the Hopi gods. Home, too, go the Kachinas. All winter they have danced for the people's pleasure, the people's aid, and now they must return until *Soyal* summons them forth once more.

Every other year, in August, the Blue and Gray Flute

Societies (in Oraibi led by chiefs of the Spider and Patki Clans) re-enact the Hopi emergence in order to bring late summer rains. On alternate years the Snake and Antelope Societies perform, running races, dancing with live rattle-snakes held in their mouths. Members of the Snake Clan, it is said, are born without the fear of snakes, those harbingers of lightning and of rain, but in any case, no snake will harm members of other clans who belong to the Snake Society. They have been chosen for their pure hearts. Always, say the Hopi, snakes honor the pure in heart.

Through October and November the three women's so-cieties, each led by a male priest of the Parrot, Lizard, or Sand Clans, distribute harvest gifts in a world grown cold and look forward to the germination to come.

In all ceremonies some dances are performed for the delight of all. Much, however, takes place secretly in the various kivas. Many of the ceremonies are as much a mystery to some Hopis as they are to the outside world, for no man holds all religious wisdom, however much he tries to par-ticipate. Though each ceremony is controlled by a certain clan or clans and is led by the leaders of these clans, it may enroll in its ceremonial society many men from other clans. Each man may thus be a member of four or five societies and a habitué of perhaps two kivas. But it is impossible to belong to all.

In the minor rituals of everyday living, as in the great ceremonies, the fundamental realities of Hopi existence are repeated. Water and corn, corn and water in a hundred different ways sanctify the smallest act. Pinches of corn meal are cast into the air with every prayer. Corn-meal paths are strewn on every hopeful journey. Corn meal is con-stantly given and received with every family obligation ful-filled. Corn Mothers, ears of perfect corn, ending in four kernels, are carefully saved to bless every newborn child and every ritual in the kiva or in the home.

Water is ritually drunk, sprinkled, and mixed with yucca

suds for ritual baths and ritual shampoos. These last are most important of all. In every crisis or transition in life, the head must be washed. Bride and groom are married in a joint shampoo, during which their hair is mingled in the suds. Even young hawks, trapped in spring, must be shampooed and renamed before they can be entrusted with messages to the skies.

Above all else, above all symbols, acts, and songs, the Hopi puts his faith in the power of positive thinking. Hopi language itself makes such faith possible. It is a language without verb tenses, with no past and no future. All things belong in one of two categories: they are, like the mesa, the village, the clan, forever available to the senses, there to be seen, touched, known; or they are in the process of becoming and are therefore present though unseen, untouched, unknown. Plants in germination, rain clouds over the horizon are yet in process, and process depends on prayer, happy thoughts, and serene temper. For every ceremony, therefore, the town crier circles the plaza advising all to put their thoughts in tune with the celebrants hidden away in their kiva, preparing for the work at hand. Dissension and worry are thought to spoil the work of bringing rain; they curdle a mother's milk and bring on illness and death. Always the sick person is advised by one and all to set his thoughts in order, to confess to a doctor or an uncle, to brace up and get well. So firm is the belief in thought that the patient who languishes in spite of all advice may be roundly scolded, or even deserted. "After all," say his relatives, "he *could* save himself if he just weren't so stubborn and willful!"

Hopi ceremonies extend over many days because the men in charge need time in which to order and purify their thoughts. They sit together in the kiva or clan house, preparing the ritual regalia, making prayer sticks—those beautiful feathered symbols of sky and earth, man and woman, corn, breath, and the sweetness of life. Over and over they address one another by kinship titles, for to be one in blood is to be one also in spirit and in religion.

As women constituted the family core on which Iroquois political life was based, so Hopi women constitute the family core from which religion flowers. Hopi women own more and do less than did their Iroquois sisters. They are also, in some ways, more dependent. They must turn to their brothers, mothers' brothers, and sons for their spiritual support and to their husbands, fathers, and sons-in-law for their material support. As among the Iroquois, Hopi lands, clan membership, and ceremonial heritage descend through the mother. A man's proper home is his mother's house. There he entertains, there he stores his ceremonial property, and there he returns for weddings and festivals and after a divorce. It is his responsibility to admonish his sister's children and keep their behavior up to snuff. He formally welcomes a new bride or groom into the family. He weaves the wedding robe for his nephew's bride and chooses one of his nephews as his ceremonial and family successor. He is head of the house but does not live in it.

He lives in his wife's house with her mother and sisters. He is a guest there—but a paying guest. For, unlike the Iroquois, it is the Hopi man who farms, though he does it on land that belongs to his wife's clan. What he raises belongs to her. He also hunts, herds sheep (first brought by Spanish missionaries), brings firewood, weaves cotton and woolen cloth (in his kiva), and makes silver jewelry. His wife guards the stored corn and grinds it, cooks, cleans, minds the children, tends kitchen gardens, makes pottery and basketry, helps to build and repair the apartment, and trades. It is she who must make the offerings of food and perform the ritual hand washing over fire that will send rabbits, slain in the hunt, "home" to the Mistress of the Beasts.

Dr. Fred Eggan thinks that Hopi women once farmed but

abdicated in favor of their husbands when corn became the
vital, indispensable food and perhaps also when raiders made
farm fields dangerous places to be.

There may possibly be another, or at least an additional,
reason. Specialists believe that women are so often the
farmers in communities new to the ways of planting, because
of their long connection with gathering. The transition from
wild plants to domesticated ones seems easy for women to
make. You will recall, however, that among desert people
like the Utes and Paiutes, men often shared gathering chores
with their womenfolk. So perhaps when some desert people
of the Southwest, once very like the Paiutes in their customs
and habits, took to planting corn, the work may have been

shared in the same casual way with no hard-and-fast rules about who was to do what. Hopi women still help out at harvest time when they are needed, but the balance has shifted. Farming is now a man's job, a job he still insists on doing with a hoe, however easily plows may be had. It is by now tradition. And the Hopi is a traditionalist first, last, and always.

Tradition requires a man to teach his sons to herd and farm, but he never scolds, never threatens, never punishes them. He must hold their loyalty with love alone. It is Uncle, Mother's brother, whose authority is backed by blood ties and a common name. He may punish, he may scold. Certainly he must see that his nephew hardens himself for the hazards of manhood with long races and icy baths. Members of Father's clan have special roles to play in a boy's life, different from those that the blood clan plays. It is Father's mother and sisters who care for the newborn baby and give him his first names. The child calls Father's people by special kinship terms and behaves toward them in special, joking ways. The children of his father's sisters (his cross cousins) he calls "Father" or "Father's sister," in a way honoring them by a promotion in generation level. Mother's brother's children (also cross cousins) are addressed as "children" and "grandchildren," a demotion which may help to offset a little the awe and respect that Uncle commands around the house. That kinship titles do not always mean what they say causes no puzzlement. Every tot very quickly learns to respond with grave courtesy when addressed as "Grandfather" by some graying old gentleman.

The bonds of kin are extended far into unrelated clans. For each child a ceremonial father and mother are chosen (very like our own habit of choosing godparents). These sponsor the child in his initiations and see that he has entrée into the kiva and all the societies to which the ceremonial parent belongs. And if the child suffers a severe illness and is cured, he gets still another honorary parent, his "doctor father," and takes on an additional set of obligations, privileges, and restrictions in his eventual choice of a wife.

Somehow these extended bonds of kin were never used by the Hopi to unite villages in the Iroquois way. Maybe it was because the Hopi were just never interested in politics. They were always content to leave the management of disputes to clan chiefs and clan mothers and the regulation of village activities to the controlling clan leaders of the various ceremonial societies. Neither were the Hopi interested in war, though they defended their villages ably enough when threatened or attacked. In the long run, each village was and still is an entity unto itself, wrapped up in its own ceremonial cycle.

Only once did the Hopi villages unite, acting in concert with every other pueblo all the way to the Rio Grande. That was in 1680 when the Pueblo people, led by Popé of Taos, rose against the hated Spanish padres and soldiers, killing many and driving the rest completely out of the Pueblo territory and south past Sante Fe.

They came back, of course, harassing the Rio Grande people as they had done before. But this time the Hopi towns escaped the pressure, for the Navajos had come. Though the new raiders intimidated the Hopi, they also sealed them off from Spanish interference. The eastern pueblos in time and under pressure learned to share much of their ceremonial life with the group as a whole and to concentrate their loyalties less on the family and more on the village.

The isolated Hopi, however, intensified their clannishness and developed feuds and factions, and, faced by the newer, subtler threat of American missionaries and officials, quarreled and split. Suspicions of witchcraft multiplied and festered. Witches—those dreaded Two-hearts who each possessed an animal heart in addition to their own and were able to assume animal form—met, said the Hopi, in secret kivas. There they condemned their own relatives to death so that they might prolong their own wicked lives. Witches, so the Hopi believed (and believe still), were everywhere. They were to be found among the Americans, the Mexicans, and every other foreign people—a sort of United Nations of witchdom, but led, of course, by the Hopi Two-hearts themselves.

It is odd and even a little sad. Hopi means "peaceable." To be violent, argumentative, ambitious, competitive is to be *ka-hopi*, everything Hopi is not. There has never been a murder in a Hopi village. No man lifts his hand against another—even if he is suspected of being a Two-heart. Since properly one always waits to be struck first before going into defensive action, there are no blows struck at all. Hopi did not and do not drink alcohol. They do not often smoke save on ceremonial occasions when tobacco is required. There are no curse words in the Hopi language; the frustrated man must turn to English or Spanish when he wants to blow off steam. Actually, he is not supposed to *want* to. Among the

Hopi, strong feelings of any kind are distrusted. Better always to wear a calm and smiling face, no matter what storms rage within.

There seem to be storms in plenty, more than the Hopi understand or can cope with. And yet now, more than ever, the Hopi—all Hopi, all the clans in all the villages of the three mesas—need to bind their hearts together and hold fast. They must if they are to inherit as a people the promised new world ahead.

The way of Hopi housebuilding—many-storied, multi-family structures of stone crowning mesa tops—does anticipate the modern penchant for high-rise apartment buildings. But the Hopi and their Anasazi ancestors were not the only American Indians to like rooms with a view. In northwest Argentina there once lived the Diaguita, a people whose way of life seems, at least superficially, to have mirrored the Hopi way, to have been a cultural identical twin. I say "once" because they are in northwest Argentina no more. Long ago the Spaniards simply moved the entire Diaguita people away from the mesas to some other, now unknown corner of the continent, where they faded from view. There remained behind only their fortified mesa-top apartment buildings and the records of Spanish priests, governors, and soldiers who had good cause to remember the Diaguita.

Like the Hopi, the Diaguita built on mesas, drawing water from springs below and storing it in rock-hewn cisterns above. Like the Hopi, the Diaguita wore woven clothing and devoted much attention to their hair. It was not so much the shampooing process that fascinated the Diaguita, however, as the decorative possibilities inherent in hair—and feathers, copper wire, baubles, and beads. Men spent hours constructing ingenious coiffures, and considered the time well spent. There was definitely status in hair. A haircut announced an immediate loss of rank, particularly in the case of a chief.

The unimaginative Spanish conquerors earned the enmity of the Diaguita by forcibly shaving male heads. Diaguita women were not shorn. No doubt it was because they cared less for their plumage than their husbands and could not be punished with barbering tools. They simply parted their hair in the middle and rolled it in side whorls surprisingly like a Hopi squash-blossom hairdo.

Like the Hopi, the Diaguita farmed "dry." They did not irrigate but trapped what moisture there was on fields made flat by careful terracing. Unlike the Hopi, they do not appear to have farmed by faith or depended much on the nourishing effect of prayer. Here, in fact, is where all the similarities fade away. For the Hopi, of course, there is no separation of the sacred and secular sides of life. All life and living is rooted in good thought and in quietness. All men are priests as well as farmers and, when they wear the Kachina masks, even a bit divine. The Diaguita set their priests and curing shamans apart from the farmers. Their religious services were not dedicated to bringing hearts into tune but instead encouraged frenzy with alcohol and with wild feasts which shocked the solemn Spanish padres. For, to Diaguita thinking, extravagant behavior would prompt the heavens to send rain in abundance. Hopi, on the other hand, placed their faith in self-denial.

The Diaguita were definitely *not* peaceable folk. They were warriors dedicated to the warrior's ideal: better death than dishonor. All their time, effort, and organization were directed to the business of war. Chiefs were generals, inheriting the position from their fathers and retaining it by frequent acts of bravado. From long experience in defensive warfare, in fighting off the incursions of wild nomads, the Diaguita knew all there was to know about strongholds under siege. They are reported once to have rerouted a small river—the sole water supply of a Spanish garrison—thereby forcing surrender.

Hopi of the old days, particularly the initiates of the one

Hopi warrior society then in existence, occasionally took scalps but always released prisoners. The Diaguita preferred trophy heads and were as ingenious as the Iroquois in torturing captives.

Mesa top and apartment house, dry farming in a dry land: the stage setting is the same, north and south. Actors move into place wearing similar costumes, bearing similar props. But they are acting different plays. One is solemn, ceremonious, serene. The other is wild and martial, ending in violent dispossession. The play—the play of custom and behavior and belief—is, after all, the thing. Somehow culture plays are never written entirely to suit the available setting and its limitations, but depend as often on the accidents of history and on the moods and modes of the players themselves, the wishful dreams of individual men.

Chibcha and Natchez
The Importance of Being Noble

The map of New World political orders (on page 156) presents the Caribbean as a lake virtually surrounded by chiefdoms and developing states. There are, of course, gaps where northern Mexico and southwest Texas would one day be, lands occupied right up to Conquest times by hunting-gathering peoples. There are other gaps in Venezuela and in the Lesser Antilles, where farmers tended their gardens and seldom cast a thought beyond the boundaries of their own villages. The small group—its enrichment and defense—was care enough. Elsewhere, whenever weather, terrain, and human skills permitted larger groups to congregate, ideas out of Mexico and Peru took root.

At the crossroads of these two civilized centers lay Colombia. And in Colombia there once lived the Chibcha. Of all the American high cultures, that of the Chibcha has most often been rated third in greatness, just behind those of Mexico and Peru. And yet it is fair to say that the archaeological evidence for this greatness is slight. The Chibcha did not build in stone but in perishable wattle, daub, and thatch. Remaining products of their art and manufacture are few, of little skill, of even less antiquity. The Chibcha were, it seems, new to the business of empire building. They had no on-the-spot tradition to follow, no preceding people on whose knowledge they could build. The Chibcha seem to have been relative newcomers to the land they occupied and displaced no one—at least, no one of accomplishments greater than their own. Whatever the character of Chibcha cultural luggage, it traveled with them from their original home—wherever in Colombia that might have been (Chibcha language relatives can be found all the way north into Central America).

The new homeland stretched along the Cordillera Oriental, the most easterly of Colombia's three great mountain chains. Unlike the other ranges, it offered many fertile valleys, streams, lakes, and one broad plateau, just right for the intensive maize cultivation that Chibcha farmers (men *and* women) practiced. So many crops were raised, in fact, and in such quantity, that the whole area in its heyday supported a very dense population. It was a population that Chibcha rulers knew very well how to organize and how to tax. For though they were neither artists nor builders in stone, the Chibcha were political artists and builders of states. It was this that so struck their Spanish conquerors and chroniclers, this that prompted all the glowing descriptions that give us cause, in turn, to grant the Chibcha high marks for achievement.

Certainly there was nothing democratic about the Chibcha political formula. There was no electorate (as among the Iroquois). There were no elections, no provision for the removal of rulers inept or despotic. Chibcha peoples were rigidly organized in classes that were almost castes, so difficult it was to rise in degree. Chibcha were nobles, commoners, or slaves. Only nobles held sacred or secular offices, and one arrived at nobility by birth—birth, that is, to the sister of a noble, a chief, or a priest. For the Chibcha nobility reckoned descent through the mother's line as did the Hopi and Iroquois. Commoners, apparently, were content to pass name and property on from father to son. Families kept to themselves and cared little or nothing for clan membership. The tenuous, sometimes artificial ties of clan had long since loosened in the more compelling grip of government. A man was not appointed to political office because of clan affiliation. But family membership did figure in the determination of individual rank.

Rank was a matter of aching concern in the Chibcha realm. To be bigger, to be better than one's neighbor has always been, it seems, a major interest since man became human. Only during hard times or by heroic effort can the urge to play one-upmanship be downed or, at any rate, balanced. And nobody tried to do either in Colombia. The burials and memorial idols of San Agustín (just two hundred or so miles south of Bogotá) are testaments in stone to the ancient importance of being important, which (in San Agustín terms, perhaps, and in Chibcha terms, certainly) meant being noble.

The Chibcha of lesser or greater nobility must have been conscious every waking moment of his position in the pecking order. The supreme ruler at the top had near-deity status, and the nobility shared his aura of divinity in lessening degrees. A supreme ruler traveled in a litter draped with clashing sheets of gold. Flowers or beautifully painted cotton cloth was strewn along the road between palace and temple so that his bearers' feet would not touch the common dust. Men bowed low before him, even while they received the gifts he bestowed, and spoke to him with head averted. No one wanted to look his dread sovereign in the face. As Professor Alfred Kroeber tells us, the favorite punishment for theft was to make the culprit stand eye to eye with the ruler. Such a confrontation was considered a humiliation far worse than death. Of course, close association with a ruler (whether visually close or not) always carried with it a certain risk. Wives and retainers of a sovereign needs must be slain at their master's death to provide service and diversion in the hereafter.

There were (the Spanish records tell us) two large Chibcha states. One, called Zaque and ruled by a king also titled the Zaque, was centered around the modern Colombian city of Tunja (which still bears the name of its Chibcha predecessor). The other, called Zipa and ruled by the Zipa, was centered around what is now modern Bogotá, the capital of the country. In Chibcha times Bogotá was merely the capital of a Zipa province and was called Teusaquillo. Several tiny states, some independent, some not, orbited the two large realms. There was also a religious state ruled by a high priest. Both priest and state were called Iraca. The boundaries of this one state and the person of its ruler were always secure, since Iraca was a sort of Chibcha Vatican. Its great man, however, was a pontiff more in influence than in actual authority. Each state organized and maintained its own priestly hierarchy. But when Iraca (the man) spoke, most Chibcha listened.

Each of the larger states was divided into six or more provinces. Each of these was ruled by its own chief who, in his turn, parceled out authority (and territory) among several lesser chiefs. It all sounds thoroughly bureaucratic but actually amounted to the sort of high-level anarchy common among the feudal kingdoms of medieval Europe. Provincial chiefs might bow reverently to each other at the king's court but were forever contending with one another behind the king's back. There were always little hit-and-run wars, sieges, and petty border disputes in progress. A supreme ruler could only compose his near-deified self and hope for the best.

This, then, was the Chibcha realm when it was discovered by the Spaniards in 1536. How glad the Spanish soldiers were to find it! Whatever it was—the dry, rarified air so like Castile, the sense of order, the docile peasants (at first they were docile)—the Spaniards felt right at home. Conquest of the Chibcha was easy, besides. The various states could not agree on war policy and went down one by one. Later rebellions quickly failed. During the few years necessary for complete subjugation, however, the Spaniards found much to admire and understand in Chibcha culture.

They understood the feudal nature of the Chibcha states. Something of the same sort was part of Spain's immediate past. They appreciated the elaborate pomp surrounding the supreme ruler. "After all, a king *must* be regal," they said. The solemn religious character of the state, the nobility of the priesthood, the fact that priests were required to be celibate, all seemed eminently proper to Spanish eyes. The twelve-year preparation for the priesthood and the six-year training of a ruler-to-be—all in monastic solitude—met with similar approval. The nature of the religion, of course, sun worship and human sacrifice, was highly barbaric and would have to be banned (and was, in short order). But the religious organization itself seemed quite civilized.

The Chibcha were warlike, and the Spanish understood that too. They admired Chibcha tactics and wondered at the predominant use of spear and spear-thrower instead of bow and arrow. Two Chibcha motivations for war—particularly when directed against jungle tribesmen of the lowlands— were to acquire land and to capture slaves. The Spanish understood that. They took slaves themselves, as many and as fast as they could. But they never really fathomed the connection between Chibcha war and Chibcha religion. The Spaniards preferred the tactful pretense of a gentle religion, one set apart from war and strife. The Chibcha had no pretenses. Their sun god demanded the blood of human sacrifice, and Chibcha captives taken in war were used to satisfy this demand. Sacrifices were purchased as well as captured. Small children from the lowlands were bought cheap by Chibcha agents and sold dear at the great temples. There they were brought up spiritually pure, free of outside contact or common stain, so that their hearts, destined to be torn from their living bodies, would be especially pleasing to the gods. Children, noble or otherwise, were regularly slain to avert drought. And maidens were pounded into the earth to support with their dying breaths the foundation posts of Chibcha palaces and temples.

No, the Spaniards never understood these things (for all the saintly horrors of their own Inquisition). They much preferred other Chibcha interests, pleasanter interests, like the market days held twice weekly at major Chibcha settlements and the lovely things traded there. The Chibcha had much produce, of course. They had salt and fine cotton cloth and beautiful emeralds. But their land had no seams of gold, and gold they very much needed. Gold imported from afar had become necessary in the pecking order. Without gold how could one tell the chiefs from the commoners? Gold had also become necessary for religious offerings. Votive urns constantly had to be filled and refilled, for their contents were secretly drained and buried by temple priests. So it was that the Chibcha continually wove fine cloth, continually mined salt and emeralds. These things could be traded for gold, and somehow the Chibcha managed to have gold enough, enough to dazzle and inflame the gullible, greedy Spaniards.

Never was the use of gold more spectacular than in the ceremony of investiture during which supreme rulers were confirmed. The records do not indicate *which* of the supreme rulers, whether the Zaque, the Zipa, or the Iraca. We must assume that Guatavita, the blue lake high in the mountains near what is now Bogotá, was sacred to all the Chibcha. At this lake on the night of investiture the people of a ruler-to-be gathered in a great multitude. Bonfires blazed on surrounding peaks, and bonfires lined the lake shores, flickering yellow in the darkness. Many golden offerings were cast into the lake. Many more were heaped on a raft moored at lakeside. Priests, intoxicated from chewing coca leaves, sang wildly and sent tobacco smoke like incense puffing across the lake. Then into the firelight stepped the ruler-to-be, his nakedness coated with a sticky resin. Onto the resin his priests applied gold dust and more gold dust until he gleamed like a gilded statue. He stepped onto the raft, which was cut loose to drift into the middle of the lake. Suddenly he dived into the black water. When he emerged, the gold was gone, washed clean from his body. And he was king.

Dr. G. Reichel-Dolmatoff, a leading Colombian anthropologist, thinks this scene may have served to dramatize the folk memory of an event which happened centuries or even millennia before ever there was farming in the Andes, back in a time when wandering hunters still pursued the great wild beasts of an earlier age. In that time, he says, a meteor fell to earth in the Colombian Andes, burying itself in or near Lake Guatavita. For miles around the fireball must have been visible. How many legends must have begun with this cosmic accident, legends that would come to dominate the imaginations of all who came to these highlands. It may be that the Chibcha investiture ceremony was meant to re-enact the ancient legends, meant to show the bright god (in the golden person of the king) in his descent to earth. Or perhaps the king was meant to be an emissary, bringing on his body some of the drowned god's lost fire and receiving, in exchange, the god's own power. Nobody knows.

What does seem very likely, says Dr. Reichel-Dolmatoff, is that here, among the Chibcha and at Lake Guatavita, was the beginning of a Spanish myth, the myth of El Dorado (the place of gold) and of the Gilded Man. It was a myth which sent conquistadors ravaging through two continents— more often angry, and therefore cruel, than content with found riches. It sent them into Hopi country, confident that the pueblos would prove to be El Dorado. It sent Hernando de Soto scouring a path from Florida to South Carolina, across the Mississippi, and finally to his death. He was given tribute of river pearls by the people he encountered, but no gold. He found chiefdoms whose rulers were tattooed from head to foot, but no Gilded Man. In all of North America, no one ever did.

In 1542, while de Soto was tramping up and down and around the land between the Mississippi and Ouachita rivers, he heard of a great chief said to be overlord of all the surrounding territory. This chief lived (so the story went) on a high mound built on a bluff on the east bank of the Great River (the Mississippi). The chief's people or their relatives were said to occupy both banks of this river, from the entry of the Arkansas south to where the Red River joined the main stream and west along the Ouachita, whose lower and middle reaches they had settled. On a later foray into the territory of this unseen chief—or king—de Soto's expedition was considerably harassed by royal canoemen. He never saw the great man himself, never even knew the name of the king's people—Natchez, they would be called by later Spanish and French. And of course he could not know that the Natchez and their relatives were living representatives of the old Temple Mound Culture.

The Natchez were not seen again by Europeans for a hundred years and more—not until Frenchmen in the north decided to explore the Mississippi to its mouth. By then Natchez numbers and Natchez might had dwindled. They now occupied ten settlements clustering near the capital that would one day be the city of Natchez, Mississippi. During this hundred-year gap, there had been great movements and migrations and uprootings of peoples—not all attributable to the white man's presence or his guns (though perhaps owing something to the white man's diseases). The old Temple Mound Culture was dying out. Choctaws, Chickasaws, and Creeks were large tribes occupying the Southeast. They spoke Muskogean languages, which represent one family of the Gulf group. The Natchez language represents another family of this same Gulf group, which itself belongs in the Hokan-Siouan major group.

The large tribes lived around the old mound sites and even built low mounds of their own. But they seemed to have forgotten much of what the mounds had meant or where the older people—their ancestors—had gone. Even the Iroquoian-speaking Cherokees, relative newcomers to the Southeast, became fond of the mounds, though they were as ignorant of their meaning as the others. Only the Natchez seem to have remembered, to have been a living link with the past, to offer an approximation, at least, of what life in Temple Mound times must have been.

The focus and center of Natchez life was the Great Emerald Mound. The old French records are not clear as to whether *this* mound was used as a base for palace or for temple, but all agree on the use of *mounds*—presumably other mounds, and big ones at that—for worship and for the royal residence. This structure was regularly demolished at the death of its royal owner and built anew with each coronation. Some sources suggest that even the mound base was destroyed and rebuilt.

In describing most other aspects of Natchez life, the old French sources agree on so many points that one must consider them to be largely accurate. The king's house, they tell us, was built to look very much like the temple and was nearly as large. In it was the king's enormous bed, which could be shared only with the chief royal wife. Only she could share his meals. All others, the royal relatives included, maintained a distance of four feet, averting their faces and saluting their lord with howls. (Every observer seemed to find this particular greeting worthy of note.) The king responded with gifts and with food from his own dish, graciously pushed to the kneeling servitor by the royal foot.

Every morning the king was awakened by his staff—his war chiefs, the temple priests, the treaty makers, the inspectors of works, the masters of feasts. They awoke him with the usual howls and brought his royal cap of net adorned with white feathers and white beads. Crown on head and pipe in hand, the king arose and moved to the eastern door. There he greeted the celestial sun, his brother (or, as some held, his grandfather), with the same reverent howls that had awakened him earlier, and sent aloft in the sun's honor three puffs of smoke from the royal pipe.

The son of the most high sun god was to the Natchez a divine hero who had brought them all they knew of farming, religion, and the good things of life. Once this hero had distributed his gifts of knowledge, he had retired into a sacred stone which was reverently placed on the temple altar, enshrined there behind a perpetual flame. Through all the reigns of all the Natchez kings a godling in stone ruled the temple and was served there only by priests and kings.

The great temple, it was said, also contained idols of fantastic snakes and birds. Perhaps they were like the Mexican-inspired figures on the artifacts recovered from temple mounds elsewhere in the Southeast. There is in Natchez legend a curious tale of origins in the west, of long travels, and of a sojourn in Mexico. This may be merely a poetic recollection of ancient visitors *from* Mexico. Nevertheless, the ties were there, faint and tenuous, but in myth unforgotten. Neither were the ancient burial customs of the Hopewell and Adena people forgotten. For the king's bones, after a stay in temple ground, were always retrieved, cleaned, and collected for a great secondary burial in the temple itself.

When the king died, he did not die alone. All his wives, all his slaves, and many of his retainers willingly accompanied him. For he was, after all, both descendant and brother of the sun. He was called the Great Sun, and his royal relatives were Suns as well—his brothers, his sisters, and his sisters' children. Among the Natchez, as among the Chibcha, royal sisters provided the candidates for Sun-heir. The chief royal sister was honored nearly as highly as the

king himself. She married whom she chose, and her poor spouse had to stand always at attention in her presence and accompany her in death. The chief sister also disposed of whom she would, exactly as the Great Sun might do. "Rid me of that dog!" she might demand, pointing at some hapless subject or a tiresome spouse. Somebody immediately obliged her with whatever club happened to be handy. Victims, it is reported, always went meekly to their deaths. Fortunately there was the restraining influence of a council composed of settlement chiefs and elders. Left uncurbed, the royal whim might well have made severe inroads in the population.

It was clear to French visitors that class lines among the Natchez were very tightly drawn. Slaves were at the bottom, then the Stinkards (which is how the French translated *miche-miche-quipy*, the Natchez term). Stinkards were said to speak a different dialect, presumably one more vulgar than that of the gentry—the Honoreds, Nobles, and Suns. The lines were tightly drawn, to be sure, but they were not inflexible. There was actually a good deal of upward movement in Natchez society. Stinkards could improve their rank by bravery in battle, and a really determined Stinkard pair could rise to the rank of Honored by sacrificing their own baby on the bier of a dead king.

Pride ever goeth before a fall, and so it was among the Natchez. While some went up in rank, others came down. They had to; among Natchez males the social seesaw permitted no exceptions. No Sun could marry another Sun, for Suns could never be slain for any reason, certainly not to provide company for a dead spouse. Suns themselves required such company, and as the nobility were inclined to be reluctant mates, Suns of either sex always married Stinkards, who were only too happy to accompany a royal spouse in death. While the children of female Suns (and those of lesser female nobility as well) took their mothers' rank, children of male Suns (and male nobility) were demoted one step in rank. Like leader, like followers; members of the lesser gentry also married beneath their station. Because of the compulsory downward drift, a living Great Sun might see his own great-grandchild brought up as a Stinkard. No matter. Attractive Stinkards, male and female, nearly always married above *their* station to set the seesaw bobbing once again.

The Natchez system came to an end with the Natchez themselves. In 1730 they warred with the French and lost. More than four hundred were sent as slaves to the West Indies. Other hardy souls lingered on to harry and hold back the incoming French, then took refuge with the Creeks, the Chickasaws, and the Cherokees. They helped the host tribes in their own struggles against French, English, and Americans and finally merged with them entirely. In 1907 anthropologist John R. Swanton was able to meet and know the last surviving speakers of the Natchez tongue, to learn from them something of a tradition by then near extinction.

Their memories, together with the old French records, tell us that, in many particulars, the Natchez were very like other tribes of the Southeast. They warred and took captives whom they adopted, enslaved, or tormented. They indulged in competitive ball games, captained by the Great Sun on one side and the War Chief on the other. They farmed in similar ways, raised the same crops, hunted and fished using similar techniques. Their bodies were tattooed and painted in the interests of status or beauty or both. (One of the Great Sun's titles was "Tattooed Serpent.") Feather and bead ornaments were much admired. They considered the handsome face to be one plucked clean of hair, a notion shared by most of the tribes of the North American Southeast and of South America as well. Like other Southeastern tribes (and the Chibcha, too), the Natchez reckoned descent through the mother, a similarity which may go back to early times when many peoples were adjusting in much the same manner to the new farming way of life.

Unlike other Southeastern tribes, the Natchez were less clan-conscious than class-conscious. Like the Chibcha they made much of the business of rank and royalty and all the trappings thereof—stools, carrying litters, sacrifices, obeisances. These were notions popular all around the Gulf. That they came originally from Mexico and flourished among people rich enough, complex enough to receive them is certain. How the ideas came and by what routes they traveled is something else again. We know only that they were contagious. All around the Gulf, on the outskirts of the two great civilizations, chiefdoms were beginning to look like states—until the Europeans came.

What would have happened in the Americas, north and south, had Europeans been less curious about the earth or less concerned with charting trade routes around it? Would the Natchez eventually have blossomed into a true civilization? Already, by the time of de Soto's expedition, they were incising on wooden plaques the pictographic record of battle exploits. Would the Chibcha, like barbarous Macedon poised above the Greek city-states, have expanded one day to engulf Peru or even Mexico? Would there ever have developed on the two continents an expanded, civilized realm, broad enough and strong enough to meet the European challenge at a later time?

We must leave these questions to the writers of fiction and fantasy. Fact reminds us that, when the Spaniards did arrive, there were in the New World only two small centers of true civilization—quickly shattered, irretrievably lost.

Part V

EMPIRE BUILDERS

16

Sacred Stones, Calendar Stones,
and Stones of Sacrifice

Corn was first planted in the dry uplands of south central
Mexico, and the heartbeat of New World life quickened.
Slowly the upland people gathered into hamlets and remained
settled for at least part of the year. To them, sometime
around 2300 B.C., came pottery and the cult of figurines.
Everywhere in the various farming hubs people devoted
themselves to the new little goddesses—some of them squat
and clumsy; some three-headed monstrosities; some graceful
and amusing, pretty little ladies with flaring legs and saucy
faces. Who knows but what they may simply have represented the good things, the sweet things of life? Certainly
early villagers were no foreigners to fun. In the graves where
little goddesses were deposited in such numbers, other sorts
of figures have been found—figures carrying balls and
wearing protective padding. Already, it seems, the highland
people were fond of ball games.

But it was not in upland villages that New World civilization began, but down in the far less likely lowlands, in the
steamy, jungly lowlands that the first temple mounds suddenly sprang into being and the first high art flowered. It
was in the lowlands that there first appeared the themes,
beliefs, forms destined to mark Middle American civilizations

◀ *Clockwise from top center: Toltec warrior; temple of Quetzalcoatl at
Teotihuacán; Aztec pottery; sun stone; sacrificial vessel; monumental
Olmec head; Inca monarch; and Moche pottery.*

to follow. And not only those of Middle America. Slowly they were to spread north and south, influencing people who would never themselves develop true civilization but who would be drawn, all the same, into the orbit of new ideas.

Specialists have long known about this lowland culture, but only a few recognized its antiquity and were willing to call it "first" and "oldest." In 1966, however, its priority was established beyond all doubt. In that year three neighboring sites in the Mexican state of Veracruz, sites known collectively as San Lorenzo, were fully excavated. Tests of charcoal fragments associated with great stone monuments already known in that area indicated an occupation of the sites beginning around 1200 B.C. and continuing to 900 B.C. There are in Middle America village sites of greater antiquity, but nowhere among them has there yet been found anything quite like San Lorenzo.

The people who once lived in San Lorenzo—or perhaps simply worshiped and built there—carefully mounded one of the centers into what archaeologist Michael D. Coe (an excavator of the site) thinks was meant to represent a huge animal whose enormous outlines could be fully appreciated only from a sky view. On top of this artificial plateau there must once have been pools, perhaps reserved for ceremonial use, for the excavators have uncovered a drainage system nearly a thousand feet in length and of surprising sophistication.

The artists of San Lorenzo made some figures of clay and many more of stone, precious jade, and serpentine. Often these were equipped with inlaid mirrors of hematite, highly polished—to reflect? to shine? to invoke—what? We do not know. The heads of the figures are usually deformed, flattened both fore and aft in the manner that was—or later became—universal high fashion throughout the Americas. (Such flattening is achieved by the application of wooden slats to a newborn baby's forehead and by the pressure of the cradleboard behind.)

There was yet more in San Lorenzo. Its artists, its sculptors also made great carved altars and mighty round heads of basalt, some looming nine feet high and weighing many tons. The faces on altars and monuments are sometimes bearded, hawk-nosed, and sharp, but those of the great heads are flat, fleshy, and powerful. They wear a conviction of strength that goes quite beyond the weight of stone. Were the heads meant to be portraits, true likenesses of great lords? Perhaps. There seems to be more of the soldier than of the priest about them, for all the popular belief that early Middle American cultures were priest-ridden and priest-run. Their headgear reminds us of the modern football helmet and may have been as thoroughly practical in construction and intent; rock carvings elsewhere show us that the chief weapon of these people was a stout cudgel.

That the colossal heads are where they are is something of a wonder. No basalt is to be found in the San Lorenzo area, the nearest source being fifty miles away in the Tuxtla Mountains. The stone must have been floated on rafts downriver to the sea, along the coast to the Coatzacoalcos River, then up to the San Lorenzo ceremonial centers. Many willing hands would have been needed for such labor, and much able direction, too. Think of the labor involved in building the Egyptian pyramids or in erecting Stonehenge. The creation of the stone heads of San Lorenzo is not so very different a proposition.

Who were these people of the stone heads, the mammoth altars? Nobody really knows. Their culture has been named Olmec after a historic (but apparently unrelated) people who lived in these lowlands in later times, people whom the Aztecs called Olmeca—"people of the rubber country." But surely their direct ancestors had nothing to do with the great heads. Possession of the Gulf coast was to change hands any number of times over the long years. Whoever the sculptors of San Lorenzo were, they seem to have had a penchant for destruction as well as creation. Sometime

around 900 B.C., many of the heads and altars were deliberately defaced, the altars toppled over offerings, the heads
pushed into ravines—much in the way statues of great men
in other times have been toppled from their pedestals when
the winds of admiration shifted. After 900 B.C. San Lorenzo
was abandoned, not to be used again for a thousand years,
this time by people whose tastes in art had changed with the
influence of newer arbiters of elegance.

The priests, the rulers, the sculptors fled. Perhaps some,
as Dr. Coe suggests, mounted the plateau and crossed it to
settle in Mexico's Pacific coastal area. Others doubtless went
in search of land for a new ceremonial center. They found
it on the island of La Venta, eighteen miles from the Gulf
in what is now the state of Tabasco. La Venta lies in the
middle of a swamp. It is tiny; only a small corps of priests
could have made it their home. The farmers who supported
the center surely lived far away where there were tillable
lands. Perhaps isolation and secrecy were exactly what the
builders of La Venta wanted. But what magnificence was
invested in this hidden shrine, this temple compound, this
grand architectural design! The whole is built on a base of
stone and varicolored clays—hand-shaped bricks in mortar
covered by caps of clay plaster. It is oriented to a point
slightly east of north. (All later temple complexes in Middle
America are so oriented.) At one end is a pyramid of clay
240 feet by 420 feet at the base and 103 feet high. The top
is flat; perhaps it once held a temple of wattle and daub.
And the sides are fluted, ridged, deliberately scarred, as one
specialist believes, to represent a volcanic cone. A memory
of the Tuxtlas? Perhaps. Flanking the pyramid are two long,
low mounds, the whole enclosing a sort of plaza, its outlines
once further marked by a fence of basalt columns seven
feet tall. Opposite the pyramid is a round mound and behind
that a terraced mound complex arranged, some think, to
represent the stylized mask of a jaguar.

GULF OF MEXICO

Chichén Itzá

Tula

VALLEY
OF
MEXICO

Teotihuacán
Tenochtitlán
Veracruz
Tres Zapotes
La Venta
San Lorenzo

Monte
Alban

Tikal

▬▬▬▬ Huastec area

ᴧᴧᴧᴧᴧᴧᴧ Aztec empire in 1518

■■■■■ Olmec heartland

═══════ Maya area

*Cultures of
Middle America*

The basalt, the clays, the jade for the many offerings of
figurines had to be imported into La Venta, as into San
Lorenzo. A whole network of trade must have supported
Olmec art which, in its turn, both expressed and supported
Olmec religion—as among the Hopewell mound builders,
miles and years away. Traders no doubt went out to discover
and exploit sources of necessary raw material. And wherever
they went, some settled or at least left behind a record of
their passing. Artifacts of Olmec type have been found
among the collections of highland village figurines. And
there are rock carvings as far south as Guatemala and San
Salvador on which are depicted Olmec warriors brandishing
clubs (the traders may have been at least partly pirates after
all).

In the Mexican states of Morelos and Guerrero, figurines, large rock carvings, and even paintings deep in caves have been discovered, all bearing the unique marks of Olmec design and Olmec belief. And what are these marks? Curves, first of all; curved heads, clouds, faces. There are serpent figures and there are bird figures. Most importantly, there is the jaguar. Or rather, there is a god who is part human, part jaguar—a baby or a baby-god, child of a woman and a jaguar; a baby with toothless gums (or sometimes sprouting curious bifurcated fangs); a baby with flamelike eyebrows, fat body, cleft head; a baby whose full, soft mouth with its swollen upper lip is perpetually drawn down in an expression that is part cry, part snarl. This peculiar mouth, this baby face, stamps all Olmec figures (no matter how realistic the artist's original intent) with the mark of the were-jaguar and of the eternal infant.

The Olmec seem to have been obsessed with babies, all kinds of babies, everyday garden-variety babies as well as

*Olmec figure,
showing jaguar-baby god*

those of the celestial sort. Carved on many altars, squalling babes in the arms of priests are shown emerging from niches or caves (another Olmec interest). Perhaps they represent the sort of worship familiar to Christians today and renewed with the crèches every year at Christmas. Perhaps, as Dr. Coe reminds us, the baby figures may have some curious connection with sacrifice. The Aztecs, two thousand years later, regularly slew babies to invoke and propitiate Tlaloc, the rain god, and the more the sacrificial children cried, the better; tear drops would summon rain drops. Now, the crying Olmec babies may be proof of just such a rite among the Olmec. But there is more to the symbolism than that. The baby-god, after all, is part jaguar, and the jaguar, among peoples of Middle America, has always meant rain, meant water. Jaguars range the lowland jungles and are water animals (though lone old males have been reported occasionally in desert country); they swim well and like to ambush their prey along watercourses. There is still more. The great Mexican artist, Miguel Covarrubias, once traced the manner in which every rain god in Middle America—from Mexican Tlaloc to Chac of the Maya—owes its artistic origins to the Olmec were-jaguar-baby. Even though Dr. Coe and his students believe they have now found among Olmec sacred figures the protypes of still other gods of later Middle America, the point still holds good: Olmec religion was built around rain.

But why? Who needed rain in the lowlands of the Gulf coast? A hundred inches a year fall in Veracruz and Tabasco and always have. Why would people whose lives were spent clearing forests so that the errant sun could fall on their fields pray incessantly for rain? And not only pray for it but build a whole religion around rain? One would think, on grounds of simple logic (admittedly, man is not always logical), that a rain god would have had dry highland beginnings. And maybe he did.

Dr. Coe confesses the real mystery of San Lorenzo: it lacks antecedents. When the great monuments, the colossal heads were carved in the lowlands, there were, everywhere on the central plateau, only hamlets of small farmers, devoted to their pretty figurines. The great art of San Lorenzo seems to have sprung into being fully formed. Nowhere are its humble beginnings to be found. Or, at least, nowhere so far.

Some specialists wonder whether influences from across the Pacific can be credited for the beginnings of Olmec styles and ideas. Those who disagree point out that in 1500 B.C. or so, Chinese civilization was just getting under way and the urban centers of India had not yet begun to build the great seafaring craft they would sail in later years. This does not, of course, rule out the introduction of Oriental ideas at later times. Dr. Gordon Ekholm and others remind us of certain small animal figures that have been found throughout Veracruz. Made of clay and equipped with clay wheels, they can be dated around 200 B.C. and after. Except for its use on these little figures—so reminiscent of the pull toy familiar to our modern children—the wheel was unused and unknown in Middle America or, for that matter, anywhere else in the New World before the Europeans brought it with them. The "toys" of Veracruz are very like ceremonial objects used in India and China from earliest times. Perhaps their use was ceremonial in the New World, too, for they are usually found in graves. There are many other themes in American art and architecture that are strikingly paralleled across the Pacific. The fact remains, however, that whatever traveled from the Old World after 1000 B.C. could not have provided much more than frills and trimmings to a pattern already shaped. But shaped where?

Perhaps we might look closer to home. Remember that while the first highland farmers were struggling with the land, living in small family groups, not even truly settled the whole year through, gatherers in the lush lowlands were

Huastec wheeled toy

already living in permanent villages. Perhaps they were already inventing the sorts of devotions and myths that leisure makes possible. To these villages came corn from the highlands. With the corn may have come ideas and even specific symbols, less tangible than food but just as powerful; some sense of the hazards surrounding the cultivation of corn, perhaps; some sense of corn's need for water—a need so desperate, so urgent, and in the highlands so often un- fulfilled that the lowlanders were themselves shaken and impressed. If one accepted corn, grew corn, then one also accepted the possible droughts and hazards that went with it. One had to develop images and formulas that would forestall the expected dangers. One learned to manage celes- tial beings of a newer sort, elaborating in the process a religion of rain in a land that was never without it.

Perhaps this is the sort of thing Dr. MacNeish had in mind when he spoke of the continued interplay in Middle America between wet land and dry land, high land and low. In the Olmec case this interplay may have involved the Tuxtla Mountains rather than the plateau of central Mexico. It is where archaeologists will look next in the search for Olmec beginnings.

About 400 B.C. La Venta suffered the same sort of destruction visited earlier upon San Lorenzo. Most carefully the heads and altars were scarred—always the heavy, stolid faces suffering the most damage. Again the priests departed. Never more would La Venta be a grand cathedral, though right up through Spanish times quiet people left small, secret offerings in its precincts. After this catastrophe the Olmec seemed not to recover their old vigor. There was in later times a modest revival in San Lorenzo, at Tres Zapotes (a site in the Tuxtla Mountains), and at various other places in southern Veracruz. But new people were coming in, new influences, and the Olmec heartland changed in time with both.

By 400 B.C., however, other civilized centers were coming into bloom, other people were picking up what the Olmec had so auspiciously begun. There were, for example, the Maya, whose territory lay in the Yucatán Peninsula. Late in getting started, peripheral to the northern centers until well into A.D. times, they began after 400 B.C. to increase in population. Little by little they developed in architecture and in art until they eventually built the intellectual capitals of the New World. It was among the Maya that hieroglyphic writing was brought to its most sophisticated expression, among the Maya that the calendar—so typical of Middle American cultures—took its most complex forms. There was a calendar for the 260-day "sacred year," another for the 365-day solar year, and still others based on the revolutions of the moon and of the planet Venus. Most complicated of all was the Maya Long Count. Our absolute reckoning of the passage of time has a B.C.–A.D. division, modern times dating from the birth of Christ. The Maya Long Count was also calculated from a beginning point (an unknown but surely important event) which works out to have been 3113 B.C. by our correlations. On monuments, then, the date of carving represented a certain length of time since the

Maya beginning. And that period was rendered in cycles of days. Cycles included the *baktun*, which had 144,000 days, the *katun*, which had 7,200 days, and several others down to the *kin*, which was one day only. Thus, a Long Count date would be expressed in terms of the number of *baktun*, *katun*, and finally *kin* involved.

The earliest Maya Long Count date yet discovered in Yucatán is, by our reckoning, 292 A.D. In Tres Zapotes, however, there has been found an Olmec stele bearing in recognizably Maya Long Count symbols a date equivalent to our 31 B.C. If we may trust the testimony of chronology, it would seem that the Long Count is of Olmec, not Mayan, invention.

Perhaps New World writing also had its beginning in the Veracruz lowlands. There are many Olmec symbols—obviously picture signs or idea signs, perhaps of sacred meaning —whose mysteries can be unraveled at least partially by using similar Mayan signs of known meaning. One wonders whether the Olmec were, after all, really Maya, or rather whether the Maya were latter-day descendants of people we call the Olmec. Did the Olmec heartland at one time stretch without a break into Yucatán? Some specialists think this may have been so. In northern Veracruz today there live the Huastecs, people who speak a Mayan language though all around them unrelated languages abound. Perhaps the Huastecs were separated from the Maya of Yucatán by newcomers pushing into the coastal area, sending Olmec (Maya?) inhabitants fleeing into the Huasteca or into Yucatán. And there is one more clue. The Aztecs loved to tell of an ancient land on the Gulf coast, where

> in a certain era
> which no one can reckon,
> which no one can remember,
> there was a government for a long time.

The name used by the Aztecs for this place is Tamoanchan.

Late Mayan miniature figurine

The word means "land of rain or mist," but it is not an Aztec word. It is a Maya word.

In the lowland state of Chiapas there is a site called Izapa (at its height around 100 B.C.) whose people seem to have had a foot in both cultural doors, Olmec and Maya. There is a temple complex, even a ball park on the site. There are also many monuments, one of which bears a Long Count date equivalent to our 36 A.D. The sculptural style in Izapa is clearly Olmec-derived, though without the Olmec appreciation for simplicity. The designs are involved and intricate, with that avoidance of empty spaces that would mark Mayan art of later times.

In the state of Oaxaca can be found the remains of yet another civilized center, called Monte Alban. Its earliest monuments (dating to about 400 B.C.) and its writing signs are clearly Olmec-inspired. Located in an out-of-the-way mountain spot, Monte Alban remained undisturbed for centuries while other temple centers fell and rose and fell again.

After 400 B.C., as temple centers multiplied, the marks of Olmec art and inspiration were less pronounced. The original ideas had become patterns to be modified and cut to suit place, time, and sentiment. While variations were being played elsewhere on the Olmec theme, the Valley of Mexico, where some of the earliest farming-village remains have been found, lingered in a backwater. For all the trekking back and forth of Olmec merchants, for their exposure to art and ideas, the little farmers had not been moved to undertake any great building projects.

And then suddenly, beginning around 100 B.C. in a side pocket of the Valley of Mexico, there was a city, a city called Teotihuacán. Now, this phrase may not strike you as startling. History-minded students have become accustomed to linking cities with civilization. Old World civilization, after all, had its clear beginnings in the little Mesopotamian cities of Sumer. These had developed as residential clumps around shrines and temples and had supported their growing populations on land wrested from the marshes and maintained by constant attention to irrigation. New World civilization also began in temple centers, but they were centers around which no dense crowds gathered to live. Occupied by priests only, the centers were supported, it seems, by farmers who came trooping in to help with the building projects and to observe the holy days.

Archaeologists used to rate the remains of certain societies as "civilized" primarily on the basis of art, architecture, and writing—all signs that are eminently clear to the investigator. Today's judgment is more often made on the basis of evidence not so easy to uncover but perhaps fairer in the long run. How big was the population? How complex was the economy? How varied were the experiences and residence patterns of the people? Were there specialists, and of what sort? What was the nature of organization, motivation, leadership? Now, the evidence of the temple centers in Middle America indicates very clearly that all the essential

criteria for civilization were met plus most of the bonus
items. In these centers complex planning was organized.
From them went forth the leadership and direction that kept
a large populace busily working toward common goals. But
it was also a populace that was scattered about and dispersed,
not one that lived forever under the noses of rulers and
priests, or priest-rulers, as the case may have been.

And that is why Teotihuacán is a word with which to
conjure. It represents something out of the pattern. It is the
name of a city, the only real city in all of Middle America
of its time and probably the largest ever to be built there in
any time before the Conquest. In its heyday around 500 A.D.
it supported a population of close to 100,000. It covered an
area of eight square miles laid out on a careful grid plan of
streets and avenues, all oriented to that slightly east-of-north
point established in Olmec times, all organized in units
about the size of our city blocks. Citizens lived in one-story
apartment complexes, windowless on the street but opening
within onto patios. Each apartment house had its own small
chapels. Each block was perhaps occupied by kinfolk or
even fellow guild members. For in Teotihuacán, the followers of the various arts and crafts—the obsidian artificers,
the potters, weavers, painters, builders—seemed to occupy
separate quarters. So did foreign merchants. In certain parts
of Teotihuacán can be found remains that are clearly
Mayan, others just as clearly from Veracruz or Oaxaca.

The upper classes—rulers, priests, maybe even military
leaders—lived in exquisite palaces built of stone and a con-
crete made of crushed volcanic rock mixed with lime. Interior palace walls were painted with beautiful murals, for
the Teotihuacános seemed to appreciate painting rather
more than they did sculpture. Many people—the ruling
classes, certainly—were literate. Glyphs on pottery and in
wall paintings tell us so. In Teotihuacán murals, people are
invariably shown with cloudlike figures issuing from their

mouths—rather reminiscent of the balloons which in our comic strips carry the dialogue and story along. Books have not been found, but they may have been written on screen-folded bark paper or deerskin, perishable, like those of the later Aztecs and Maya.

One wonders why and how a little side-pocket community became the first and largest city of pre-Conquest Middle America. Probably, says Dr. René Millon, because the area abounded in rich sources of obsidian, and obsidian was, right up to Conquest times, the primary raw material for tools and weapons. The location of the little side-pocket valley may also have had something to do with its success. It was the gateway into the larger Valley of Puebla which, in its turn, opened into the lowlands. But there was another reason, and it very likely had to do with an improved method of farming, one that would permit the permanent residence impossible to a people who must shift to new fields when the soil grows poor.

The whole Valley of Mexico is rich in springs which feed a central lake (actually a series of connecting basins without drainage) which was much larger in ancient times than it is today. Around this lake and in its shallower, marshy parts there have been built since Aztec times, at least, artificial islands called *chinampas*. The islands are made from mud dredged from the lake bottom and piled up with reeds, the whole held together with stakes and growing trees. They serve a dual purpose: they drain the swamp into a network of canals and create close-packed, tiny, but very fertile fields, capable of producing several crops a year almost indefinitely. *Chinampas* are in use today near Mexico City. The islands and canals are still laid out in a grid pattern oriented slightly east of north, exactly like the city plan of Teotihuacán. It has long been supposed that some sort of irrigation system must have been used to support the farms of Teotihuacán, though no evidence for such a system has yet been found. Perhaps that old city was supported instead by the produce of *chinampas* established in the southern portions of the lake. Many of the figurines still being dredged up from the canal bottoms of modern *chinampas* in the area are old, as old as Teotihuacán itself, and are made in the Teotihuacán style.

However Teotihuacán began, it quickly attracted trade and pilgrims, too. Along its central avenue ran a procession of religious shrines, temples, and monuments bounded at one end by the Pyramid of the Moon and at the other by the much grander Pyramid of the Sun (as large at the base as that of Cheops in Egypt). Beyond the Sun pyramid was yet another building complex, a set of platforms flanking an enormous plaza which may well have been the central market place of Teotihuacán. Across a thoroughfare which the Aztecs dubbed the Street of the Dead there was yet another great compound, perhaps the royal palace, containing a beautiful temple of Quetzalcoatl, the Feathered Serpent. Just such a creature had often been carved and painted by the Olmec, but what it meant to them we do not know. Judging by the records of Aztec times, we can suppose that Teotihuacán's Quetzalcoatl represented in reptile guise the god of agriculture, he who had stolen corn from the ants and given it to men. Like the Aztec Quetzalcoatl, he was probably also the god of artificers in jade and of all the arts and blessings of civilized life. Always, it seems, he was a kind god, one who tormented his own body but received from mankind only serpents and butterflies in sacrifice. What a world of difference from the bloodthirsty deities of later times!

So great was the influence of Teotihuacán that its art styles, its buildings, its fashions were copied from Veracruz to Maya land. At great Tikal, the largest and most breathtakingly beautiful of all the Mayan temple centers, there has been found a statue of Teotihuacán's rain god—recognizably the bespectacled and ancient Tlaloc. The Mayan highland

The rain god Tlaloc

center of Kaminaljuyu (near modern Guatemala City) was little more than a provincial outpost of the great Mexican city to the north. Some scholars have thought it a conquered state, administered by the soldiers of Teotihuacán. This may well be so, though military might seems not to have been in those days a matter of supreme importance—not the way it would be after 900 A.D. when so-called Classic times had ended. While Teotihuacán flourished, temple centers were not fortified. Even the great city itself was undefended, unprepared for the disasters that were to come.

Sometime between 600 and 760 A.D., the Valley of Mexico and areas to the north seem to have become increasingly dry. Crops failed. Slopes, long since shorn of their trees, eroded. Teotihuacán's population shrank. After natural hardships came man-made disasters. Raiders entered, burned, demolished Teotihuacán. They were, more likely than not, food-gathering tribes of the desert, grown wild with thirst and hunger, who pushed through the northern frontier and attacked the city. There seems to have followed a short interlude during which squatters lived and built amid the ruins. Then the city was deserted.

Perhaps not deserted altogether, however. The great nations that developed after Teotihuacán's fall held even the ruins in awe. It is said that Aztec kings made pilgrimage there on foot. For it was considered not only the successor to ancient, mythical Tamoanchan, but the holy spot on which the gods had immolated themselves to achieve the rebirth of the sun and a new era on earth.

Whatever its subsequent transformation in legend, its earthly demise had repercussions all around Middle America. Other great temple centers declined, some were abandoned. In the great Mayan centers, art work and temple construction stopped for half a century but were then resumed, to flower as never before—this time without central Mexican influence anywhere in evidence. Tall, steep pyramids crowned with narrow temples rose above the lowland jungles in Mayan territory. Older centers were heightened, enlarged, refurbished. Though complexes often included palaces of corbeled arches and pillared porticoes, the temple sites were always oriented as of old—rectangular plazas enclosed by mounds and pyramids. If the Olmec penchant for trade and travel had been reborn in Teotihuacán, surely the Olmec religious dedication was recaptured among the Maya, though even they were not above trade.

Sometime before 900 A.D. the fervor faltered. Ideas from the Valley of Mexico, newer ideas from newer people, began once more to find their way into Maya land. On the pillars and monuments there began to appear scenes of warriors and captives and human sacrifice. And then suddenly the temple centers were overthrown, defaced, and deserted, much as San Lorenzo and La Venta had been deserted, each in its own time. If only the stately Mayan glyphs could be fully translated! Some specialists believe they detail only astronomical observations and calculations, prayers, and invocations. Others, however, insist the writings are concerned with historical events and with the birth and death of kings. If so, we may yet hope to learn how and why Classic Mayan centers came to their end.

When next the old patterns quickened in Middle America it was to the sound of marching feet, the blare of war songs, and the screams of captives sacrificed to please the gods. For after 900 A.D. the time of empire dawned in Middle America, and it is in war and suffering that empires are built. It seems to have been about this time that strong Mexican influences began to penetrate North America and temple mound building along the Mississippi was begun. Perhaps there came along many less tangible notions about the nature of war and sacrifice, for never in Middle America's past had war and sacrifice been so popular or so compelling.

Waves of wild desert folk who settled in the Valley of Mexico learned from survivors of Teotihuacán the ways and gods of older, wiser times and grew strong in their turn. They were, as well, the recipients of a new technology unknown to their predecessors. The knowledge of metallurgy, transmitted northward from Peru, spread into Middle America sometime around 900 A.D., and the desert invaders were quick to adopt the new process. It must be said, however, that products of the smelter ran more often to ornament than to weaponry. The warriors of Middle America preferred obsidian blades and points and would follow the preference right up to the time when the Spaniards arrived in Mexico.

After an initial settling in, the newcomers began to fan out and to found little states along the Gulf coast and elsewhere. But the crucial central valley was dominated by a people known as the Toltecs. They did not live in Teotihuacán but built their own strongly fortified capital north of the valley (in what is now the state of Hidalgo) and called it Tollan, or Tula. In Tula the old emblems of eagle, jaguar, and serpent, plus new ones depicting human skulls and hearts, ornamented pillars and walls. In Tula the fighting men also had their day in art. They appear everywhere in friezes as gigantic, grim-faced columns and in portrait heads as knights wearing the totemic gear of their military orders. Signs of Quetzalcoatl are also evident, but it seems he was honored far more in art than he was in act. For it was at Tula, so the traditions and later written records tell us, that there began the blood worship of Tezcatlipoca of the Smoking Mirror, black god of night and war.

His followers, the living warriors of Tula, went everywhere, *atlatl* and darts in hand. Some conquered even into Yucatán, which saw the old and waning Maya culture reborn in a mixed Mexican image centered on Chichén Itzá, reminiscent of Toltec Tula in its buildings and art. But nothing lasts forever, and what had begun in conquest ended so. The Toltecs in their turn were overcome by newer desert tribes. They were dispersed or dispatched, and around 1156 A.D. Tula was burned to the ground.

In time the new invaders forgot the circumstances of their arrival and made of the vanished Toltecs a race of heroes. Each tribe longed to repeat the legendary exploits, to reclaim the captured land, to succeed to the Toltec empire. One tribe did. They were the Aztecs.

Since the civilization of Middle America had their beginning along the eastern coastline, it seems only proper that the second center of New World civilization should have developed in the west, along Pacific shores. Sometime after 1500 B.C., you will recall, the Olmecs appeared suddenly in Mexico, bringing with them high art and the skill to bind to themselves peoples numerous and diverse. It was not too long after this initial date that the first great Andean civilization came to flower, itself possessing the power of imagination and the skill to bind. Unlike the Olmec phenomenon, its way had been prepared. Behind it lay a long record of change and growth and elaboration, of temples and towns from their very beginnings along the arid coast of Peru.

Peru—meaning the whole of the area that the last Andean civilization, that of the Incas, would one day occupy—is called so because of a misunderstanding so old as to be by now almost forgotten. The Inca name for the land was *Tehuantinsuyu*, "the four quarters," but the Spaniards first to drop anchor off Tumbes could not have known the proper name. They made inquiry of a native fisherman in his boat. "Pelu," he said in answer to their unintelligible questions. And whether Pelu was the river in which he was fishing or his own name no one knows. And, really, it does not matter after all. Either one would seem entirely appropriate to describe a land in which civilization found its beginnings in the labor and imagination of fisherfolk.

The narrow coast of Peru is a cool, mist-hung desert punctuated by some forty tiny rivers. Each is barred from its neighbors, not only by sand, but by mountain spurs and desolate rocks. Communication between valleys—if there is to be communication at all—must be by sea or a little way back from the sea amid the slopes. (It was here, or higher still in the mountains themselves, that later Andean people would build their famous roads.)

Dividing the Andes chains are three long river systems running from north to south. Their valleys broaden in only six or seven spots to provide room for farming, room in which people could congregate in large numbers. But everywhere, except for a high pass now and then, the narrow valleys do nicely for travel. There are just such inter-mountain valleys in the Ecuadorian Andes and in those of Colombia, too. It was perhaps by way of these river highways that maize arrived in Peru. Anthropologist Edward P. Lanning, who has done perhaps the most recent excavating of early Peruvian sites, and certainly the most up-to-date survey of Peruvian archaeology in general, believes that even the idea of cultivating squash may have traveled to Peru from Mexico.

You will recall (in Chapter Six) the ancient fishermen of Peru, people who had earlier hunted and gathered on the *lomas*, those fog-nourished vegetation zones between some coastal rivers. With the drying of the *lomas*, their people moved to settle permanently on the little river deltas and to gather from the sea. By 3600 B.C. some of the fishermen had become squash farmers as well. By 2500 B.C. most were also cultivating cotton. Between 2500 and 1800 (the time after which pottery began to come into general use) people in one of the north central sites, a collection of shell-mound villages around the Culebras River, had learned to cultivate maize. And not only maize has been found in the site, but the bones of a domesticated animal—the little guinea pig, which compensates for its small size by its dependable numbers. Some time later the llama and the alpaca—cousins to the wild guanaco—would be domesticated in the highlands, but always they would be important as much for wool and sacrifice as for their meat.

Predictably, the Culebras population was large, larger than any to be found at other villages of the same pre-pottery period. The Culebras people had acquired some of the comforts and graces of prosperous farmers everywhere. Most of them occupied homes no longer dug into the shell-refuse mound but situated airily on terraces and constructed of substantial basalt blocks and clay bricks set in clay mortar. Each was equipped with an elaborate guinea-pig hutch, complete with stone-lined tunnels. Even the Culebras dead were no longer deposited in the middens as before but were laid to rest in cemeteries with a variety of rich offerings, with the

exquisite textiles for which Peruvians would become famous
—whether they were twined as in those early days or loom-
woven as in later times. All in all, the Culebras people were
certainly building for comfort and convenience, but they
were not building a civilization.

That was to be the invention—at least in part—of people
farther south near the area where the city of Lima would
one day rise. The people there, along the Chillón River, had
no maize (though they might possibly have cultivated potatoes), and they had no guinea pigs. Neither could they boast
a large, concentrated population. What they did have, apparently, was an idea, and because of the idea, they were
moved to create a temple center. Built sometime after 2500
B.C., it seems to have been the first such center in Peru. The
complex consisted of nine stone-faced buildings enclosing a
central plaza and covered, in all, an area of 900 by 650 yards
—quite an impressive size for a first attempt. What was worshiped there we cannot know, but it must have been compelling enough to attract the effort of the fishermen and
squash farmers from many separate groups. The temple itself
with its wings was a simple, blocky affair. Later, however, in
a neighboring valley, the Río Seco folk were a bit more
ambitious. Apparently they began their temple as a simple
stone house structure. Then somebody had a brilliant idea.
Fill it in! Fill in all the rooms with boulders and build another, somewhat smaller house on top. Fill *that* in, and what
results? A sort of pyramid, small and crude, to be sure, but
mark the date of building: sometime between 2000 and
1800 B.C., long before pyramids rose anywhere else in the
New World. The Río Seco people covered their construction with sand and placed long blocks of stone on top. Then
they built another pyramid exactly like the first. Surely the
twin monuments of Río Seco were something to elicit awe
and wonder and the pride of accomplishment that, in itself,
carries the seeds of religious conviction.

Slowly temple building spread north. By the time pottery came into use a certain pattern had already been set along the central coast. There were temple centers in most of the river valleys—pyramid, wings, and plaza. Sometimes these stood alone, isolated on sterile land, useless for farming. Sometimes they rose in the middle of villages, but always the plan of construction was the same. There were cemeteries in the valleys, filled with grave goods—baskets, fabrics, flutes, mirrors, needles, slings. In the dry desert air, cemetery inhabitants quickly mummified. Their remains clearly tell us that pointed heads were in high fashion. Some heads show evidence of trepanning, of openings cut in the skull for the relief of pressure or the release of demons. That the surgeons were skilled is proved by the numbers of skulls showing signs of regrowth around the original opening. Some hardy patients lived long enough to undergo yet another session under knife and saw.

The head was, in fact, to become as symbolically special in the Andes as scalps were to be in North America. Even in those early times, trophy heads were taken, and the habit would intensify with time.

The cemeteries do not give much evidence of trade—except for the presence of coca quids, which surely came from the jungly highlands on the eastern slopes of the Andes. Coca in Peru, then and in later times, was chewed with lime obtained from certain burned woods or burned shells. The lime was stored in special gourd bottles and spooned out with special bone spatulas.

To all the elementary patterns of Peruvian life of early times, suddenly around 900 B.C. something new was added. Again, it was an idea, powerful enough this time to bring most of Peru very quickly under its sway, or at least under its influence, since it did not reflect a governing body of any sort. What kind of idea? Archaeologists are at a loss except for one thing. At its heart was a god, a supreme god who wore the fangs of the jaguar set in a mouth drawn down in a jaguar's snarl. So pervasive were these attributes that even the familiar snakes and eagles—which had decorated fabrics since fiber twining began—were given the jaguar's fangs. The supreme being was not a local river god grown mighty and tall. He had arrived, it seems, by way of the highlands, the northern highlands, more likely than not.

Now, the jaguar is a creature of the jungles, and some specialists have claimed a jungle origin for the jaguar deity—perhaps in the eastern slopes of the Andes, the jungly Montaña. But no, say others; the cultures of the Montaña have never been complex enough to produce such a god, and its men have always firmly rejected every introduction of civilization up to and including those of modern times. Specialists in Middle American cultures have had other notions and origins in mind. They note how very much the Peruvian deity resembles the Olmec were-jaguar-baby with his down-drawn mouth, flat nose, and curious eyes.

Certainly not, objects Dr. Lanning, pointing out that elements of the new art—prototypes, so to speak—can be found in early temples on the coastal rivers. And he reminds us that little cat faces were often worked into the first Peruvian textiles and gourds. Dr. Lanning's primary objection, however, is based on chronology, on the fact that the Olmec La Venta site with its feline god is clearly later in time than the first appearance of a feline god in Peru.

Claims and rebuttals are to be found in Dr. Lanning's fine book, *Peru Before the Incas,* which went to press in 1967 at about the same time that reports describing the San Lorenzo excavations were published. Dr. Lanning could not have known about this site, so much older than La Venta. Now, of course, given the recognized antiquity of these Olmec remains, a journey for the Mexican were-jaguar-baby through mountain valleys or even by sea voyage to Peru seems more and more possible.

But if the god came from Mexico, the impetus to temple building certainly did not. Clearly such building was a

Peruvian invention, turned after 900 B.C. to the new god's purpose. The most imposing of the temples clearly dedicated to the jaguar god was found in the highlands behind the Santa River at a site called Chavin de Huantar, and from this comes the name we give the religion and even occasionally the period in which it flourished—Chavin.

At Chavin de Huantar the rough, solid little pyramids and platforms of the river valleys have metamorphosed into a three-story castle of dressed stone built without mortar, its windowless exterior studded with stone heads of manlike beasts and beastlike men. Inside, the secret corridors are dark, but they are not dank. Fresh air still circulates through the ancient ventilating system, and all moisture is removed by drainage tubes in operation to this day. By ramps and stairs one moves slowly to the building's heart. There in the center, rising from a well, stands the jaguar god himself, fashioned of white granite, fifteen feet tall, smiling as he smiles in no other representation. For here he is enclosed in the secret kernel of the mystery. Here we feel an intimation of his power and his truth, a truth so foreign to our own world view, so removed that we can never penetrate its meaning.

Outside, the main temple is flanked by wings and outbuildings and terraces. On one terrace stands a shaft of stone cut again in the image of the jaguar god adorned with a curious headdress composed of his own repeated muzzle alive with writhing snakes. His taloned hands encircle a pair of elaborate supports that have given the figure a name—"the Staff God."

It was during Chavin times that metals—first gold, then copper, hammered cold from nuggets—first came into use. Suddenly there appeared metal pendants, ear spools, plaques, necklaces, and rings. All the signs of Chavin myth were beaten into golden sheets. Strips of metal were placed in the mouths of the dead—gold for important folk, copper for commoners. Exactly what anxious hopes for the hereafter

Chavin temple-wall sculpture

went into these little strips we cannot know. A similar mortuary custom, common throughout Aztec Mexico, may give us at least a glimmer of the Peruvian meaning. In Mexico, small lumps of jade were placed in the mouths of the dead, for wild beasts were believed to wait along the road eternal, beasts that longed to feast on the human heart but could be satisfied by a counterfeit of jade. Perhaps the metal strips given Peruvian dead served similarly as guarantee or payment for entrance to the world beyond.

After 200 B.C., metal smelting had been discovered and the harder alloys were used prominently in weapons. There were many more weapons now and more opportunities for using them. Cemeteries in the river valleys began to receive the corpses of young men whose heads were missing, no doubt carried elsewhere for display as trophies in enemy halls. For this was a time of war, one valley against the next. Perhaps, as Dr. Lanning suggests, the pinch for arable land—always at a premium in Peru—was beginning to be felt. The population was certainly growing everywhere, that is plain enough. It had arrived at a figure of roughly half the six million there would be in Inca times. There were cities being built in the high, cool basin of Lake Titicaca and in the intermountain valley of the Mantaro River as well. Cities were rising, too, in the little coastal valleys of the south—always, as in the days of the temple centers, on barren ground.

One of these coastal cities, located on the Nazca River, expanded into neighboring valleys to form a small state and a culture which has become famous among archaeologists and art historians for its pots and ponchos of many exquisite colors. The Nazca world view went quite beyond kiln and loom, however, to include the stars. Peruvians never developed the obsession for calendars common to Middle America, but they were not without their sky watchers. Eastward, behind the areas of Nazca influence, is a long tableland, high, bare, and bone-dry. It is strewn with Nazca potsherds; strewn, too, with rocks. Some of these, the dark ones, glittering and rich with ore, have been arranged in huge formations, in lines so arrow-straight one wonders how they could have been made by earthbound men. Certainly the patterns can be fully appreciated only by the modern man in an airplane—appreciated but never understood. For where the arrows point and why is not known as yet. Perhaps to rising stars or the sun's position at the solstices and equinoxes. Perhaps it is all, as archaeologist J. Alden Mason suggests, a gigantic farmer's almanac.

Far to the north of the Nazca farmer-craftsmen were quite another sort of Peruvian folk, much less interested in the skies above than in the land below—how to use it, make it bear, and get more of it. No city people were to be found at this time in the north, but these land-hungry people of the Moche Valley did build marvelous temple centers and irrigation systems. They had even learned to apply fertilizer to their fields. Birds in countless numbers, drawn by the rich fishing of the Peruvian Current, have for millennia visited the rocky coves and offshore islands, depositing there such immense quantities of fertilizing guano that men can mine for it. The Moche people did. The Incas did also, and later the Spanish would set their Indian slaves to the task. Guano is still being mined, still being used on fields today in Peru and all over the world.

Whether it was superior production, surplus grain, and subsequent leisure that gave the farmers of the Moche Valley a taste for power; whether it was overpopulation, or simply the trend of the times, they overran the five or six little river valleys south to the Nepena and north to the Chicama. Conquered territory was held by fortresses and connected by roads provided, in the Roman manner, with well-built posthouses for the convenience of runners. Territory and people were governed by an arrogant ruling class whose punishments for infractions of the rules were immediate and harsh: mutilations of lips, noses, and feet, or exposure on crags for the attention of vultures, much as Prometheus in the Greek myth was punished by an enraged Zeus.

How do we know all these things of a people without decipherable written records? We know from Moche pottery, because Moche potters were intensely interested in what they saw around them every day and reproduced the scenes on pots and jars, sometimes modeling the vessels themselves into houses and portrait heads. The toys children played with, the foods families ate at dinner, even the intimate details of private life—details which most American Indians would have considered shockingly crude—did not escape the potters' interest. They show us in line and color the sorts of dishes used at table (plates of gourd, pottery, or silver) and the accompanying table utensils (silver spoons and pointed objects rather resembling overlarge toothpicks). Real plates, spoons, and toothpicks found in graves support the information on Moche pots. We see ordinary men dressed in ordinary clothes convivially drinking a beverage that could only have been *chicha*. Coca, by the testimony of the jars, seems to have been reserved for the upper crust. We see that men were always more elegantly dressed, coiffed, and ornamented than women. We can even examine the details of masculine apparel: the thin cotton undershirt (verifiable by way of tomb-preserved fabrics), the plush overshirt and poncho, the skirt or breechcloth, the boots painted on bare skin, the ear spools and nail guards of golden foil.

We watch men tilling fields (women occasionally helped, as was the pattern in Mexico), building roads, mining metals, and working them at forge and kiln. We see them fishing in reed boats very like those still in use on Lake Titicaca. In later years the Spanish would be astonished to see just such boats, equipped with sturdy sails, making confidently out to sea.

Women, we learn from the Moche pots, stayed close to home. They did not participate in government or religious ceremonies or even attend social events—dinner parties among the Moche were strictly stag affairs. The one professional field women could enter was that of the doctor. It was a profession as much magical as medical (and would remain so into Inca times), and it was certainly a high-ranking one. We can tell that from the chiefly robes which the doctors on Moche pottery wear.

The details of war were not neglected. We see actual

Moche figures in pottery decoration

battles, the taking of prisoners and their disposal, hurled live and naked from precipices. Often waiting underneath to receive the offering is the Moche god—a man with cat whiskers and great cat fangs set in a wrinkled, human face. Sometimes he appears as a warrior fighting monstrous fish and dragons; sometimes as a doctor, a musician, a hunter; sometimes as a ruler surrounded by a retinue of attendants straight out of Aesop. There is the lizard-slave, the dog as faithful friend, the doctor-owl and the fox-savant, the falcon-shield-bearer and the messenger-eagle bearing pouches of beans inscribed with strange symbols. The Moche, it is believed, may actually have had a system of writing—ideographic, perhaps merely memory-jogging. Whatever the beans had to say, they are unreadable today. Indeed, they were not readable for very long after the Moche demise. By Inca times bean writing had been forgotten, replaced by a recording device called the quipu—a skein of cords which could be knotted in certain ways to represent numbers.

The old fanged god of the Moche was also seen as an emblem of fertility, both human and agricultural, and this theme can be traced beyond pottery and into the cemetery. In one hasty grave bearing sacrificed women and headless llamas, there were found the mummies of an old man and a young boy. The man wore a copper mask set with fangs. Around him lay the wherewithal of battle—slings, clubs, darts—and one single digging stick. Carved on the stick (as archaeologist G. H. S. Bushnell describes) is the figure of the fanged god accompanied by a little helper who scatters from his hand bits of turquoise representing seed corn. Whoever the dead man was—war leader, priest, representative of the god on the digging stick—he had died as the Moche state was itself coming to an end sometime around 600 A.D., swallowed up in the expansion of another empire.

By 600 A.D. the cities of the highlands had sent out their armies, had spread their wings to encompass nearly all of

Peru and a good chunk of highland Bolivia as well. Tiahuanaco on the southern shore of Lake Titicaca seems to have
sent religious emissaries as well as warriors, and the belief
they preached was that of the old cat god reborn. If you
travel today to the ruins of Tiahuanaco, you will see a great
gate carved of a single stone. Over its portal, surrounded by
"angels," sits the god, looking for all the world like the old
Staff God at Chavin de Huantar. You will see there, too, the
Aymara people, llama and alpaca herders who may be
descendants of Tiahuanaco's founders.

The power of Tiahuanacan religion influenced the folk
of the highland city of Huari, who presently embarked on
their own career of conquest. The ideas and politics of
Huari seem to have been much focused on Pachacamac, a
town near the river Rímac, Lima's future location. The pottery and artifacts of Pachacamac reflect Tiahuanacan religious themes, but its real claim to fame was an oracle.
Housed in a beautiful temple, that oracle had drawn pilgrims
long before Huari rose and would still draw pilgrims long
after Huari was no more. Even the powerful Incas would
revere it. Pachacamac ("Maker of the World") is an Inca
word, perhaps the translation of an earlier title framed in a
language no longer known to us.

Neither empire—Huari or Tiahuanaco—lasted much beyond its formation. By 800 A.D., according to Dr. Lanning,
dissolution had set in, and by 1000 it was all over, all the
glory, the marching troops, the trade, the expansion. There
were no empires, no large states, and in the south no cities
either. These had been utterly deserted—not because of inva-
sion but because, it would seem, people could no longer bear
to live in them. The inhabitants had long since retreated into
small rural villages and towns and were content with that.

Northern Peru, the stronghold of the ceremonial center, had
picked up an interest in city building during the spread of
the Huari empire and after a time, particularly in the old

Moche area, revived statecraft as well. But the recycling had barely got under way when the Incas appeared. They were not themselves city-loving folk, though Cuzco, their capital, of necessity became a city. So they shifted and separated their subjects until the desired degree of rural life had been restored. But though people were scattered, they were never again to be culturally isolated one from another, nor were they ever again to cultivate personalities, governments, or even art forms, unique unto themselves. The Incas preferred a homogeneous state and homogeneous people, all alike, all manageable. Therefore their own Quechua language was imposed, and imposed so thoroughly that, even before the Conquest, the individual speech of each valley had already become extinct. Whether Inca or Spanish, the many peoples of Andean Peru were to be forevermore one.

The Aztecs

Inheritors and Dispossessed

The Aztecs, whose empire was last to rule Indian Mexico, had a word for the desert nomads beyond their frontiers. Chichimecas, they were called, "lineage of the dog." The modern reader will at once translate the term into an insult, another example of the social climber snooting his humble beginnings. For the Aztecs, however, Chichimeca carried no such implication. They knew very well from whence they had come and were, on the whole, rather proud of what they had made of themselves. They knew that they themselves had once hunted rabbits with bows and arrows, had lived in caves, had eaten grasshoppers. That way of life had been discarded, true, but it was not forgotten. In point of fact, the Aztecs could not very well forget, for out in the hinterland there were many groups of Chichimecas still following the old habits. (Aztec merchants who traveled among them were often exhorted not to abandon these "younger brethren" but to take them by the hand and teach them the ways of civilization.)

Some Chichimecas spoke languages of the Otomanguean group and had civilized linguistic relatives all the way down to old Monte Alban. Others spoke Nahua dialects related to the Aztec Nahuatl (which belongs to the Azteco-Tanoan group, Macro-Penutian major group). Actually, there were

PENUTIAN (Zoque, Huave, etc.)
TARASCAN
AZTECO-TANOAN (Nahuatl, etc.)
OTOMANGUEAN (Otomi,
  Mixtec, Zapotec, etc.)
MAYOID (Maya, Huastec, etc.)
TOTONAC
CUITLATEC

*Language Groups
of Middle America*

*(Sources: G. L. Traeger
and M. Coe)*

many others. The affinities (which weaken with the miles) can nevertheless be traced all the way to Oregon, to where the desert country comes to an end. Certainly the Aztecs of the Valley of Mexico couldn't have known about Chichimecas of North America—the Utes, the Paiutes, and the Shoshoni. Aztec merchants, however, foot-loose and venturesome as they were, must have been acquainted with the Pima and Papago, farmers settled in what is now southern Arizona. They may even have been able to catch the drift of Piman conversations, though just barely. Perhaps they had heard of the Pueblo people farther north, also related to them by language—Chichimecas who, like the Pima, had profited by the example of farming folk.

The awesome Toltecs of Tula had themselves once been

Nahua-speaking Chichimecas. There was no telling then and there is no telling now how far back in time the Nahua connections went and how widespread they had been. At the time of the Conquest, Aztec priests were intoning prayers in a Nahua language so ancient that it could not be fully understood—rather as old Anglo-Saxon is unintelligible to speakers of modern English. Just what the old form was could not be told. Perhaps it was the language as it had once been spoken in Tula. Perhaps it harked back to even earlier times in Teotihuacán.

What is certain is that the Aztecs, last of the desert tribes to enter the Valley of Mexico, readily absorbed the general civilized heritage of Middle America without a struggle or even without much modification. General heritage means, more than anything else, religious heritage, for it was belief, worship, and ritual which both sustained and motivated Middle American life. All the daily business of living—marriage, mercantile ventures, art, ball games, and games of chance—was rooted firmly in religion, and had been for as long as anyone could remember.

The Aztecs accepted that. They accepted old Tlaloc, the god of rain, and an even older god of fire. They accepted the dual gods of beneficence and destruction, of light and dark, Quetzalcoatl and Tezcatlipoca. They accepted the old earth goddess of birth and death, and the dim creator figures, Two-Lord and Two-Lady, beings of "our flesh and substance," embodiments of corn, growth, and fertility. They accepted all, the leading players of an established pantheon, plus an ever-expanding retinue of local divinities associated with stars, streams, and volcanoes.

Aztec priests, with their greater appreciation of theological abstraction, gloried in the interweaving of gods and attributes. They gloried in the order of the four cardinal directions, with a fifth to represent the celestial "up." They gloried in the concept of dualism, of two in one, good in evil, death in life—which, if the old village figurines with heads half grinning skull, half smiling face, are any indication, was a notion as old as settled life in the Valley of Mexico. The priests reveled in a cosmology involving successive creations and destructions during which various gods commanded the sun, were in fact the sun, only to be deposed in great upheavals. It was during these repeated "suns" (there were to be five in all) that man had developed successively from a swimming fish to a cultivator of corn. Here was the heart of a belief whose echo still can be heard in Hopi pueblos.

The only new personage added to the ancient pantheon was the Aztecs' own tribal god, Huitzilopochtli, "Hummingbird-on-the-Left," who led his people in their painful journeys until they arrived in the promised land—a land marked by an eagle sitting on a cactus and devouring a snake. (This emblem now decorates the flag of modern Mexico.) Huitzilopochtli, like the Toltec Tezcatlipoca before him, was a god of war. He was born, it was said, fully armed to slay his mother's enemies, the stars and planets who were his own sisters and brothers. Huitzilopochtli promised his chosen people conquest and destruction and riches beyond dreaming, and he kept his word. But he demanded something in return. Somehow in the course of time he had become associated with the sun and so had daily to fight the forces of night and evil. In this fight he needed the support of virtue and required his people to live lives of purity and austerity, free from sin. In this fight he also required sustenance—a special sustenance, human blood, which daily had to be supplied.

It was a command the Aztecs loved to obey. Their wars were fought not only to conquer land and to amass tribute, but to take captives, captives for the sacrificial knife. In time there came into being a special kind of war waged with specially chosen adversaries. It was called "flowery war"— perhaps the most outrageous of all the poetic euphemisms Aztecs were wont to apply to barbarous activities. Flowery war was *not* fought with bouquets, and its purpose was the collection of captives, not blooms. In all fairness it must be said that flowery war was fought with enthusiasm.

> There is nothing like death in war,
> nothing like the flowery death
> so precious to Him who gives life:
> far off I see it: my heart yearns for it!

Death was thought to bring to ordinary folk a dismal array of trials before eternal peace could be attained: wild beasts to elude, mountains to climb, freezing winds to withstand, a frightful river which could be crossed only with the aid of little red dogs. (Every Aztec, needless to say, kept such pets handy for company in cremation.) Warriors and sacrificial victims, on the other hand, could anticipate immediate entry into the highest paradise, the House of the Sun. So could women who died in childbirth, for they too had fought a kind of battle and died taking captive a prisoner. Nowhere is the connection between warfare and religion —a connection to be so often repeated in the Americas— more clearly drawn than in Aztec belief and practice.

And yet it was not the Aztecs alone who sustained the gods with sacrifice. With one or two minor exceptions, the custom was shared throughout Middle America for reasons which had little to do with Huitzilopochtli's specific need. All the gods, it was said, had sacrificed themselves for man, shed their own blood for man, died for man. Was man to give nothing in return? The conquistadors accompanying Hernando Cortés were shocked to find even small towns ornamented with racks of sacrificial skulls and to discover that every time they appeared in battle array before a new settlement, frightened townsmen rushed fresh victims to the stone. Said Bernal Díaz del Castillo, a plain, bluff soldier who seems to have accompanied Cortés everywhere:

> Every day we saw sacrificed before us three, four, or five Indians whose hearts were offered to the idols and their blood plastered on the walls, and the feet, arms, and legs

of the victims were cut off and eaten, just as in our country we buy beef from the butcher.

He was to be even more horrified when captured Spanish soldiers and even Spanish horses were so sacrificed.

How the small towns of Mexico acquired their victims is difficult to imagine. They must have relied on slave traders to supply them with offerings from the hinterlands. They themselves were often required to furnish from among their own citizenry victims for the great temples of Tenochtitlán, the capital city of the Aztecs. The greatest of these were the twin temples of Huitzilopochtli and Tlaloc, mounted on a single pyramid. The chief priests of these deities were the twin pontiffs of Tenochtitlán and dominated most of the religious life around the capital, just as the market of Tenochtitlán dominated economic life in the realm.

The great city itself was built on an island in Lake Texcoco. Surrounded by its *chinampas*, it had about it something of the look of Venice, at least to those of the conquistadors who had traveled in Europe and could make the comparison. They saw Tenochtitlán from afar, and of that first vision Díaz del Castillo wrote:

> When we saw so many cities and villages built in the waters of the lake and other large towns on dry land, and that straight, level causeway leading into Mexico City, we were amazed and we said it was like the enchanted things related in the book of Amadis because of the great towers, temples, and buildings rising from the water, and all of masonry....

And again,

> Gazing on such wonderful sights, we did not know what to say or whether what appeared before us was real, for on one side, on the land, there were great cities, and in the lake ever so many more, and the lake itself was crowded with canoes, and in the causeway were many bridges at intervals, and in front of us stood the great City of Mexico, and we—we did not number even 400 soldiers!

Having been greeted on the way to Tenochtitlán by

several royal embassies, all led by nephews to the great Montezuma II, the soldiers were not surprised at the pomp with which the monarch eventually presented himself. They had already learned to expect royal personages to be carried in litters adorned with gold and precious feathers, their way strewn with costly cotton cloths, and their noble persons treated with great deference. The conquistadors were astonished, however, at the amenities of royal life in Mexico. They goggled at Montezuma's huge, airy palace, his orchards and gardens (every noble had extensive gardens, but Montezuma's were best of all). They gaped at his aviary, his tanks of tropical fish, his private zoo (where the carnivores, it was whispered, were fed with meat from the sacrific[al

stone). They craned their necks to see the corps of royal entertainers—jugglers, acrobats, hunchbacks, dwarfs, and mountebanks. And they fairly gasped at the appearance of the royal dinner (which they saw but did not eat, as it was reserved for the royal appetite alone). Seated before a snowy table, Montezuma was offered his choice of hundreds of different dishes: various pastries; small roasted dogs, turkeys, wild deer; pure-white tortillas; fruits—all served by beautiful noblewomen on special ware from Cholula. For drink he was brought gold cups full of frothy chocolate sweetened with honey and flavored with vanilla and nutmeg. This meant he was literally drinking money, for the cacao bean

was used (and sometimes counterfeited) as currency. Spaniards saw that, too, in the great market of Tenochtitlán.

It was bigger than the biggest markets anyone had ever
seen in Europe, said the soldiers, marveling at the variety of
goods offered for sale: foods of all kinds, spices, gold dust in
hollow turkey quills, tobacco in tubes for smoking (surely
the prototype for today's cigars and cigarettes). They saw
fine woven fabrics and ready-made clothing as well—loose
blouses and skirts for women, breechcloths and capes for
men. The capes came in many expensive and gorgeous styles.
Some were bordered with precious stones or precious
feathers, some painted or embroidered with designs, some
made all of fur. There were even outer capes to keep the
fancy ones dry and clean. The market also had its slave
quarters in which were held poor creatures hooked to long
poles and driven in from outlying towns. There one might
buy victims for sacrifice or, more rarely, for service; slave
workers were more often chosen from among families who
had voluntarily assumed the yoke to escape the wrath of
creditors. Everywhere the streets were polished clean and
free of filth, for there were garbage collectors constantly
busy at their rounds. Everywhere were flowers to refresh
the eye. The people of Tenochtitlán loved bright blooms
above all else.

The Spaniards knew Tenochtitlán was something of an
achievement but could never have appreciated just how
much of an achievement it really was. Barely two hundred
years before the Conquest, its people had been ragtail wanderers, scratching for a foothold in the Valley of Mexico.
One great lord after another had employed them as mercenaries and then, disgusted by their rude ways, had thrown
them bodily out of the territory. Eventually they took
refuge in a small, swampy island in Lake Texcoco and began
to gather strength. In 1367 or thereabouts they were again
invited to serve as mercenaries, this time for a particularly
powerful ruler who considered himself representative of the

vanished Toltecs. The Aztecs (sometimes also called the Mexica) proved so helpful in his wars of conquest that, in gratitude, he gave them one of his relatives for their king. Thus provided with legitimate connections, the Aztecs began to think of themselves as heirs to Toltec greatness, entitled to everything they could take.

They took first the city of their benefactor and then, led by shrewd rulers, they proceeded to extend their domains. Garrisons were scattered through the land to secure their winnings, and tax collectors were sent to extract the proper tribute (carefully listed in special, folded deerskin books). It was all very efficient and very ruthless, and the Aztecs were cordially hated as a result—a state of affairs that eventually permitted Cortés to draw willing allies to his cause and to turn the Conquest into something that resembled a popular revolution.

In the course of expansion, the Aztecs had appropriated Tlatiluco, their sister town on a neighboring island. Tlatiluco seems to have been already in existence when the Aztecs first fled to the swamp. (Some experts maintain that Tlatiluco was founded, instead, by Aztec contingents.) In any case, it was the home of an exceptionally aggressive and astute collection of merchants, merchants who were possessed of long experience and expertise. They honored the god of merchants, Yacatecuhtli, a being so ancient that his image can be traced back to Teotihuacán, and their special rites (involving always the use of liquid rubber) hint of even older connections, perhaps with the heartland of ancient Olmec civilization. Merchants were accustomed to travel far afield, accustomed to trips lasting years at a time. They knew how to open up new territories, how to spy out the terrain, when it was safe to approach a new settlement, and when the trader must enter in disguise.

After the Aztecs took over Tlatiluco, the merchants seem to have turned these talents to the service of their new lord. They learned to open new territory, not only for trade, but

for Aztec occupation. They went about armed and learned
to foment trouble so that Aztec armies would have to come
to their aid and remain to conquer. Their fearlessness was
proverbial. One merchant group endured a siege of four
years in Anahuac and, before the rescuing armies arrived,
took so many captives that the military was quite put in the
shade.

The old rulers of Tlatiluco had always honored the merchant princes, and so did the Aztec kings who followed.
Travelers just home from successful expeditions were hailed:

> O my beloved uncles, O Merchants, O Vanguard
> Merchants—seat yourselves, rest!

and were then placed among the lords and nobles and war
leaders (who may or may not have been correspondingly
cordial).

Aztecs of Tenochtitlán were divided roughly into twenty
calpulli—clans, or perhaps simply residence groups organized at least nominally along kinship lines. Each *calpulli* had
its own area in the town, its own land, subject to the dis-
pensation of its own leaders. These tended to be hereditary
in their offices and wealthier than the commoners in the clan.
And as some lineages in each *calpulli* were more socially
prominent than others, so some *calpulli* ranked higher than
others, were wealthier, possessed more land and slaves and
bondsmen, were allowed several wives instead of the common man's one, and were closer to the palace grandees who
belonged to the royal clan—naturally, at the very top of the
social ladder.

In terms of the merchants and the honored slave dealers,
the old records are not entirely clear. Sometimes it seems
they were members of various *calpulli*. Elsewhere one gets
the impression that they formed their own *calpulli*—seven
are mentioned in one source—located mostly in Tlatiluco.
Like all other *calpulli*, each seems to have had its leading
families and its chief men, the "principal merchants." Each

had its own temple around the great temple square of Tenochtitlán. Certainly there was one special shrine in which all merchants honored Yacatecuhtli. Each merchant *calpulli* was responsible for the training of its young men in the preparatory school for commoners. Each fielded its own military contingents. But the merchants apparently owned no more than living space and were forbidden admission to the prestigious military orders of the Jaguar and the Eagle.

In compensation they were permitted to govern themselves, regulating the market, punishing infractions of rules, even meting out the death penalty. And the lack of land proved to be no great drawback. They grew rich with trade —so rich that they took care after long journeys to enter their town by night, never going straight home but depositing their earnings with an uncle or sister. Though they sold gaudy garb, they never wore it themselves, preferring the meanest sort of cloak woven of agave fiber. They gave generously to the poor and the powerful alike and never, never called attention to themselves in any way. In spite of all their care, they ran afoul of the other self-made men of the Aztec system—the knights, chieftains, and war leaders of common birth who had, through bravery, won personal land. Still, in spite of all these winnings, warlords envied the merchants their wealth and secret powers, and some time before the Spanish came they managed with false testimony "of imagined deeds to condemn innocent merchants to death so that they, the war leaders, might be sustained." It is an episode that smacks of the pogrom.

What we know of the merchants and their persecution, indeed what we know of Aztec life in general, we owe in large part to a Franciscan teaching friar, Bernardino de Sahagun, who came to Mexico ten years after the Conquest. Given his background and piety, given also the bizarre religious practices of the Aztecs, one might well have expected from him a biased account. But this was not the case. No ethnologist today could fault the friar's methods or his eagerness to understand. First of all, he learned perfect Nahuatl. Next he settled in a town near Tenochtitlán and gathered about him a group of reputable informants. He wrote down their words phonetically in their own language, had them make accompanying drawings, and learned from them the decipherment of their rebus writing. After several years and the accumulation of books of information, he had everything checked by a second group of informants in another town. Only then did he begin the translation into Spanish. After many years the books numbered thirteen. In one, Fra Bernardino was injudicious enough to describe the Conquest from the Aztec point of view and was forced by the religious hierarchy to make "corrections." Even after complying he was suspected and then denounced. Worst of all, his books were confiscated and scattered. Somehow they were reassembled and survive today as *The Florentine Codex*, perhaps the most reliable of all the sources describing life in Aztec Mexico.

Nothing escaped Fra Bernardino's sympathetic interest or his searching questions. He wanted to know, for example, about the Aztec family and how the roles were ideally to be played. Here is what he was told: *Father*: "source of the lineage . . . sincere . . . diligent . . . thrifty." *Mother*: "diligent . . . solicitous . . . constantly at work." *Grandparents*: "reprimanders." *Good Youths and Maidens*: "obedient . . . reverent . . . modest . . . pure in heart." *A Bad Youth*: "drunk, a sot . . . goes about eating mushrooms [Aztecs knew of one variety which induces hallucinations] . . . impudent . . . lewd . . . a vile brute." (It should be mentioned that bad youths, if they were also clever, took care not to drink *pulque* [fermented maguey sap] in public. This was the privilege of age, and drunken young people were subject to summary execution as an example to others. In Aztec society all lapses of virtue were punished with the severity reserved by other peoples for murder and theft.)

The Aztecs were quite specific about the behavior ap-

propriate to every station in life. *The Good Woman*: "reso-
lute . . . brave, like a man . . . gives of herself . . . goes in
humility . . . one who chews chicle" (but if she is a wife,
not in public). *The Bad Woman*: "quite publicly [she] goes
about chewing chicle along the roads, in the market place,
clacking like castanets." *The Good Noble* (there is much
about this character): "of noble birth . . . eloquent . . . of
noble bearing . . . sets an example for the exemplary life."
The Wise Man: "he owns books."

Fra Bernardino learned much about Aztec professional
people. *The Judge*: "a hearer of both sides." *The Attorney*:
"discreet, able . . . he appeals . . . pleads . . . ensnares . . .
accuses . . . collects tribute [for his client] and consumes a
tenth of it." *The Bad Physician*: "a quack [who] draws
paper, flint, obsidian, worms from [patients] . . . deceives
them . . . perverts them, makes them believe . . . a giver of
overdoses." *The Good Physician*: "[he or she] is a restorer
. . . a giver of potions . . . lances . . . rubs . . . massages . . .
provides splints . . . an adviser, counselor . . . worthy of confidence." The magical cures of simple folk, the reliance on
spirits and trance were, it seems, fast giving way before
practical observation. The good Aztec physician relied on
homely remedies. He or she prescribed pine resin rubbed
about the nostrils for stuffy noses, steam baths and honey for
coughs, turkey broth and fried lizard for stomach-ache.
Knowing very well the causes of tooth decay, the physician
advised against hot drinks followed too closely by cold ones
and against leaving the teeth unbrushed after meals. Fra
Bernardino reports that even lopped-off noses could be restored to the face by suturing with hair and bathing with
plenty of salt and bees' honey.

Fra Bernardino dutifully listed the Aztec descriptions of
the parts of the body and their uses and abuses; the omens
of dread; the activities of sorcerers. Most of all, however, he
enjoyed detailing the Aztec calendric system, which was
very like all those in use in Middle America though it lacked

the complexities of the Maya Long Count. The annual round by itself was complex enough. There was the religious year of 260 days, divided into twenty months. The days were named according to twenty rotating day-signs. The first month of thirteen days, ticked off, would therefore read: one-crocodile, two-wind, three-house, four-lizard, five-serpent, six-death, seven-deer, eight-rabbit, nine-water, ten-dog, eleven-monkey, twelve-grass, thirteen-reed. The first day of the next month would begin with the jaguar, which was the fourteenth day-sign on the wheel, and would be called one-jaguar. No two days in the year had the same name and number, which was convenient since each person was given as his own name the day-name of his birth. If it happened to be one of evil omen, parents would simply put off the naming ceremony until a more propitious day dawned.

Each of the religious months had its special feast day—"movable feasts," Fra Bernardino called them, because they never appeared in exactly the same seasons year by year. Only once every fifty-two years did the fixed solar calendar and the religious calendar conjoin. At that time, at the "binding of our years," everyone fasted and did penance by piercing his tongue and ears with cactus spines. Household rubbish and all the pots and pans were thrown out. Hearth fires were extinguished, as were the temple fires that had burned without cease for fifty-two years, for the time of new fire had come. At midnight the priests kindled a blaze in the breast of a sacrificial victim newly deprived of his heart, and from this all lit their torches and started the cycles all over again.

The solar year had eighteen months of twenty days each —360 days in all, with an intercalary period of five special days of fast and sacrifice. There were festivals for each month of the solar year, too. There were rain rituals which called for the slaying of children. There were fire rituals which required the burning alive of slaves. There was an arrow ceremony during which a captive bound to a post was pierced at dawn by many arrows. (Curiously, the Pawnees of the Great Plains practiced a similar ceremony until it was stopped by a chief's son who had seen it performed once too often.) There were ceremonies of first fruits and first flowers, ceremonies to the deities of maize and fertility, and a rite of spring during which the new green of vegetation was represented by the suit of skin newly flayed from a captive and worn by the proper priest.

> Put on thy mask,
> Put on thy golden garments. . . .
> Like unto the precious jade
> My heart is green . . .

Among the Aztecs it was considered an honor to provide slaves for the sacrifices and even, in a curious way, an honor to *be* the sacrifice. Fra Bernardino suggests that some victims were given a drug to deprive them of fear, but it could not have been given to all. The fact remains that, with or without drugs, victims danced, sang, and participated in nightlong ceremonies with their sponsors as they awaited death. Most walked to the stone without coercion, playing along the way the role assigned to them. It is a realm of belief beyond our comprehension and perhaps beyond Fra Bernardino's as well. But he seldom said so, presenting his accounts without comment.

It was in 1518, as the good friar relates, that Montezuma began to hear of evil omens. People reported wonders in the skies. The lake boiled without wind to stir it. At night was heard the sound of a woman weeping through the streets of Tenochtitlán. A dead woman rose and prophesied the end of the Aztecs. Montezuma played a sacred ball game with the tributary king of Texcoco to learn whether the prophecy would be fulfilled. He lost. And then the messengers arrived to tell of the castles with wings which had been sighted in the Gulf, drawing near to land, and of the pale, bearded men who inhabited them.

Cortés's ships arrived on the day two-reed, and here was yet another omen. For in the long-ago time of Toltec Tula, the kingdom had been rent between Quetzalcoatl as man and god and Tezcatlipoca, also god in man. Quetzalcoatl, said to have been pale and black of beard, had been forced to depart from Tula and make his slow, sad way to the Gulf coast. There (in one version of the legend) he boarded a raft of serpents, vowing to return on the day of two-reed sometime in the misty future. Mayan history and modern archaeology date the departure at 987 A.D., suggesting that the legend had its kernel of truth. For it was about this time that Toltec entry into Maya land took place, about this time that the temple center of Chichén Itzá began to resemble Tula, about this time that Mayan stories speak most pointedly of Kulkulkan, their word for the plumed serpent.

The myth of the returning pale god was more powerful than historical circumstance, however. It was to spread far and wide in both Americas, all the way to Inca Peru. The Hopi cherished such a belief. They called it the Return of the Lost White Brother and were just as immobilized as Montezuma when the supposed brother, the supposed godman, turned up in Spanish armor, demanding their all. Montezuma sent the costume of Quetzalcoatl to Cortés and, when the truth began to dawn on him, offered him gold and jewels but could not stay his hand. The Aztec king died, stoned by his own people, who had long since ceased to believe in a Second Coming, and shortly thereafter the Aztec realm, the independent Empire of the Mexica, itself became a legend.

With the end of the empire, the old gods toppled too, right down the steps of their temples. And when no bolts of lightning struck the impious Spaniards, when the earth remained quiet, accepting the sacrilege, the Aztecs ceased to believe entirely. It was relatively easy for them to embrace Catholicism with its disciplines and rituals so often reminiscent of the old ways. They were familiar with confession and penances (more painful than those the friars were wont to prescribe). They were accustomed to holy water, incense (copal in Mexico), and genuflections on entering the holy places. They expected priests to be celibate and to wear black robes and cowls (though the new ones unaccountably preferred shorn heads to the bloody and matted hair cultivated by Aztec clergy). They expected to see monasteries in which monks told the hours with prayer. They expected nuns and nunneries and even hermits in the woods. The attributes of their many gods were transferred to the Catholic sainthood. Even Quetzalcoatl became affiliated for them with St. Thomas. In time the elite—what was left of it after war and smallpox—vanished into Spanish ranks by way of intermarriage and conversion. Nahuatl was spoken only by village peasants who managed to preserve and cherish the old beliefs in their folk plays and dances.

Sometime around 1472 A.D., before the Aztecs had yet achieved their final dominion over central Mexico, they were allied with the kingdom of Texcoco. Its king, a very wise and gentle man, perhaps foreseeing that his own realm would one day be engulfed by his fierce allies, wrote a poem ending in these words:

> Vanished are these glories,
> just as the fearful smoke vanishes
> that belches forth from the infernal fires
> of Popocatepetl.
> Nothing recalls them but the written page.

Like the people of Texcoco and all the people of all the proud cities of Mexico, the Aztecs had inherited the wealth of those that had gone before. Like them all, the Aztecs were finally dispossessed. But this time no one picked up the traditions and carried on. The long skein stretching from the Olmec heartland had been cut at last and for all time. And, truly, only the written page remained.

18

The Incas
Once and Future Kings

A first quick look at Inca civilization in Peru puts the student at once in mind of Egypt. He reads of mummies, of the concern with preservation of the body as a condition of happy, useful afterlife. He notes the reverence paid mummies of rulers past and of the elaborate provisions made for their perpetual care. He discovers a people who, like the Egyptians, worshiped the sun and saw in their ruler on earth, sun-descended and headed sunward at his end, merely another aspect of the solar divinity above. A ruler so connected must naturally be blood-proud and blood-pure, and (again in the Egyptian manner) the king, *The* Inca, insured divinity by taking as chief wife his own royal sister. Like the Egyptians, Incas built monumentally to the gods' honor, built in stone so marvelously hewn, dressed, and set that not even the sharp blade of a knife can be driven between the mortarless blocks.

Here the similarity blurs. For Inca architectural genius did not confine itself to temples and tombs, was neither god-obsessed nor death-obsessed, but was directed instead to the business of the state. The Incas built roads (sometimes ornamentally walled), roadhouses, bridges, aqueducts, and canals. They built fortresses and towns of refuge so minutely planned that (it is said) scale models were constructed beforehand. In this, Inca civilization reminds us of Rome. Like the Romans, Incas were practical planners, born to organize and born to rule. But their rule extended into secret places of the human heart, areas that Roman law would never have touched, was never intended to touch. In all the Inca empire no one starved, no one went unclothed—and no one had so much as a thought he could truly call his own. Certainly he never made a personal decision. For the Inca empire was regimented to a degree no Communist nation of modern times has succeeded in achieving. And with it all, Inca subjects seem to have been reasonably contented—a claim surely *no* state today can make.

Exaggeration! you might protest, and with reason. The most prestigious record of Inca days and ways has long been (until recent disaffection set in) *The Royal Commentaries* by Garcilaso de la Vega, himself the son of a noble conquistador and an Inca princess of the blood royal. Disinherited by a law that required Spaniards to put aside their Indian wives, he became a savant instead of a wealthy landholder and spent most of his life in Spain valiantly trying to demonstrate the intellectual capacity and finer feelings of his Inca forbears. Forgivably, he may well have exaggerated the extent of Inca political organization, may well have forgotten, may well have erred. But not the grandees themselves, some of whom saw all too well the havoc they had wrought. Note the following excerpt from the deathbed confession dictated by Mancío Serra de Leguiçamo and addressed to Philip II, King of Spain:

> We found these lands in such a state that there was not even a robber or a vicious or idle man, or adulterous or immoral woman: all such conduct was forbidden. . . . Everything from the most important to the least was ordered and harmonized with great wisdom. The Incas were feared, obeyed, respected, and venerated by their subjects, who considered them to be most capable lords. . . . I desire his majesty to understand why I have set down this account; it is to unburden my conscience and confess

my guilt, for we have transformed the Indians who had such wisdom and committed so few crimes, excesses, or extravagances. . . . This kingdom has fallen into such disorder . . . it has passed from one extreme to another. There was no evil: now there is almost no good.

Whatever the true workings of the Inca state, it was certainly nothing at all like the Spanish state. The individual Peruvian, collectivist in inclination and by careful Inca nurture, was not like the Spanish conquistador—brash, brave, out to grab what he could in any way he could get it. Nor were Incas very much like the Aztecs to the north. In spite of a shared continental home, an ancient background of shared themes and ideas, and certainly many plants and techniques shared over the long years, there was no common outlook on the world, and in personality there was all the world in difference.

Just how the Incas came to be what they were by the time of the Conquest is something of a puzzle. Surely they owed much to the Andean civilizations that had preceded them. Their roads and use of runners, their buildings and irrigation projects, even their marks of status—litters, parasols, gold, coca—can be traced back to prototypes plain to see on Moche pottery. Surely the Incas borrowed much from the remnants of the old Tiahuanaco empire. (Indians around Lake Titicaca were wont to sniff haughtily at the new state and claim it was merely the old days warmed over.) Exactly what the indebtedness was neither archaeology nor old traditions can tell us. We do know that trade during Tiahuanaco times was far more vital and active than it would ever be under the Incas, who slowed it to a mere trickle of luxury goods meant for aristocratic consumption. We do know that cities had flourished in the south during the time of empires, cities which the Incas never revived or wanted to revive. One is tempted to suppose that, though the ancient forms and patterns were inherited, Inca regimentation was unique, something new. How it came into being is anybody's guess.

It is just possible that the creation of the Inca state with all its complex orchestration may ultimately be traceable to one organizing genius, the great general Yupanqui, who was called "Pachacuti Inca." Now, as a people the Incas seem to have come into being around 1200. Their traditions name twelve Inca kings, and indeed, as late as 1539 there were in the Sun Temple in Cuzco or in their private palace-mausoleums twelve royal mummies to prove the claim. The Incas seem to have begun their tribal career as raiders pushing and being pushed back by the developing mountain groups around the home base, which became Cuzco. Sometime around 1430 one of these groups threatened the stronghold itself. The old Inca king fled with his favorite son, whom he named heir. Prince Yupanqui remained to defend Cuzco successfully and afterward found himself strong enough not only to replace the king's named heir, but to replace the king himself. He was crowned with the fillet of gold and the scarlet fringe in 1438, the first reliable date obtainable for Inca history, and he took the name Pachacuti, literally "cataclysm."

His armies, swelled by conscription from among peoples he gradually overcame, moved farther and farther afield, consolidating as they conquered. Pachacuti's son, Topa Inca, collaborated in his father's plans and methods and continued them later on his own, always with similar success. By the end of his reign in 1493, the empire had very nearly reached its ultimate extent—about 3000 miles from north to south. A world, said Garcilaso de la Vega, in the shape of a man with Cuzco at his navel. It was probably during Topa Inca's reign that the Diaguita were incorporated and their Hopi-like pueblos garrisoned with Inca troops. There are rumors that this king sailed into the Pacific and returned. To this day on the island of Mangareva, people tell of an ancient

visit by men on balsa rafts, men from the east led by a chief named Tupa. He is also said to have sailed in the other direction, leading a flotilla of canoes down one of the rivers of the Montaña into the eastern jungles. There (so the story goes) he met the Mojos, whom he admired and did not subdue, and other, more simply organized jungle folk whom he did not admire and also did not subdue. The Incas were never successful against jungle tribesmen. Devoted to their bows and arrows, the jungle warriors insisted on waging furtive guerrilla warfare when the Incas were trained for stand-up battle. Slings and bolas were used by Inca troops as distance weapons, but, by and large, they preferred hand-to-hand matches with wooden swords and maces. The forest people refused to cooperate in any way. Back over the mountains went the Inca expedition. "They do not deserve to be ruled by us," observed Topa Inca with dignity.

All along the western hills and mountains, all through the desert oases of the shore, it was a very different story. People after people and, in the north, city after city (even the big ones like Chanchan of the Chimu kingdom) capitulated and accepted Inca rule. For the Incas had learned the power of advance publicity, and they had learned also the power of clemency. Always they tried diplomacy before battle, sending messages to persuade the target area and its people of the superior advantage of Inca management. Defecting and rebellious subjects were usually pardoned for a first

offense. No Inca soldier raped or looted in conquered towns or even foraged for himself on the line of march, as instant death was the punishment. In battle, some trophy heads were taken, some few prisoners sacrificed to the sun god and their skins made up into war drums. For the most part, however, prisoners were quickly released and sent home. Clemency on the Incas' part was not proof of superior virtue. Neither was it an indication of squeamishness. Incas were perfectly capable of destroying a village or a people warned once too often. It was, rather, a matter of sober policy. "We must spare our enemies," one of the Inca princes is said to have explained, "or it will be our loss, since they and all that belongs to them must soon be ours."

Invariably the Incas inaugurated their annexation of a new territory with a complete survey of the sort we might call topographic, demographic, economic, and ethnographic. They noted how the great north-south highways (coastal and mountain) should be extended and where trunk lines should be added. They inspected the irrigation systems in valley areas, building aqueducts and canals where needed to increase production. In the highlands, they demonstrated terrace farming to those not already in possession of the knowledge. "In some provinces remote from Cuzco [and] still not well disciplined by the Inca kings," Garcilaso de la Vega tells us, "the women tilled the fields and the men sat at home spinning and weaving." A people so barbarous, in his opinion, "do not deserve to be remembered."

In addition to the agricultural surveys, Inca inspectors took stock of the llama herds. They also inquired as to wild animals of the region. Henceforth hunting would be prohibited to all except when the king decreed a great surround. In any given province, this occurred but once in each four years. Only thus could wild life be conserved and the silky wool of the wild vicuña guaranteed for the emperor's clothing and counterpanes.

Other resources of a new region were not neglected. Inspectors noted the special skills of the inhabitants along with the local availability of copper mines, salt mines, and islands where guano could be found. They observed the local religious system in operation and made provision for the maintenance of its priesthood. They brought in teachers of the Quechua language, enough to staff each village. Lastly, they took a census, recording the result on their quipus.

Like Africans of the old kingdom of Dahomey, Incas might not have written, but they could certainly count—a fact which both explains and underlines their special genius. (Said Pachacuti Inca on one occasion, "He who seeks to count the stars before he can count the scores and knots of the quipus deserves derision.") Inca arithmetic was, like ours, based on a decimal system. Quipu strands were arranged so that place value could be indicated. One fixed a number by tying knots on the proper strands. Zero (always a difficult concept) was designated by the absence of a knot. By using cords of various colors (yellow for gold, white for silver, red for war, etc.), many kinds of information could be recorded. Some sources claim that even nonnumerical knowledge—king lists, historical accounts, poetry—could be brought to mind with the aid of special quipus, properly used. Others (perhaps over-enthusiastically) insist that quipus could be used in computing with all the speed and accuracy of the Chinese abacus.

Armed with all possible information, surveyors of a new territory knew exactly what to recommend to their superiors. They knew exactly what to change and what to leave alone, how much could be required in labor and tribute without exciting anger or revolt. This is what made the Inca system work: this balance, this care. For though the obligations were great and Inca laws severe, both were eminently clear, eminently predictable, eminently exact—which, as anthropologist John H. Rowe suggests, was at least better than what the Spanish brought: unpredictable demands, and justice reserved for the conquerors themselves.

In every new territory, the Incas built temples to their sun god to give presence to the official religion, but they never changed or banned any of the local faiths. The alien gods were sometimes carted off to Cuzco to add to the Inca pantheon—a great honor, the locals were told. Actually, the images were divine hostages to encourage good behavior back home. In the same way, local leaders were carted off to Cuzco, but only to be given there a quick cram course in Inca methods and management. They were then restored to their former estates and rule with, if anything, greater prestige than before. They were, of course, answerable to Inca provincial governors who reported in turn to one of the four royal viceroys in ultimate charge of the administrative quarters of the empire. These tried, however, to remain unobtrusively in the background, leaving day-to-day management up to the old leaders and rulers, now called *curacas*. They represented an aristocratic caste, just below true Inca nobility on the status ladder. Their good behavior was guaranteed by the presence of their children and gods in Cuzco. Indoctrinated in Inca ways, the children would one day be permitted to succeed their fathers in provincial offices.

In spite of the care and forethought given to the amalgamation of new territories, some occasionally proved indigestible. In such cases, the Inca masters would order whole tribes and villages to be transferred to other regions where they would live among happy Inca subjects. Loyal colonists were then sent to fill the gaps. But again, in the careful Inca manner, never were highlanders (adjusted by long heredity to the thin air of the mountains) sent permanently to the shore or seamen to the mountains; never were transferred people set to raising unfamiliar crops or to work in crafts they did not know.

Perhaps the oldest institution throughout the Andean zone was the *ayllu*, the extended kin group or community which owned land in common. The Incas never touched or altered these *ayllus* but made them instead the basic governing units of the empire. Each *ayllu* everywhere remained in possession of its land, and the land was allocated as before, family by family according to numbers and need. The fields of widows, the sick, or the afflicted were worked by the community as before. (The Incas added the fields of army conscripts to this list.) The lands were not touched nor the method of their working altered. Presumably some of the produce had always gone in tribute to the local chieftain; Inca law simply applied the same principle in making their own demands. Some portion of *ayllu* land—about a third of it, generally—was to be planted with crops destined for the royal storehouses. Another portion was to be used for support of the state religion. Llama and alpaca herds were likewise divided. This was not quite so outrageous as it seems at first glance. For, though the stores from the royal treasuries helped provide for the noble and official classes, for soldiers on march (there was always a convenient storehouse at the end of each day's hike), and for craftsmen on duty with Inca or provincial nobility, there were also storehouses of national insurance. Wherever natural disasters struck, wherever crops failed or shortages threatened, the royal storehouses could provide. Think of our income taxes, and the law of land tribute comes into sharper focus.

Inca rulers demanded yet another sort of tribute. Each person in each *ayllu* was liable to service which he alone could provide. Skilled metal craftsmen (supplied with tools and raw materials) spent certain months of the year at work producing weapons and implements, objects of ritual offering and objects of adornment. Some *ayllus* provided special services—singers and dancers for the royal court. Most, however, rendered tribute in the form of ordinary work hours. Women and children spun and wove rough cloth for the storehouses or made sandals of llama hide and plaited rush. Even the old and the sick were not exempt. They rendered tribute, if we may believe Garcilaso de la Vega, in lice plucked from their bodies and stored in hollow reeds. No useful purpose was served thereby (except, perhaps, that of personal cleanliness), but the Incas were firm believers in the virtues of industry. Idleness, they held, was nothing short of vice.

Men might labor in mines if these were located near home. Copper went into weapons and implements, gold and silver into decorations for church and palace. There was no money in the Inca scheme of things nor any need for it, so mine labor was neither arduous nor intense, and it was never extended beyond a stipulated period of time for anyone. Of course, gold was a royal monopoly. So was coca, the drug of dreams and divining. Grown only on The Inca's personal plantations by serf or convict labor, it was doled out to the general public on feast days. Coca chewing never became the national habit as it did later under Spanish rule when the bans were removed. But it was at that time, too, that hunger and fatigue became for the first time national afflictions. Since coca dulls hunger pangs and allays fatigue, who could expect otherwise?

Where there were no mines, men of the *ayllus* rendered labor tribute in construction projects or in the maintenance of roads and bridges in their neighborhoods. Suspension bridges had to be completely replaced every two years—no mean task considering the dizzying heights across which some were strung. The *ayllus* were also required to provide for official travelers in the resthouses of their areas and to man the relay stations with two-runner teams.

These runners, called *chasquis*, were the lifeline of the nation. Like the pony express of our American West (without the ponies, of course), they took pride in speed. The runner approaching a relay station yelled ahead to warn those within. Immediately a fresh *chasqui* dashed out, and the two ran on together without breaking stride until message, quipus, or packages had been transferred. There was no pause to chat or rest, no halt at nightfall to await the dawn. The mail must go through!

Actually, the fine Inca roads were used only by the *chasquis*, by soldiers, or by persons on official business. Occasionally pack trains of llamas, each with its hundred-pound load, might wind slowly over the road from one warehouse to another. There were no traveling salesmen on Inca roads, for there was scarcely any trade. Luxury items intended for aristocratic use were carried by *chasquis*. It was The Inca's boast that fresh fish from the river Rímac would reach him —several hundred miles away in Cuzco—before two days had gone by. (One must assume that the cold, dry Peruvian air maintained freshness the while.)

Otherwise there was no travel. It was not only discouraged, it was positively forbidden. Apart from local market fairs, people stayed put and married always within their own *ayllus*. And they married, what is more, by the time they reached twenty-five. Inca officialdom saw to that, too, for men were minors, exempt from labor tribute, until they married. A public betrothal was held every two years. The Inca or his local representative presided, formalizing unions already arranged and making the final decision when any girl had two suitors seeking her hand. Marriages for commoners were monogamous. If mistakes were made at betrothal time, it was too bad. Divorce was difficult and adultery punishable by death. Whom The Inca hath joined together, let no man put asunder.

Throughout the Inca empire there seems to have been very little hanky-panky of any sort. Unlike the ancient Moche, Incas had rather puritanical notions about what constituted proper behavior, public and private, and these were translated into civil laws and punishments. To these the clergy added the awful weight of sin. Now, in Inca terms as in our own, the wages of sin were death, and if the law didn't catch the sinner, the hereafter certainly would. There might even be discomforts on earth. All sorts of misfortunes and bad luck were regularly attributed to sin. A dangerous accumulation of sin among the general public was thought to bring illness to The Inca himself, so everybody took pains to make frequent confessions. Little sins were confessed to the priests of local shrines. Big sins like sorcery had to be taken to more impressive priests at temples and the penances were correspondingly severe.

In many ways the general Inca public seems to have been more sinned against than sinning, for opportunities to err were slim indeed. Everyone lived under the watchful eye of some monitor or other. The Inca governor watched the captain of ten thousand, who watched his ten captains of a thousand, who, in their turn, each had two captains of five hundred in charge. The captains of five hundred supervised the captains of one hundred who were heads of *ayllus*. Each *ayllu* was composed (ideally but not always) of one hundred families and was supposed to be the basic governing unit. And even the *ayllu* was subdivided into groups of ten men with their families, each ten with its captain. This captain was responsible for his charges, for the way they rendered tribute or tilled their lands, for the orderliness of their homes and the way they brought up their children. Any breach of discipline on their part brought double punishment to him, and he took care to be watchful.

There were not only the various "captains" forever nosing about, but also at any given time there were likely to be all sorts of "visitors"—the private eyes and ears of The Inca, making sure everyone did his or her job. There were, as well, the regular circuit officials who came around to receive quipu records and oral reports. These officials received other things as well. Regularly they took away clever boys and girls to serve as *yanacona*, serfs in a sense (there was no slavery in Inca Peru), to be assigned to aristocratic fields and households. Also they removed all girls of ten or so whose faces gave promise of great beauty to come. These were destined to be *acllacuna*, "chosen women," attached to provincial convents where they learned fine weaving and the proper deportment for church and palace. There they remained, awaiting

The Inca's pleasure—like the contents of the royal store-houses, another sort of surplus, a surplus of beauty to be distributed in concubinage to outstanding generals or to be chosen by The Inca himself. The leftovers became priestesses in service to the local sun temple.

Cuzco had its own convent but, says Garcilaso de la Vega, of a very different sort. Girls who entered its gates or were given into its service were of the blood royal and became Virgins of the Sun. They were, rather, virgins on earth and Brides of the Sun in all his brilliant eminence. Apart from the queen and her daughters, they saw and spoke to no one from the outside world. Violation of their sanctuary meant death to the man so reckless of cost. Death by strangulation was decreed for him and his entire village along with him. As for the object of his daring, the beautiful sun-virgin whom he loved, she was doomed to burial alive.

Like the vestal virgins of ancient Rome, the *acllacuna* of Cuzco had to guarantee in their way of life the purity and strength of the state. Like the vestals, they kept the sacred fire burning. They also wove the exquisite cloths of sacrifice, baked the sacrificial bread, and brewed the sacramental *chicha*, the intoxicating drink poured in libation to the sun and to his greater glory.

Serving the sun was not the only privilege reserved to Inca nobility. (These, of course, consisted of members of the twelve royal *ayllus*, lineal descendants of each of the former kings. Pachacuti Inca had, during his reign, extended honorary Incahood to all persons who spoke Quechua as a native tongue, but everyone of pedigree knew exactly who was who.) Only noble Incas could function as high priests in Cuzco or even enter the priesthood there. In the provinces, of course, members of the *curaca* caste performed the religious offices. Even there, however, it was deemed desirable to have at least a visiting priest of the blood royal, for the blood royal was the blood of the sun and therefore imbued the provincial temple with genuine divinity.

Members of the royal *ayllus* possessed lands and servants. They enjoyed as well the marks of royal favor—litters, parasols, and adornments only a little smaller, a little less gorgeous than those worn by the great Inca himself. Men of royal blood were permitted many wives, and while they might not marry full sisters as the king did, they could marry half-sisters if they chose. No commoner might do that. They were, moreover, exempt from taxation, protected in most cases from the harsh punishments that might be visited upon commoners for infractions of the rules. Nobles were expected to be models of deportment. (And why not? asks one source. After all, what had they to covet or to complain of?)

Young members of Inca nobility were expected to demonstrate fitness and courage in initiation ordeals. The Inca himself awarded the breechcloths of manhood. The young nobles were also privileged to attend, with the sons of provincial nobility, a four-year "college" where they learned Inca language and oratory, Inca religion and ritual, the art of using the quipu, and Inca history. Since there were no books to be studied, all learning was transmitted in lecture form by the *amautas*, the learned professors. Each was a walking book who had memorized his lore and could repeat it on demand.

The older Inca nobility constituted a sort of management pool, each one ready at any time to serve as priest, governor, inspector, judge, or army general. Closeness to The Inca, however, did not permit presumption. No one entered The Inca's presence shod or without bearing some light burden. Few saw him face to face. Personal initiative among subjects was discouraged, however necessary action might be. Pachacuti Inca's general, his own full brother, was executed for going beyond orders even though he had scored a resounding military victory by so doing. The Inca's word had been given, and the word was a divine decree. In this sense, disobedience was more than indiscretion; it was outright sin. It could be said that Inca government and society was like a pyramid with The Inca at its peak. But it would be closer to the truth to call him the pyramid entire. He was, at least, the spirit giving animation to the state. Without him, it could not exist.

Given all the sober emphasis on practical administration and the proper chain of command, given the lack of mysticism and passion, Inca civilization was nevertheless religious at its core and in its every expression. It was not everywhere the same religion, but everywhere the moving spirit was to be found. Peasants of the highlands put their faith in Mother Earth, patroness of fields and herds. Peasants of the shore honored Mother Sea. For both there were the sacred caves from which the ancestors had emerged, and there were as well all the various *huacas*—sacred things and places, mummies, heirlooms, even piles of rocks crowning hills hard to climb and difficult of access. Here the pious climber added to the pile a tuft of straw or blew into the wind some of his own eyebrows plucked in token of thanks.

In the great temple centers there was, of course, the official cult of the sun, whose sanctuaries were spread with sheets of bright gold. The sun's image was exactly the one we use today in ads and cartoons—a man's face in an aureole of rays. It was to the sun, to thunder, or to the sun's wife the silver moon that libations were poured, to whom in times of special stress sacrifices were dedicated—sacrifices of beautiful young boys and girls. But never would the practical Incas, ever mindful of value, provide their gods with the rivers of human blood thought necessary by the Aztecs. Generally, fine cloth and still-beating llama hearts sufficed.

Beyond the worship of *huacas* and images, beyond the little gods of the fields and the great gods of the temples, was another divinity, the Creator. Called by many names, he was ancient in Andean tradition. It may have his carven figure that guarded the stone gate at Tiahuanaco, that smiled in the secret well at Chavin de Huantar. However omnipotent this Creator, the common folk in time found him unsympathetic and remote. They built him no shrines, and his worship among them faded until two royal Incas chose to associate this god with themselves. One of these two, Pachacuti Inca, is said to have wondered how it was that the sun must go forever up and down, up and down, so that night follows day, always on schedule. Surely, he said, the sun could not be his own master but must have behind him some higher power, a power that was the spirit, the animation in all reality. Pachacuti Inca and others addressed this higher power as Viracocha—"Lord." Garcilaso de la Vega called the Creator "Pachacamac," identifying him with the famous oracle of the seacoast which even the Incas praised and honored. Here is a fragment of prayer which uses the two names:

> To Viracocha, power over all that exists, be it male or female,
> Saint, Lord, Creator of newborn light. Why art Thou? Where art Thou?
> Is it not possible for me to see Thee? In the world above, or in the world below,
> Or wheresoever in the world Thy mighty throne is to be found?
> In the heavenly ocean or the seas of the earth, where is Thy habitation? O Pachacamac,
> Creator of man,
> Lord, Thy servants desire that their feeble eyes may behold Thee . . .

Origin myths are just as diverse. Some held that the first Inca *ayllu*—four brothers and four sisters—emerged from a cave and came down to Cuzco. Three brothers were disposed of en route. The other siblings became the ancestors of Incas to come. Other myths picture a beginning with only one brother and one sister sent directly to earth by the sun god himself. Some have them landing near Cuzco; others set them down on an island in Lake Titicaca whose corn has ever since been considered sacred to corn cultivators throughout Peru.

Still another origin myth, recounted by anthropologist Alfred Métraux, reminds us of Aztec cosmological beliefs, depicting as it does a world begun in fits and starts, in creative "suns" each followed by its own special cataclysm— war and pestilence, withdrawal of light, floods, and the fatal "softening" of man. In this myth, the coming of the Incas signaled the regeneration of life and the fifth and final "sun."

Through all the myths—except for those devoted solely to the Inca dynasty—there appears the misty, remote figure of Viracocha, the Creator. He makes, he molds, he causes life to be. And then, in one of the quick transformations that only myth can achieve, he becomes a culture hero bringing the gifts of husbandry and order to a fully peopled world. Transformed into a pale and bearded man, he is seen moving in slow progress toward Quito until he reaches the western sea, mounts upon its waves, and walks calmly into the sunset.

This last tradition was to bring disaster to the Incas, as the Quetzalcoatl myth had earlier immobilized the Aztecs. For when the Spaniards—having heard tales of Peruvian gold—at last crossed the Isthmus of Panama to sail westward into the Pacific, they were everywhere addressed as Viracocha, sometimes as Children of the Sun. Did they not, after all, wear shiny garments and carry in their arms sticks that made thunder, the servant of the sun?

The Spanish arrival was not entirely unannounced. Dreadful signs and portents had troubled The Inca—meteors and rainbows, eagles falling dead in the great square at Cuzco. Spanish ships had been sighted from afar. And Spanish pestilence, carried southward from Middle America, arrived before ever a conquistador set foot on Peruvian soil. Huayna Capac, son of Topa Inca, died of it—whether measles or smallpox, we can't be sure. Certainly he died inopportunely, leaving the empire in turmoil. Had he lived, or had the succession been secure, the Spaniards might well have been repulsed.

Of all his domains, Huayna Capac had loved Quito best. He married an old-line Quito princess who bore him Atahuallpa, his favorite son. However royal the maternal connections, they were not royal *Inca* and therefore Atahuallpa was not considered to have a legitimate claim to the throne. His half brothers, Huáscar and Manco, were royal through their mother as well as their father and preferred by Inca nobility. In frustrated affection, or perhaps senseless with fever, the dying Inca divided the empire, leaving the old kingdom of Quito to Atahuallpa. He also left there his most experienced troops and generals. Atahuallpa could not forbear to use them. He fought Huáscar and won the final victory just as Francisco Pizarro and his small army began their march into the heart of Peru.

Before the new reign could be consolidated, before the armies could be refitted and reformed, Atahuallpa was taken prisoner by the Spaniards. And though he paid his golden ransom (amounting to something between eight and fifteen million dollars in our terms), he was executed. It is true that he had sent from his place of confinement orders for Huáscar's assassination, but he had not really had time or opportunity to foment rebellion against the Spanish conquerors, as Pizarro charged. Death by fire was decreed for Atahuallpa, but, on taking Christian vows, he was permitted instead the boon of strangulation. His wives, in despair, took their own lives as was the custom among royal women. His people wore mourning black almost constantly thereafter. And on November 15, 1533, Pizarro entered Cuzco.

The transition was not smooth. New royal Incas arose. There were revolts and guerrilla expeditions. Cuzco was burned to the ground by her own people. Strongholds were built in the inaccessible eastern Andes, strongholds from which Indians emerged to harry the invaders in every way possible. For over two hundred years some sort of resistance was maintained. But the Spaniards did not go away. Instead they grew ever stronger, ever more prosperous. For they used Inca laws and Inca institutions to exact tribute, to exact labor of a sort and with a brutality that would have horrified careful Inca administrators in their time.

One by one the old leadership became extinct, but the people survived. As Dr. Métraux tells us, there are today in the highlands of Peru, Ecuador, and Bolivia six or seven million Indians whose ancestors were once ruled by the Incas. Many still live in their ancient communities though they are land-hungry, land-poor, and turned in on themselves. They still speak (and now can write) the ancient Quechua and Aymara. They know the ancient history which now looms grandly in the imagination as a sort of golden age, a haven of content. Poor and without power, they are yet somehow a nation, distinct from the educated elite, half Spanish, half Indian, who began to rule Peru after the European overlords were expelled.

And one day, with yet another creative "sun," that nation in its numbers may well rise to rule again.

Epilogue

The New World Growing Older

Whatever man touches is changed. For it is his nature to make for himself a world conformable to his wishes and his needs. It has always been so in the Old World. It became so in the New. From the time hunters appeared with their deadly points and burning brands, the large animals that were the hunters' meat began to dwindle and die away. Huge though they were, fleet though they were, they made no match for man.

It was perhaps in this first loss of plenty that man in the New World remembered or devised the laws of compensation, learned that for each life taken, something must be returned; learned to kill only when in need and with ceremony to insure the animal's return; learned to honor the spirit that dwells in all things.

Even so, he changed the life around him and harnessed what he found. He could not do otherwise. Some few animals were tamed, and many of the wild green things he had gathered for his food he now caused to grow where he would plant them. But in planting, the laws of compensation were not forgotten. Prayers rose for rain. Fish and guano were fed to the soil from which sprang corn and squash and beans. Men called the earth Mother, a mother who must be cared for and revered. "Would you tear at your mother's breast with plowshares?" once asked an Iroquois of other farmers who would have him learn newer ways. "No, you must only tickle her gently with digging stick and hoe." It was a sentiment widely shared. To this day there are Hopi farmers who will not use a plow. It was not in Indian America, north or south, that erosion furrowed the land and exposed its topsoil naked to the winds.

Only where cities arose in Middle America was the land deprived of its soil-binding shrubs and erosion begun. For men were by then driven not merely by the need for food but by the demands of trade and the multiplying products of their crafts. Fires were needed for kiln and forge, and to feed the fires trees were stripped from dry places that could least sustain the loss. And yet cities were few and the extortions slight, and men strove still for harmony with earth and sky, accommodating themselves to their surroundings even as they changed them, accommodating always to the rhythms nature imposed.

Later men—the men from across the Atlantic—recognized few natural rhythms and applied the laws of compensation only among their own kind. The violence, the shifting dominion that New World tribes had visited upon one another was as nothing to the iron grasp in which they now were held and would be held until they themselves were other than they once had been.

With the new dominion, the people of the land changed, and the land itself changed, too. Mines were dug, forests leveled, hillsides shorn. Cities rose on plains where once the great herds had grazed. Soon there were petroleum wells and the machines that petroleum feeds. There was power of a sort the first Americans had seen only in the lightning, power for factories with their outpouring goods and their wastes. Inexorably the changes went on until rivers were poisoned and the sweet air fouled, until the earth was herself so pruned and parceled that the look of youthful wildness, familiar to her discoverers, was very nearly gone, could scarcely be remembered.

The New World grows older. And yet the land remains —the living tie which binds us, first men and last, inheritors and dispossessed. For all our willful power and our pride, she is our mother still. Patiently she waits for us to learn in our own time what men have learned before: the laws of compensation and of respect for life in all its forms.

It is a law we must learn soon. Already we have set foot on another world, old and barren and bleak but new to us. If in time we find still other new worlds, worlds with growing things upon them, perhaps with intelligent life, will we, in the old familiar way, blast for ourselves a home on these worlds, caring little what we bring of poison or of pain? Or will we have learned in time to move softly and with respect, disturbing little and bringing much of good?

Let us try, let us learn now before some young Columbus, cruising the seas of night, makes planetfall among another people, curious, wondering, and vulnerable. Let us learn before Earth shrinks in our changing perspective to something blue and small, before the western continents of her globe, the last of her own bright lands to make a New World for man, have finally grown old.

Bibliography

PROLOGUE

Chang, K. C. "Major Aspects of the Interrelationship of Archaeology and Ethnology." *Current Anthropology*, June 1967.

Genoves, Santiago T. "Some Problems in the Physical Anthropological Study of the Peopling of America." *Current Anthropology*, October 1967.

Greenman, E. F. "The Upper Paleolithic and the New World." *Current Anthropology*, February 1963.

Hooton, Earnest A. *Up from the Ape*. Macmillan, 1947.

Howells, William W. *Mankind in the Making*. Doubleday & Co., Inc., 1959.

Jennings, Jesse D., and Norbeck, Edward, eds. *Prehistoric Man in the New World*. University of Chicago Press, 1964.

Mason, J. Alden. "Pre-Folsom Estimates of the Age of Man in America." *American Anthropologist*, Vol. 68, no. 1, 1966.

Meggers, Betty J., and Evans, Clifford. *Aboriginal Cultural Development in Latin America*. Smithsonian Miscellaneous Collections, Vol. 146, no. 1, Smithsonian Institution, 1963.

Owen, Roger C.; Deetz, James J. F.; and Fisher, Anthony D., eds. *The North American Indians, A Sourcebook*. Macmillan, 1967.

Steward, Julian H., and Faron, Louis C. *Native Peoples of South America*. McGraw-Hill, 1959.

Stewart, T. D. "A Physical Anthropologist's View of the Peopling of the New World." *Southwestern Journal of Anthropology*, Autumn 1960.

Swadesh, Morris. "A Linguistic Overview." In *Prehistoric Man in the New World, op. cit.*

Trager, G. L. "Languages of the World." In *Colliers Encyclopedia*, Vol. 14. Crowell-Collier-Macmillan, 1965.

Willey, Gordon R. *An Introduction to American Archaeology*. Vol. 1, *North and Middle America*. Prentice-Hall, 1966.

CHAPTER I

Bird, Junius. "The Archaeology of Patagonia." In J. Steward, ed., *Handbook of South American Indians*, Vol. 1. Bureau of American Ethnology, Bulletin 143, Smithsonian Institution, 1946.

Caldwell, Joseph R. *Trend and Tradition in the Prehistory of the Eastern United States*. American Anthropological Association, Memoir no. 88, 1958.

Evans, Clifford. "Lowland South America." In *Prehistoric Man in the New World, op. cit.*

Griffin, James B. "Northeast Woodlands Area." In *Prehistoric Man in the New World, op. cit.*

Haynes, C. Vance. "Fluted Projectile Points: Their Age and Dispersal." *Science*, September 25, 1964.

———. "Elephant Hunting in North America." *Scientific American*, June 1966.

Humphrey, Robert L. "The Prehistory of the Utukok River Region, Arctic Alaska: Early Fluted Point Tradition with Old World Relationships." *Current Anthropology*, December 1966.

Krieger, Alex D. "Early Man in the New World." In *Prehistoric Man in the New World, op. cit.*

Lanning, Edward P., and Patterson, Thomas C. "Early Man in South America." *Scientific American*, November 1967.

Martin, Paul S. "Pleistocene Overkill." *Natural History Magazine*, December 1967.

Montane, Julio. "Paleo-Indian Remains from Laguna de Tagua, Central Chile." *Science*, Sept. 13, 1968.

Wedel, Waldo R. "The Great Plains." In *Prehistoric Man in the New World, op. cit.*

Willey, Gordon. "The Archaeology of the Greater Pampa." In *Handbook of South America Indians*, Vol. 1, *op. cit.*

———. *An Introduction to American Archaeology.* Prentice-Hall, 1966.

CHAPTER 2

Ewers, John C. *The Horse in Blackfoot Culture.* Bureau of American Ethnology, Smithsonian Institution, 1955.

———. *The Blackfeet: Raiders of the Northwestern Plains.* University of Oklahoma Press, 1958.

Grinnell, G. B. "Coup and Scalp Among the Plains Indians." *American Anthropologist*, Vol. 12, 1910.

Jablow, Joseph. *The Cheyenne in Plains Trade Relations, 1795–1840.* Monograph of the American Ethnological Society, 1950.

Lewis, Oscar. *The Effects of White Contact upon Blackfoot Culture, with Special Reference to the Role of the Fur Trade.* Monograph of the American Ethnological Society, 1942.

Lowie, Robert H. *Indians of the Plains.* McGraw-Hill, 1954.

Mishkin, Bernard. *Rank and Warfare Among the Plains Indians.* Monograph of the American Ethnological Society, 1940.

Richardson, Jane. *Law and Status Among the Kiowa Indians.* Monograph of the American Ethnological Society, 1940.

Secoy, Frank Raymond. *Changing Military Patterns on the Great Plains (17th Century Through Early 19th Century).* Monograph of the American Ethnological Society, 1953.

Spier, Leslie. "The Sun Dance of the Plains Indians: Its Development and Diffusion." In Clark Wissler, ed., *The Sun Dance of the Plains Indians.* Anthropological Papers of the American Museum of Natural History, no. 16, 1921.

Wissler, Clark. "The Influence of the Horse in the Development of Plains Culture." *American Anthropologist*, Vol. 16, 1914.

———. *North American Indians of the Plains.* American Museum of Natural History Handbook Series, 1941.

Reference Note

The quotations on pages 33 and 34 are from George Parker Winship, *The*

Journey of Coronado, 1540–1542, as cited in Wissler, *Indians of the Plains*.

CHAPTER 3

Alexander, Hartley Burr. "Latin American Myth." In L. H. Gray, ed., *The Mythology of All Races*. Marshall Jones Co., 1920.
Bridges, E. Lucas. *Uttermost Parts of the Earth*. Dutton, 1949.
Cooper, John M. "The Patagonian and Pampean Hunters." In *Handbook of South American Indians*, Vol. 1, *op. cit.*
Lothrop, Samuel Kirkland. *The Indians of Tierra del Fuego*. The Heye Foundation, 1928.
Musters, George Chaworth. *At Home with the Patagonians*. John Murray, 1871.
Nordenskiold, Erland. "Origin of the Indian Civilizations in South America." *Comparative Ethnological Studies*, Vol. 9, Erlanders Boktryckeri Aktiebolag, 1931.
Steward, Julian H., and Faron, Louis C. *Native Peoples of South America*. McGraw-Hill, 1959.

CHAPTER 4

Greenman, E. F. "The Upper Paleolithic and the New World." *Current Anthropology*, February 1963.
Hallowell, A. Irving. "Ojibwa World View." In *The North American Indians. A Sourcebook*, *op. cit.*
Hickerson, Harold. "Some Implications of the Theory of the Particularity, or 'Atomism,' of Northern Algonkians." *Current Anthropology*, October 1967.
Jenness, Diamond. *The Ojibwa Indians of Parry Island: Their Social and Religious Life*. Department of Mines, National Museum of Canada, Bulletin no. 78, 1935.
———. "The Indians of Canada." *Bulletin of the National Museum of Canada*, no. 65, Anthropological Series no. 15, 1955.
Landes, Ruth. *Ojibwa Sociology*. Columbia University Contributions to Anthropology, Vol. 29. Columbia University Press, 1937.
———. *The Ojibwa Woman*. Columbia University Contributions to Anthropology, Vol. 31. Columbia University Press, 1938.
———. "The Ojibwa of Canada." In Margaret Mead, ed., *Cooperation and Competition Among Primitive Peoples*, Beacon Press, 1961.

Reference Note
The quotation on page 79 is from Diamond Jenness, *The Carrier Indians of the Bulkley River*. Bureau of American Ethnology, Bulletin 133, Smithsonian Institution, 1943.

CHAPTER 5

Holmberg, Allan R. "The Siriono." In *Handbook of South American Indians*, Vol. 1, *op. cit.*
———. *Indians of the Long Bow: The Siriono of Eastern Bolivia*. Institute of Social Anthropology, Publication no. 10, Smithsonian Institution, 1950.
———. "Adventure in Culture Change." In R. F. Spencer, ed., *Perspective in Anthropology*. University of Minnesota Press, 1954.
Steward, Julian H., and Faron, Louis C. *Native Peoples of South America*. McGraw-Hill, 1959.

CHAPTER 6

Bird, Junius. "The Archaeology of Patagonia." In *Handbook of South American Indians*, Vol. 1, *op. cit.*

Heizer, Robert F. "The Western Coast of North America." In *Prehistoric Man in the New World, op. cit.*

Lanning, Edward P. "Early Man in Peru." *Scientific American*, October 1965.

Meggers, Betty J. *Ecuador*. Praeger, 1966.

———, and Evans, Clifford. "A Transpacific Contact in 3000 B.C." *Scientific American*, January 1966.

———; Evans, Clifford; and Estrada, Emilio. *Early Formative Period of Coastal Ecuador, the Valdivia and Machalilla Phases. Smithsonian Contributions to Anthropology*, Vol. 1. Smithsonian Institution, 1965.

Noma, Seiroku. "Primitives of Japan, a Legacy in Clay." *Natural History Magazine*, March 1963.

Ray, Verne F. "The Life Cycle of the Plateau Sanpoil." In *The North American Indians, A Sourcebook, op. cit.*

Steward, Julian H., and Faron, Louis C. *Native Peoples of South America*. McGraw-Hill, 1959.

Willey, Gordon R. *An Introduction to American Archaeology*. Prentice-Hall, 1966.

CHAPTER 7

Bridges, E. Lucas. *Uttermost Parts of the Earth, op. cit.*

Cooper, John M. "The Yahgan." In *Handbook of South American Indians*, Vol. 1, *op. cit.*

Darwin, Charles. *Journal of Researches into the Natural History and Geology of the Countries Visited During the Voyage of H.M.S. Beagle Under the Command of Captain Fitzroy, R.N.* (1896) Heritage Press, 1957.

Loeb, E. M. "The Religious Organizations of North Central California and Tierra del Fuego." *American Anthropologist*, October–December 1931.

Lothrop, Samuel Kirkland. *The Indians of Tierra del Fuego*. The Heye Foundation, 1928.

Reference Note

The quotations on pages 101 and 112 are from Charles Darwin, *Journal.*

CHAPTER 8

Barnett, H. G. "The Nature of the Potlatch." *American Anthropologist*, July–September 1938.

———. "The Coast Salish of Canada." In *The North American Indians, A Sourcebook, op. cit.*

Benedict, Ruth. *Patterns of Culture*. Houghton Mifflin Co., 1934.

Boas, Franz. *Ethnology of the Kwakiutl*. Bureau of American Ethnology, 35th Annual Report, 1913.

Codere, Helen. *Fighting with Property*. Monograph of the American Ethnological Society, 1950.

———. "The Amiable Side of Kwakiutl Life: The Potlatch and the Play Potlatch." *American Anthropologist*, April 1956.

Drucker, Philip. "Rank, Wealth, and Kinship in Northwest Coastal Society." *American Anthropologist*, Vol. 41, 1939.

———. *Indians of the Northwest Coast*. McGraw-Hill, 1955.

Ford, Clellan S. *Smoke from Their Fires: The Life of a Kwakiutl Chief*. Yale University Press, 1941.

Forde, C. Daryll. *Habitat, Economy, and Society.* Dutton, 1963.
Goldman, Irving. "The Kwakiutl Indians of Vancouver Island." In *Co-operation and Competition Among Primitive Peoples, op. cit.*
Vayda, Andrew P. *A Re-examination of Northwest Coast Economic Systems.* Transactions of the New York Academy of Sciences, Series 7, May 1961.

Reference Note

The quotations on pages 122 and 123 are from Franz Boas, *Ethnology of the Kwakiutl.*

CHAPTER 9

Jennings, Jesse D. "The Desert West." In *Prehistoric Man in the New World, op. cit.*
MacNeish, Richard S. "The Food Gathering and Incipient Agriculture Stage of Prehistoric Middle America." In Robert C. West, ed., *Handbook of Middle American Indians*, Vol. 1, University of Texas Press, 1964.
———. "The Origins of New World Civilization." *Scientific American*, November 1964.
———. "Mesoamerican Archaeology." In Siegel and Beals, eds., *Biennial Review of Anthropology.* Stanford University Press, 1967.
Willey, Gordon R. *An Introduction to American Archaeology*, Prentice-Hall, 1966.

CHAPTER 10

Forde, C. Daryll. *Habitat, Economy, and Society, op. cit.*
Harris, Jack S. "The White Knife Shoshoni of Nevada." In Ralph Linton, ed., *Acculturation in Seven American Indian Tribes.* Peter Smith, 1963.
Opler, Marvin K. "The Southern Ute of Colorado." In *Acculturation in Seven American Indian Tribes, op. cit.*
Park, Willard Z. "Paviotso Shamanism." In *The North American Indians, A Sourcebook, op. cit.*
Steward, Julian H. *Basin-Plateau Aboriginal Socio-Political Groups.* Bureau of American Ethnology, Bulletin 120, 1938.
———. *Theory of Culture Change.* University of Illinois Press, 1955.
Whiting, Beatrice Blyth. *Paiute Sorcery.* Viking Fund Publications in Anthropology no. 15, 1950.

CHAPTER 11

Bennett, Wendell C. "The Archaeology of Colombia." In *Handbook of South American Indians*, Vol. 2, *op. cit.*
Caldwell, Joseph R. *Trend and Tradition in the Prehistory of the Eastern United States.* Memoir no. 88, American Anthropological Association, 1958.
Carter, George F. "Plant Evidence for Early Contacts with America." *Southwestern Journal of Anthropology*, Vol. 6, 1950.
Chard, Chester S. "Invention Versus Diffusion: The Burial Mound Complex of the Eastern United States." *Southwestern Journal of Anthropology*, Vol. 17, 1961.
Coe, Michael D. "Archaeological Linkages with North and South America at La Victoria, Guatemala." *American Anthropologist*, Vol. 63, June 1960.
Evans, Clifford. "Lowland South America." In *Prehistoric Man in the New World, op. cit.*

Gonzalez, Albert Rex. "Cultural Development in Northwestern Argentina." In Meggers and Evans, eds., *Aboriginal Cultural Development in Latin America*. Smithsonian Miscellaneous Collections, Vol. 146, no. 1, Smithsonian Institution, U.S. Government Printing Office, 1963.

Griffin, James B. "Northeastern Woodlands." In *Prehistoric Man in the New World, op. cit.*

————. "Mesoamerica and the Eastern United States in Prehistoric Times." In Ekholm and Willey, eds., *Handbook of Middle American Indians*, Vol. 4. University of Texas Press, 1966.

Kidder, Alfred, II; Lumbreras S., Luis G.; and Smith, David B. "Cultural Development in the Central Andes, Peru and Bolivia." In *Aboriginal Cultural Development in Latin America, op. cit.*

Kidder, Alfred, II. "South American High Cultures." In *Prehistoric Man in the New World, op. cit.*

Lanning, Edward P. "Early Man in Peru." *Scientific American*, October 1965.

MacNeish, Richard S. "The Origins of New World Civilization." *Scientific American*, November 1964.

————. "Mesoamerican Archaeology." In *Biennial Review of Anthropology, op. cit.*

Mangelsdorf, Paul C.; MacNeish, Richard S.; and Willey, Gordon R. "The Origins of Agriculture in Middle America." In *Handbook of Middle American Indians*, Vol. 1, *op. cit.*

Meggers, Betty J. "Cultural Development in Latin America: An Interpretive Overview." In *Aboriginal Cultural Development in Latin America, op. cit.*

————. "North and South American Cultural Connections and Convergences," in *Prehistoric Man in the New World, op. cit.*

Miranda, Ferando Marquez. "The Diaguita of Argentina." In *Handbook of South American Indians*, Vol. 2, *op. cit.*

Parsons, James L., and Deneven, William M. "Precolumbian Ridged Fields." *Scientific American*, July 1967.

Prufer, Olaf H. "The Hopewell Cult." *Scientific American*, December 1964.

Reichel-Dolmatoff, Gerardo, "Jungle Gods of San Agustin." *Natural History Magazine*, December 1966.

————. *Colombia*. Praeger, 1965.

Rouse, Irving. "The Caribbean Area." In *Prehistoric Man in the New World, op. cit.*

Spaulding, Albert. "The Origin of the Adena Culture of the Ohio Valley." *Southwestern Journal of Anthropology*, Vol. 8, 1952.

————. "Prehistoric Cultures of the East." In *The North American Indians, A Sourcebook, op. cit.*

Steward, Julian H. "American Culture History in the Light of South America." *Southwestern Journal of Anthropology*, Vol. 3, 1947.

Valdes, Carlos Angulo. "Cultural Development in Colombia." In *Aboriginal Cultural Development in Latin America, op. cit.*

Willey, Gordon R. *An Introduction to American Archaeology*. Vol. 1, *North and Middle America*. Prentice-Hall, 1966.

Wormington, H. M. *Prehistoric Indians of the Southwest*. The Denver Museum of Natural History, 1961.

CHAPTER 12

Chagnon, Napoleon A. "Yanomamö—The Fierce People." *Natural History Magazine*, January 1967.

————. "Yanomamö Social Organization and Warfare." *Natural History Magazine,* December 1967.
————. "The Feast." *Natural History Magazine,* April 1968.
————. *Yanomamö: The Fierce People.* Holt, Rinehart, 1968.
DeForest, John W. *History of the Indians of Connecticut.* William James Hamersley, 1852.
Goldman, Irving. *The Cubeo: Indians of the Northwest Amazon.* University of Illinois Press, 1963.
Steward, Julian H., and Faron, Louis C. *Native Peoples of South America.* McGraw-Hill, 1959.

CHAPTER 13

Fenton, William N. "Locality as a Basic Factor in the Development of Iroquois Social Structure." In *Symposium on Local Diversity in Iroquois Culture.* Bureau of American Ethnology Bulletin no. 149, Smithsonian Institution, 1951.
Fenton, William N., and Gulick, John. *Symposium on Cherokee and Iroquois Culture.* Bureau of American Ethnology, Bulletin no. 180, Smithsonian Institution, 1961.
Goldenweiser, Alexander A. "Iroquois Social Organization." In *The North American Indians, A Sourcebook, op. cit.*
Hale, Horatio, ed. *The Iroquois Book of Rites.* D. G. Brinton, 1883.
Métraux, Alfred. *The Native Tribes of Eastern Bolivia and Western Matto Grosso.* Bureau of American Ethnology, Bulletin 134, Smithsonian Institution, 1942.
————. "Tribes of Eastern Bolivia and the Madeira Headwaters." In *Handbook of South American Indians,* Vol. 3, *op. cit.*
Morgan, Lewis H. *League of the Ho-De-No-Sau-Nee, or Iroquois.* Dodd, Mead, 1851 (2nd ed., 1902).
Otterbein, Keith F. "An Analysis of Iroquois Military Tactics." In Paul Bohannon, ed., *Law and Welfare.* Natural History Press, 1967.
Quain, B. H. "The Iroquois." In *Cooperation and Competition Among Primitive Peoples, op. cit.*
Stern, Theodore. *Rubber-Ball Games of the Americas.* Monograph of the American Ethnological Society, 1948.
Steward, Julian, and Faron, Louis C. *Native Peoples of South America.* McGraw-Hill, 1959.
Wallace, Anthony F. C. "Dreams and Wishes of the Soul, A Type of Psychoanalytic Theory Among the Seventeenth Century Iroquois." *American Anthropologist,* Vol. 70, April 1958.

Reference Notes

The quotations on pages 184 and 189 are from Chief Elias Johnson, *Legends, Traditions and Laws of the Iroquois, of Six Nations,* 1881.
The quotation on page 186 is from Horatio Hale, ed., *The Iroquois Book of Rites.*
The quotation on page 194 is from Lewis H. Morgan, *League of the Ho-De-No-Sau-Nee.*

CHAPTER 14

Beaglehole, Ernest and Pearl. *Hopi of the Second Mesa.* Memoir no. 44, American Anthropological Association, 1935.
Carroll, John B. *Language, Thought, and Reality: Selected Writings of Benjamin Lee Whorf.* John Wiley, 1956.
Dozier, Edward P. "The Pueblo Indians of the Southwest." *Current Anthropology,* Vol. 5, April 1964.
Eggan, Fred. *Social Organization of the Western Pueblos.* University of Chicago Press, 1950.

Gonzalez, Alberto Rex. "Cultural Development in Northwestern Argentina." In Meggers and Evans, eds. *Aboriginal Cultural Development in Latin America. Smithsonian Miscellaneous Collections*, Vol. 146, no. 1, Smithsonian Institution, 1963.

Kirchhoff, Paul. "Gatherers and Farmers in the Greater Southwest: A Problem in Classification." *American Anthropologist*, Vol. 56, 1954.

Miranda, Fernando Marquez. "The Diaguita of Argentina." In *Handbook of South American Indians*, Vol. 2, *op. cit.*

Simmons, Leo W. *Sun Chief: The Autobiography of a Hopi Indian.* Yale University Press, 1942.

Titiev, Mischa. *Old Oraibi. Papers of the Peabody Museum of American Archaeology and Ethnology, Harvard University*, Vol. XXII, no. 1, 1944.

Waters, Frank. *The Book of the Hopi.* The Viking Press, 1963.

CHAPTER 15

Bennett, Wendell C. "Colombia: The Environment and Tribes." In *Handbook of South American Indians*, Vol. 2, *op. cit.*

Caldwell, Joseph R. *Trend and Tradition in the Prehistory of the Eastern United States.* Memoir no. 88, American Anthropological Association, 1958.

Kroeber, Alfred L. "The Chibcha." In *Handbook of South American Indians*, Vol. 2, *op. cit.*

Reichel-Dolmatoff, Gerardo. *Colombia.* Praeger, 1965.

Steward, Julian H. "American Culture History in the Light of South America." *Southwestern Journal of Anthropology*, Vol. 3, 1947.

Steward, Julian H., and Faron, Louis C. *Native Peoples of South America.* McGraw-Hill, 1959.

Sturtevant, William C. *The Significance of Ethnological Similarities Between Southeastern North America and the Antilles. Yale University Publications in Anthropology*, no. 64, 1960.

Swanton, John R. *Indian Tribes of the Lower Mississippi Valley and Adjacent Coast of the Gulf of Mexico.* Bureau of American Ethnology, Bulletin 43, Smithsonian Institution, 1911.

――――. *Aboriginal Culture of the Southeast.* Bureau of American Ethnology, 42nd Annual Report, 1924–25.

――――. *The Indians of the Southeastern United States.* Bureau of American Ethnology, Bulletin 137, Smithsonian Institution, 1946.

CHAPTER 16

Mexico

Coe, Michael D. *Mexico.* Praeger, 1962.

――――. "The Chinampas of Mexico." *Scientific American*, July 1964.

――――. "Archaeological Synthesis of Southern Vera Cruz and Tabasco." In G. Willey, ed., *Handbook of Middle American Indians*, Vol. 3, Part 2. University of Texas Press, 1965.

――――. "The Olmec Style and Its Distribution." In *Handbook of Middle American Indians*, Vol. 3, Part 2, *op. cit.*

――――. *The Jaguar's Children: Pre-Classic Central Mexico.* The Museum of Primitive Art, New York Graphic Society, 1965.

――――. *America's First Civilization.* American Heritage, 1968.

――――. Lecture. Yale University Alumni Seminar, 1969.

――――; Diehl, Richard A.; and Stuiver, Minze. "Olmec Civilization, Vera Cruz, Mexico: Dating of the San Lorenzo Phase." *Science*, Vol. 155, March 17, 1967.

Covarrubias, Miguel. *Indian Art of Mexico and Central America*. Alfred A. Knopf, 1957.
Drucker, Philip; Heizer, Robert F.; and Squier, Robert J. *Excavations at La Venta, Tabasco, 1955*. Bureau of American Ethnology, Bulletin 170, Smithsonian Institution, 1959.
Ekholm, Gordon F. "Transpacific Contacts." In *Prehistoric Man in the New World, op. cit.*
Gay, Carlo T. E. "Rock Carvings at Chalcacingo." *Natural History Magazine*, August–September 1966.
———, "Oldest Paintings of the New World." *Natural History Magazine*, April 1967.
Grove, David C. "Olmec Cave Paintings: Discovery from Guerrero, Mexico." *Science*, April 25, 1969.
Heine-Geldern, Robert. "The Problem of Transpacific Influences in Meso-america." In *Handbook of Middle American Indians*, Vol. 4, *op. cit.*
MacNeish, Richard S. "Meso American Archaeology." In *Biennial Review of Anthropology, op. cit.*
Millon, René. "Teotihuacán." *Scientific American*, June 1967.
Parsons, Jeffrey R. "Teotihuacán, Mexico and Its Impact on Regional Demography." *Science*, Vol. 126, Nov. 22, 1968.
Phillips, Philip. "The Role of Transpacific Contacts in the Development of New World Pre-Columbian Civilization." In *Handbook of Middle American Indians*, Vol. 4, *op. cit.*
Stirling, Matthew. "Monumental Sculpture of Southern Vera Cruz and Tabasco." In *Handbook of Middle American Indians*, Vol. 3, Part 2, *op. cit.*
Vivo Escoto, Jorge A. "Weather and Climate of Mexico and Central America." In *Handbook of Middle American Indians*, Vol. 1, *op. cit.*
Willey, Gordon R. *An Introduction to American Archaeology*. Vol. 1: *North and Middle America*, Prentice-Hall, 1966.
Willey, Gordon R.; Ekholm, Gordon F.; and Millon, René F. "The Patterns of Farming Life and Civilization." In *Handbook of Middle American Indians*, Vol. 1, *op. cit.*

Reference Note

The quotation on page 241 is translated from the Spanish version of the Nahuatl text by Michael Coe in *Mexico*.

Peru

Bennett, Wendell C. "The Andean Civilizations." In *Handbook of South American Indians*, Vol. 2, *op. cit.*
———, and Bird, Junius B. *Andean Culture History*. Natural History Press, 1960.
Bushnell, G. H. S. *Peru*. Praeger, 1963.
Coe, Michael D. Lecture. Yale University Alumni Seminar, 1969.
Easby, Dudley T., Jr. "Early Metallurgy in the New World." *Scientific American*, April 1966.
Hoyle, Rafael Larco. "A Culture Sequence for the North Coast of Peru." In *Handbook of South American Indians*, Vol. 2, *op. cit.*
Kidder, Alfred, II; Lumbreras S., Luis G.; and Smith, David B. "Cultural Development in the Central Andes: Peru and Bolivia." In *Aboriginal Cultural Development in Latin America, op. cit.*
Kidder, Alfred, II. "South American High Cultures." In *Prehistoric Man in the New World, op. cit.*
Lanning, Edward P. "Early Man in Peru." *Scientific American*, October 1965.
———. *Peru Before the Incas*. Prentice-Hall, 1967.

Mason, J. Alden. *The Ancient Civilizations of Peru.* Penguin Books, 1961.
Steward, Julian H., and Faron, Louis C. *Native Peoples of South America.* McGraw-Hill, 1959.

CHAPTER 17

Caso, Alfonso. *The Aztecs: People of the Sun.* Translated by Lowell Dunham. University of Oklahoma Press, 1958.
Coe, Michael D. *Mexico.* Praeger, 1962.
Díaz del Castillo, Bernal. *The Discovery and Conquest of Mexico.* Translated by A. P. Maudslay. Farrar, Straus and Cudahy, 1956.
Peterson, Frederick. *Ancient Mexico.* Capricorn Books, 1962.
Sahagun, Bernardino de. *A History of Ancient Mexico.* Translated by Fanny R. Bandeiler from the Spanish of Carlos María de Bustamante. Fisk University Press, 1932.
———. *Florentine Codex: General History of the Things of New Spain.* Translated from the Aztec by C. E. Dibble and Arthur J. O. Anderson. Monograph of the School of American Research and The Museum of New Mexico, no. 14, Part 11, 1961.
Stern, Theodore. *The Rubber-Ball Games of the Americas.* Monograph of the American Ethnological Society, 1949.
Vaillant, G. C. *The Aztecs of Mexico.* Penguin Books, 1950.
Willey, Gordon R. *An Introduction to American Archaeology.* Prentice-Hall, 1966.
Wolf, Eric R. *Sons of the Shaking Earth.* University of Chicago Press, 1959.

Reference Notes

The quotation on page 268 is translated from Nahuatl into Spanish by A. M. Garibay, *Historia de la Literatura Nahuatl,* and from Spanish into English by Michael Coe in *Mexico.*
The quotations on pages 268 and 269 are from Bernal Díaz de Castillo, *The Discovery and Conquest of Mexico.*
The quotation on page 274 is from Bernardino de Sahagun, *The Florentine Codex.*
The quotation on page 279 is from Alfonso Caso, *The Aztecs: People of the Sun.*
The quotation on page 281 is cited in Eric R. Wolf, *Sons of the Shaking Earth.*

CHAPTER 18

Garcilaso de la Vega, El Inca. *Royal Commentaries of the Incas and General History of Peru.* University of Texas Press, 1966.
Mason, J. Alden. *The Ancient Civilization of Peru.* Penguin Books, 1961.
Métraux, Alfred. *The Incas.* Studio Vista, 1965.
Prescott, William H. *The History of the Conquest of Peru.* The Heritage Press, 1957.
Rowe, John Howland. "Inca Culture at the Time of the Spanish Conquest." In *Handbook of South American Indians,* Vol. 2, *op. cit.*
Swadesh, Morris. "A Linguistic Overview." In *Prehistoric Man in the New World, op. cit.*

Reference Notes

The quotation on pages 283–4 is cited in the Translator's Introduction to *Royal Commentaries of the Incas and General History of Peru.*
The quotation on page 298 was collected by Father Christobal de Molina in 1957 and cited in Métraux, *The Incas.*

Index

Index